Porn Chic

Dress, Body, Culture

Series Editor: **Joanne B. Eicher,** *Regents' Professor, University of Minnesota*

Advisory Board:
Ruth Barnes, *Ashmolean Museum, University of Oxford*
James Hall, *University of Illinois at Chicago*
Ted Polhemus, *Curator, "Street Style" Exhibition, Victoria and Albert Museum*
Griselda Pollock, *University of Leeds*
Valerie Steele, *The Museum at the Fashion Institute of Technology*
Lou Taylor, *University of Brighton*
John Wright, *University of Minnesota*

Books in this provocative series seek to articulate the connections between culture and dress which is defined here in its broadest possible sense as any modification or supplement to the body. Interdisciplinary in approach, the series highlights the dialogue between identity and dress, cosmetics, coiffure and body alternations as manifested in practices as varied as plastic surgery, tattooing, and ritual scarification. The series aims, in particular, to analyze the meaning of dress in relation to popular culture and gender issues and will include works grounded in anthropology, sociology, history, art history, literature, and folklore.

ISSN: 1360–466X

Previously published in the Series

Helen Bradley Foster, *"New Raiments of Self": African American Clothing in the Antebellum South*
Claudine Griggs, *S/he: Changing Sex and Changing Clothes*
Michaele Thurgood Haynes, *Dressing Up Debutantes: Pageantry and Glitz in Texas*
Anne Brydon and Sandra Niessen, *Consuming Fashion: Adorning the Transnational Body*
Dani Cavallaro and Alexandra Warwick, *Fashioning the Frame: Boundaries, Dress and the Body*
Judith Perani and Norma H. Wolff, *Cloth, Dress and Art Patronage in Africa*
Linda B. Arthur, *Religion, Dress and the Body*
Paul Jobling, *Fashion Spreads: Word and Image in Fashion Photography*
Fadwa El Guindi, *Veil: Modesty, Privacy and Resistance*
Thomas S. Abler, *Hinterland Warriors and Military Dress: European Empires and Exotic Uniforms*
Linda Welters, *Folk Dress in Europe and Anatolia: Beliefs about Protection and Fertility*
Kim K. P. Johnson and Sharron J. Lennon, *Appearance and Power*
Barbara Burman, *The Culture of Sewing*
Annette Lynch, *Dress, Gender and Cultural Change*
Antonia Young, *Women Who Become Men*
David Muggleton, *Inside Subculture: The Postmodern Meaning of Style*
Nicola White, *Reconstructing Italian Fashion: America and the Development of the Italian Fashion Industry*
Brian J. McVeigh, *Wearing Ideology: The Uniformity of Self-Presentation in Japan*
Shaun Cole, *Don We Now Our Gay Apparel: Gay Men's Dress in the Twentieth Century*
Kate Ince, *Orlan: Millennial Female*
Nicola White and Ian Griffiths, *The Fashion Business: Theory, Practice, Image*
Ali Guy, Eileen Green and Maura Banim, *Through the Wardrobe: Women's Relationships with their Clothes*
Linda B. Arthur, *Undressing Religion: Commitment and Conversion from a Cross-Cultural Perspective*
William J. F. Keenan, *Dressed to Impress: Looking the Part*
Joanne Entwistle and Elizabeth Wilson, *Body Dressing*
Leigh Summers, *Bound to Please: A History of the Victorian Corset*
Paul Hodkinson, *Goth: Identity, Style and Subculture*
Leslie W. Rabine, *The Global Circulation of African Fashion*
Michael Carter, *Fashion Classics from Carlyle to Barthes*
Sandra Niessen, Ann Marie Leshkowich and Carla Jones, *Re-Orienting Fashion: The Globalization of Asian Dress*
Kim K. P. Johnson, Susan J. Torntore and Joanne B. Eicher, *Fashion Foundations: Early Writings on Fashion and Dress*
Helen Bradley Foster and Donald Clay Johnson, *Wedding Dress Across Cultures*
Eugenia Paulicelli, *Fashion under Fascism: Beyond the Black Shirt*
Charlotte Suthrell, *Unzipping Gender: Sex, Cross-Dressing and Culture*
Irene Guenther, *Nazi Chic? Fashioning Women in the Third Reich*
Yuniya Kawamura, *The Japanese Revolution in Paris Fashion*
Patricia Calefato, *The Clothed Body*
Ruth Barcan, *Nudity: A Cultural Anatomy*
Samantha Holland, *Alternative Femininities: Body, Age and Identity*
Alexandra Palmer and Hazel Clark, *Old Clothes, New Looks: Second Hand Fashion*
Yuniya Kawamura, *Fashionology: An Introduction to Fashion Studies*
Regina A. Root, *The Latin American Fashion Reader*
Linda Welters and Patricia A. Cunningham, *Twentieth-Century American Fashion*
Jennifer Craik, *Uniforms Exposed: From Conformity to Transgression*
Alison L. Goodrum, *The National Fabric: Fashion, Britishness, Globalization*
Annette Lynch and Mitchell D. Strauss, *Changing Fashion: A Critical Introduction to Trend Analysis and Meaning*
Catherine M. Roach, *Stripping, Sex and Popular Culture*
Marybeth C. Stalp, *Quilting: The Fabric of Everyday Life*
Jonathan S. Marion, *Ballroom: Culture and Costume in Competitive Dance*
Dunja Brill, *Goth Culture: Gender, Sexuality and Style*
Joanne Entwistle, *The Aesthetic Economy of Fashion: Markets and Value in Clothing and Modelling*
Juanjuan Wu, *Chinese Fashion: From Mao to Now*
Brent Luvaas, *DIY Style: Fashion, Music and Global Digital Cultures*

Porn Chic
Exploring the Contours of Raunch Eroticism

Annette Lynch

London • New York

English edition
First published in 2012 by
Berg
Editorial offices:
50 Bedford Square, London WC1B 3DP, UK
175 Fifth Avenue, New York, NY 10010, USA

Berg is an imprint of Bloomsbury Publishing Plc.

Library of Congress Cataloging-in-Publication Data
A catalogue record for this book is available from the Library of Congress.

Library of Congress Cataloging-in-Publication Data
Lynch, Annette (Annette Ferne)
Porn chic : exploring the contours of raunch eroticism / Annette Lynch — English ed.
p. cm. — (Dress, body, culture)
Includes bibliographical references and index.
ISBN 978-1-84788-629-3 (alk. paper) — ISBN 978-1-84788-628-6 (alk. paper)
1. Pornography. 2. Erotica. 3. Pop culture. 4. Pornography–Social aspects.
5. Sex–Social aspects. I. Title.
HQ471.L985   2012
306.77—dc23   2012013130

British Library Cataloguing-in-Publication Data
A catalogue record for this book is available from the British Library.

ISBN 978-1-84788-629-3 (Cloth)
978-1-84788-628-6 (Paper)

Typeset by Apex CoVantage, LLC, Madison, WI, USA.
Printed in the UK by the MPG Books Group

www.bergpublishers.com

To Gender Justice

Contents

List of Figures and Table

Figures

Table

Porn Chic: Exploring the Contours
of Raunch Eroticism

In the fall of 2003 I was almost knocked down by riot police as I was doing field-work at a football homecoming party held in a bar district adjoining my campus. I was conducting interviews and gathering field data on the breast-flashing behaviors of college women, some of whom were enrolled in my classes at the university. A male student in one of my classes pulled me aside the following week and showed me Internet *Girls Gone Wild* (*GGW*)—style images of female students from my home campus photographed with cell phones. These images were being distributed on websites and as e-mail attachments all across the country. The following year included a visit from the official *GGW* bus at a local college bar. Our small rural campus had made it onto the *GGW* map. Not surprisingly, young men from Texas (a road trip taking a full day in the car) were driving across the country for the event the following year.

While homecoming mass flashing and related street riot conditions have been successfully curbed by local and campus police, the *GGW* bus has continued to pull into town to service the local bars for close to a decade. Just a few months ago I again followed the *GGW* camera crew as they worked the string of bars adjoining our campus, making April 2011 another *GGW* springtime for students attending this small public university. The now-customary *GGW* breast flashing is augmented with added "bootie" shots, including a shot of the exposed (and wiggling) rear end of a young woman who was a friend of a student enrolled in one my classes. Not shy and not embarrassed, the young woman turned to rear-flash the camera within an arm's length of me.

Porn chic is getting news attention in the United Kingdom as well. In 2009 a reporter working on a BBC radio investigation discovered that not only are British teenagers viewing extensive amounts of pornography, but some girls are circulating their own photographs, using poses learned from the pro websites. One sixth grader tells the somewhat startled reporter that "everyone makes porn—more people than you would expect.... Over the holidays I went to a party from my old school and one of the girls was on her bed with nothing on. She had loads and loads of makeup on, so you could see she had really thought about it" (Marshall, 2009). The sixth grader goes on to explain to the reporter that once this provocative pose was captured on her cell phone, the seventeen-year-old posing for the photograph sent the image to a list of her male friends and acquaintances. In the United States, teenage sexting turned tragic in May 2008:

> The image was blurred and the voice distorted, but the words spoken by a young Ohio woman are haunting. She had sent nude pictures of herself to a boyfriend. When they broke up, he sent them to other high school girls. The girls were harassing her, calling her a slut and a whore. She was miserable and depressed, afraid even to go to school.
>
> And now Jesse Logan was going on a Cincinnati television station to tell her story. Her purpose was simple: "I just want to make sure no one else will have to go through this again."
>
> The interview was in May 2008. Two months later, Jessica Logan hanged herself in her bedroom. She was 18. (Celizic, 2009)

In my fashion-trend analysis course my students bring up Betsey Johnson's Spring 2012 Tits and Ass runway show as an example of how sexy fashion can be used to express women's power. The burlesque-inspired collection was purposefully marketed by Betsey as a power-slut look, with the invitations featuring an illustration of tits and ass. Within Betsey's hot and grinding runway show, tits were uniformly emphasized, with each model marked by a small red heart on the full, ripe left breast. Fashion reviewer Maya Singer (2011) described the runway show as "so va-va-voom" and quoted Betsey's comments after the show stressing how proud she was to have a sexy daughter on the runway: "Backstage after the show, Johnson elaborated on her inspiration this season, saying she was especially proud to see her daughter, Lulu, back on the runway. 'After ten years and two kids,' Johnson noted, 'she's voluptuous and fabulous. And I just wanted, you know, to express this attitude of pride and confidence in your body.'" The focus of this book is an exploration, through a series of case study examples, of how the attitudes, behaviors, trends, and norms of the porn industry have worked their way into the mainstream and, ultimately, of what the mainstreaming of porn means in terms of its impact on culture and gender relations.

Beginning with Ariel Levy's 2005 book on raunch culture, a number of books have focused on the prevalence and mainstreaming of pornography as a cultural trend. Levy's work in many ways was a benchmark book in initiating a dialogue among feminists on women's active participation in the mainstreaming of pornography. Following up her work, scholars such as Rosalind Gill (2008) and I (Lynch, 2007) have further questioned the sexual agency of the women and girls who have been swept up into this all-consuming cultural phenomenon. Gail Dines (2010) and Pamela Paul (2005) have examined the prevalence, economic power and breadth, and impact of the porn industry on both consumers of pornography and their sexual partners, with Dines's book title literally arguing that "porn has hijacked our sexuality." Masculinity scholars Jackson Katz (2006) and Michael Kimmel (2008) have examined the impact of pornography on the cultural construction of masculinity, with Katz paying particular attention to its contribution to violence against women.

The focus of this book is on exploring how porn chic became the millennium style for young women, and many girls, and what this trend means in terms of the cultural transformation of sexuality and normative gender constructions for both men and women. Of particular focus will be the role of the male gaze, particularly those aspects of men's culture steeped in misogyny, in scripting expressions of female sexuality. Gill (2008, p. 42) documents the turn-of-the-century shift that has occurred in the presentation of the female sexual body in popular culture, from the late twentieth-century "passive, mute objects of male gaze" to the "actively desiring sexual subjects" of the new millennium. The question that follows is who is creating the story, and does this apparently empowering guise of female sexuality cover up escalated levels of misogyny and related white heterosexual privilege? Or, in rebuttal, do these changes constitute a move forward for women, giving them permission to express their own sexual needs and desires? In particular, the following chapters investigate the intersection of fashion and porn chic, exploring trend-based and marketed cultural constructions of gender presented in this shifting cultural landscape.

Definitions and Key Theoretical Contributions

The working definition of *porn chic* in this book includes fashions and related trend-based behaviors linked to the porn industry that have now become mainstreamed into the dress of women and girls, particularly within the United States and the United Kingdom. Similarly, the term *raunch eroticism* is used throughout the book to reference sexuality as it is constructed within the porn industry and then played out in popular culture and the mass media. Both terms are tinged with the forbidden, thus carrying the added caveat that the so-labeled behavior or look carries some degree of stigma due to its link to pornography.

The working definition of sexual agency used throughout the book is drawn from the scholarship of Marilyn Corsianos. Corsianos (2007) stipulates that expression of sexual agency requires that an individual be prepared and have the ability to evaluate sexual choices. This would include defining one's own sexual identity. It would also include making one's own choices in terms of sexual acts clear of coercion, conformity to external social norms, or force. The term *sexual objectification* is rooted in Karl Marx's theory of alienation. Within this book it refers to the process whereby a young girl learns to view her body as a separate object of the male gaze and desire. Sexual objectification also refers to the process by which men are socialized through the media and peer culture to see and treat women and girls as disposable objects. In contrast, *sexual subjectification* (sometimes referred to by scholars as *self-objectification*) refers to the more recent popular culture trend in which women and girls participate in their own objectification, experiencing a limited degree of empowerment based on their heightened ability to attract the male gaze and desire.

Theoretical Arguments

The question as to whether porn chic expresses a movement forward in terms of women's control over their bodies and sexual behaviors, or whether it reinforces in an even stronger way the power of the male gaze to direct the popular culture sexual script, is situated in a complex web of attitudes linked to the history of the women's movement and coupled in many cases with theoretical arguments. Most frequently, the argument has been oversimplified to a showdown between anti- and pro-pornography feminists. In reality the debate is both more complicated and more interesting than that. For the sake of clarity I have divided the multiple voices contributing to this discussion into three theoretical camps: (1) feminist scholarship focused on sexual objectification of women by self and others, as linked to self-policing behaviors; (2) sexy dress/behavior as empowerment; and (3) scholarship holding that gender is a continually constituted performance, wherein existing power structures are continually reified and at times challenged and transformed.

Sexual Objectification by Self and Others

Marxist feminists have used the theory of alienation to argue that sexual objectification of women's bodies alienates women from their own sexuality, in a similar sense as workers, according to Marx, are alienated from their own humanity through capitalist production methods. Sandra Bartky (1990), using the seminal work of Simone de Beauvoir, articulated the process of objectification, charting the separation of a young girl from her own body at adolescence, a time period when she learns to step out of herself and begins to see her body as a separate object of the male gaze and desire. Feminine narcissism, the pampering of the physical body resulting in pleasure linked to seeing oneself as a reflection of the male gaze, becomes, according to Bartky, a form of "repressed satisfaction" (1990, p. 42). This repressed satisfaction is what pulls women and girls into media beauty culture, a popular culture zone that gives women and girls pleasure as they use dress and other beauty methods to better prepare themselves for the male gaze and desire.

Bartky's arguments are supported by Joni Johnston, who cites the socialization of women as a problem in the construction of a healthy sexual identity: "As she learns to view her body as an object to be viewed, adorned, controlled, and changed, a dichotomy develops between her mind and her body. As she is surveyed, she learns to survey everything she does and everything she is because how she appears to others is culturally linked to what is thought to be success in her life. Her own sense of self is supplanted by a sense of being viewed, evaluated, and appreciated as herself by another" (1997, p. 67). In terms of the direct impact of this socialization and sexual objectification, Johnston goes on later to state: "She learns to 'be desired' is much more important than to 'feel desire.'" As one of her patients succinctly stated,

"'I never knew if I wanted men or not, but I sure knew that I wanted them to want me'" (1997, p. 71). Barbara Fredrickson and Tomi-Ann Roberts (1997) and Rachel Calogero (2004) used what they label *objectification theory* to argue that women self-objectify, imagining themselves as they will be seen by men, and in the process compromise their own lives and sexuality.

With a goal of understanding invisible patterns of domination, a substantial thread of Foucauldian feminism informs this approach. The focus then becomes probing women's adherence to an invisible set of rules enacted on the microlevel, creating through a related series of incremental steps a pattern of domination. Using Michel Foucault's idea that existing power structures are maintained by individuals' willing compliance with a normative set of expectations, Bartky (1990) argues that the beautifying process, although superficially pleasurable and a key part of female culture, in the end locks women more tightly into a patriarchal system as women focus their attention and energy on preparing themselves to be objects of the male gaze and desire. Catharine MacKinnon not only argues that provocative dress is locked to a patriarchal model, and therefore cannot be used to express sexual agency, but goes on to question the very existence of true female sexuality: "A woman is a being who identifies and is identified as one whose sexuality exists for someone else, who is socially male. Women's sexuality is the capacity to arouse desire in that someone. If what is sexual about a woman is what the male point of view requires for excitement, have male requirements so usurped its terms as to have become them? Considering women's sexuality in this way forces confrontation with whether there is any such thing" (1982, p. 515).

Alinor Sterling, also influenced by Foucault as well as by Susan Bordo (1991) and Frigga Haug (1987), questioned whether women are free to exercise choice within an imposed patriarchal system of modesty and sexual objectification. Bordo and Haug, in the words of Sterling,

> lean toward the position that a complex and all-encompassing system of norms leaves no room for agency. The modesty and objectifying imperatives are patriarchal rules. To the extent that women choose, they choose among rules. The tension that results involves women in a balancing act that constrains their ability to rebel. A foray into rebellion deviates from the modesty norms and thereby approaches objectification; a woman who is totally objectified risks losing her economic stability, social status, and physical safety. A violation of modesty norms both exposes a woman to the dangers of being objectified and foils her rebellion. (1995, p. 102)

Thus Sterling argues that that both modesty and sexual objectification express semiotic sexual meaning related to a system of domination based on the male gaze: "The dynamic between modesty and objectification, like the dynamic between clothing and nudity, is a relationship of covering and uncovering. Modesty describes sexuality by concealing it; objectification describes sexuality by exposing it" (1995,

p. 100). Both modest and provocative versions of female appearance, according to Sterling, are locked into a male-constructed gendered gaze, with women socialized to confine their enacted appearances to fit male-shaped reality.

Following this line of argument into more contemporary scholarship focused on female self-objectification, a substantial body of feminist scholars still question the agency of these apparently sexually empowered flesh-and-blood women and mass media icons. Included in this body of research is my own fieldwork on *GGW* flashing on American college campuses. My fieldwork and interviews with both male audience members and female flashers indicated that the *GGW* show in the street was experienced as a male-driven event, with women playing the sexually objectified roles assigned by the male audience, with little agency given to women to experiment with or express their own sexuality. Similarly, Corsianos questions the seemingly sexually experimental and liberated trend toward self-defined straight women crossing over into same-sex relationships. Is this, she asks, just another mode of satisfying the heterosexual male desire to see girl-on-girl sex, quoting some of her female students who say they do it because "the guys get a kick out of it" (2007, p. 866)?

Sexy Dress as Empowerment

Duncan Kennedy challenges the writing off of all female sexual empowerment, as argued by the preceding scholars, in his discussion of what he refers to as "sexy dress subculture," a culture within which women's sexuality is celebrated through defiant and blatantly sexual dress styles, an experimentation that he argues results in agency and in transformation of gender: "Why dismiss the vast amount of energy, imagination, and work that women put into the constant evolution of the repertoire of dress? This happens at the microlevel, where there are an indefinite number of possible combinations of clothes and body, with distinguishable finely graded meanings in the language of sex. Women produce themselves as gendered artifacts using this vast repertoire—indeed they produce gender itself" (1993, p. 169). Similarly, Linda Scott has interpreted power and agency in beauty and sexy dress culture. In discussing cosmetic culture she argues that "advertisements call up competing ideas of beauty for readers to consider and negotiate" (1993, p. 132). Elizabeth Wilson, also a proponent of this stance that appearance can be subversive, stresses that women "create individual identities by putting together [their] own self-representations" and further that "mainstream fashion...continuously changes its own definitions of masculinity and femininity and plays with gender all the time" (1990, p. 69). Molly Hite, in analyzing Madonna's enactment of flamboyant female desire, argues that the performance is subversive and turns the passive object of desire into "a producer of meanings" (1988, pp. 121–122).

In a more radical and less theoretical vein, self-labeled "do-me" and "prosex" feminists such as Debbie Stollar have directly linked assertive and experimental sexuality with feminism. Rebecca Munford uses the following quote from Stollar (1999) to illustrate the attitude and stance of the new girl "do-me" feminist: "Call us do-me feminists, call us prosex feminists, just don't call us late for the sale at Good Vibrations. In our quest for total sexual satisfaction we shall leave no sex toy unturned and no sexual avenue unexplored. Women are trying their hands (and other body parts) at everything from phone sex to cyber sex, solo sex to group sex, heterosex to homosex. Lusty feminists of the third wave, we're more than ready to drag-race down sexual roads less traveled. Ladies, start your engine" (quoted in Munford, 2009, p. 183). The central message of many "do-me" feminists is that femininity/sexuality is not in conflict with feminism and that being a "girlie feminist" is the true act of power and agency. This faction of the feminist movement often self-consciously poses itself in conflict with older second-wave feminists, who they charge have thrown away the pleasure and fun of being a girl through moralistic posturing in regard to pornography and sexual objectification. The SlutWalk movement discussed in chapter 10 is embedded within the guise of this version of feminism.

Gender as Performance and Transformation

Feminists using the later work of Foucault focusing on identity and resistance distance themselves from the idea that women are fatally locked into conformity to norms and behaviors supporting patriarchy and the primacy of the male gaze. Scholars working out of this theoretical framework view power as productive, with women's as well as men's identities in flux, formulated over and over again in local social contexts through the exercise of power. Jana Sawicki and others argue that we "become" by virtue of interacting within "a hierarchal context of power relations at the micro level of society" (Sawicki, 1991, p. 8). Social and personal relationships become political within the philosophy of Foucault (1980), as power is viewed as decentralized, with larger structures of domination fed by individual actions within unique microenvironments. The multidimensional and pluralistic nature of power as articulated by Foucault and argued by Sawicki (1991) leaves open possibilities for liberation as well as domination within a given social context.

Judith Butler has been influential in her argument that gender is a performance and that "just as a script may be enacted in various ways . . . so the gendered body acts its part in a culturally restricted corporeal space and enacts interpretations within the confines of already existing directives" (2004, p. 161). Certainly by and large what occurs in the daily performance of gender is reproduction of the social laws, but there is also the possibility for transgression. At the same time as Butler argues that "as a corporeal field of cultural play, gender is a basically innovative affair," she further stipulates that "there are strict punishments for contesting the script by performing out of turn or through unwarranted improvisations" (p. 164). Thus, while transformation is possible, it is not easy.

Point of Departure: Transformation Is Possible

My research among Hmong American and African American teenagers (Lynch, 1999a) provides evidence that dress and appearance can be used within ritual contacts to subvert dominating scripts and norms and contribute to the cultural transformation of gender identity. For Hmong American teenagers, traditional styles of dress worn to an annual New Year's ethnic festival became a means to express changing gender scripts and norms as teenagers balanced traditional Hmong gender identities with new American norms. For African American teenage girls, the annual debutante ball became a vehicle to present a positive image of African American female identity to the community, an identity in opposition to the negative stereotypes of black women that haunt American history and popular culture. Similarly, young African American men (Lynch, 1999a, 2009) found a means of positively expressing an alternative black masculinity posed in direct response to white hegemonic masculinity through performances of gender at the annual Beautillion Ball.

Fashion, while typically a force reinforcing social norms, can function subversively. The impact of subversive fashion is limited, however, with either a light level of adoption in a marginalized population or the transformation of the subversive into the mainstream by the fashion system. Once an antifashion look becomes widely adopted, it tends to modify itself to fit within the social norms. Thus, antifashion looks that defy normative social regulations begin as subversive trends, are noticed by the fashion industry, and are appropriated into marketed styles that conform to underlying social regulations supporting the existing power system. For example, Ellen Riordan's (2001) analysis of Riot Grrrls, the young feminist movement emanating out of the West Coast girl music culture of the 1990s, traced the transformative power of the early movement to its eventual commodification in the form of the Spice Girls. Riordan argued that while the early movement based in punk girl bands "inspired a lot of young women to produce subversive culture," the later manifestation as enacted by the Spice Girls diluted and changed the original subversive meaning of the movement to fit existing patriarchal patterns:

> Embedded in the Spice Girls' theme of girl power are conflicting messages about what empowerment means for girls. For the Spice Girls, scantily dressed, full-on makeup, and a lot of body adornments, the apparent message was that empowerment came in the way one dresses, looks, and uses her sexuality for a heterosexual male gaze to get what she wants.... Although their song lyrics and interviews paid lip service to girls' taking charge and engendering change, their images contradicted this, suggesting similar patterns of women's oppression: the only way for girls to achieve power is by using one's sexuality and looks. (Riordan, 2001, p. 290)

In light of these contrasting theoretical arguments, one of the points of narrative emphasis within each chapter is to examine Foucault's assertion that systems such as patriarchy continue to be powerful because most of us subconsciously follow social rules supporting the existing power structure. It takes great effort to question and then to find a stress fracture within the status quo, so most dress to fit within the system and, by so doing, support the existing power structure. Posed in opposition to this is the idea that appearance can be subversive, that dress allows us the power to continually recreate ourselves and our gender identities. The question then becomes whether the women enacting raunch erotic ideals are conforming to unwritten but strongly communicated rules serving the male gaze or demonstrating their own sexual agency in the creation of newly liberated sexual ideals.

The power of the male gaze to determine the path and form of raunch erotic cultural expressions and products places an understanding of porn chic within the world of men and boys at a central position in this discourse. The millennium emergence of a heavily marketed and widely endorsed "bad boy" popular culture ideal is built on a foundation of misogyny and sexual objectification of women dating back to the post–World War II decade in the United States and Britain. This juxtaposition sets out a path of analysis focused on disentangling apparent expressions of empowered female sexuality that are actually created to serve the male gaze and desire from authentic expressions of girls' and women's sexual agency. As a foundation, chapter 2 provides an overview of the emergence of a broadly accepted bad boy ideal in both the United States and Britain that set the stage for the development of the raunch erotic female ideal.

Figure 1.1 *Look at Me.* Courtesy of Nicola Bockelmann.

Chapters 3 through 8 are explorations of different cultural manifestations of raunch eroticism as expressed as a form of popular culture. Seven key points of inquiry are used at the end of each of these chapters to systematically analyze the contours of raunch eroticism explored by each topic area. The seven points of inquiry listed in the following can perhaps be most easily understood as potential traps signaling the likelihood of underlying patriarchal control and providing evidence that the seemingly empowered dress and behavior discussed in the chapter are in fact a well-put-together and -marketed guise, a cover-up for conformance to a minimized and often sexually objectified position for women and girls in the social order. Chapters 9 and 10 are explorations of attempts by designers, artists, musicians, performers, and, finally, social justice activists to construct identities, performances, artworks, apparel designs, and social movements that challenge us to think reflectively about the impact of porn chic on us and those who surround us.

Exploring the Contours of Raunch Eroticism

Focus on the White Heterosexual Male Gaze

A theme underlying many of the case studies that make up this volume is the dominance of and blind adherence to the white male heterosexual worldview as normative. The narrow band of acceptable female sexuality evident in mass media imagery and advertising is directed by a very particular male view, that of a white heterosexual male. Most obviously excluded are members of the homosexual community, with special scorn directed toward gay men. Girl-on-girl sex is a core element of raunch eroticism, but always depicted in the service of male desire, and typically shown in combination with a dominating male. The use of humor and, increasingly, violence to exclude women who do not conform to the narrow band of acceptable female sexuality is a common mode of policing the boundary separating "sexy" women from all the rest.

Sexual Objectification of Women

Research on male sexuality supports the gender differences in how sexuality is experienced. Bruce Ellis and Donald Symons found that "men are more likely to view *others* as the objects of their sexual desires, whereas women are more likely to view *themselves* as the objects of sexual desire" (1990, p. 529). The fundamental tie between the cultural construction of masculinity and sexual objectification has been identified by multiple researchers. Gary Brooks (1997) and Jack Litewka (1974) identified primary elements of male sexuality including sexual objectification of women, voyeurism, and a tendency toward fixation on certain portions of female anatomy, including the breasts.

Self-Objectification (Sexual Subjectification)

This analysis focuses on the role of women and girls in their own sexual objectification. A central underlying question is who is scripting the performance. Are the women and girls themselves creating versions of their own sexuality, or are they performing or adorning themselves to even more successfully compete for the male gaze and desire?

Sexual Attention and Sexualized Practice as Power

This stage of the analysis attempts to parse out the degree of female sexual agency being expressed within the case study examples. Using Corsianos's (2007) definition of sexual agency, the question will be asked, are the women participating within the case studies standing clear enough from the cultural pressures that encourage them to use their sexuality to attract the male gaze that they can make their own sexual choices and create identities and performances celebrating and exploring their own sexuality? Central to the analysis of each case study chapter will be a discussion of the cultural meaning of the presentation of sexual attention and sexualized behavior as a form of power within the case study. A key debate will be whether the display of sexual power explored in the chapter example further oppresses or in some sense allows the expression of the sexual agency of the female performers.

Private Is Public

The ability of all of us to broadcast intimate details of our lives causes the blending of what used to be the separate spheres of our public and private lives. While the greatest impact is on those actively participating in online networking sites such as Facebook, the impact is broadened to include those who either willingly or unwillingly are brought into this world through the postings of others. Working in tandem with the trends toward self-objectification and presentation of sexual behavior and sexual assertiveness as power, websites have become a means for women to self-project cyber-identities focused on sexual power. Each chapter includes a section focused on the impact of online imaging and dialogue on the case study, with a particular focus on the disappearing private world and the disappearing boundary between our public and our private selves.

Extreme, Up the Ante

The immense demand placed on our attention has resulted in an upping of the ante in terms of the scale and audacity of all cultural products in the hopes of being noticed by a targeted audience. The ante is upped not only through the multiple media modes of delivery—television, Internet, social networking sites, electronic billboards—but also by a glut of offerings of stimulating product, much of it available for free or close to free on the Internet. Dines's (2010) analysis of the porn industry points out that the result is an intensely competitive hard-core porn market characterized by increasing levels of violence and misogyny being used to move product. This theme plays out in a range of ways throughout the chapters of the book, from some popular culture icons' multiple breast-enhancement surgeries, to competing "raunch postings" on Facebook by college coeds, to male bad boy behavior, taken to extremes and validated by other male peers and the consumer marketplace.

Misogyny

The cultural landscape surrounding sexuality has been dramatically changed as a result of the invention and broad adoption of Internet technology by all sectors of the consumer market in the United States and Britain. The average age of exposure to Internet porn is 11.5 years for boys in the United States, and the content and message of the imagery are dramatically different from what their fathers experienced. Their fathers, growing up in the era of *Playboy* and *Penthouse*, were exposed to sexually objectified pictures of naked women. Certainly it could be argued that the pictures taught boys that women "existed to be looked at, objectified, used and put away until the next time," in the words of Dines (2010, p. xvii). In contrast, the images of degraded and violently assaulted women that are now being disseminated by the porn industry and used as a masturbation tool by young men teach a much more disturbing message relating sexual arousal to violence against women. A cultural tolerance for these blatant expressions of misogyny, particularly when cloaked within a humoristic exchange, has accompanied the porn chic trend.

Related to the imagery of women being degraded and violently victimized that is now a central component of the hard-core market is the use of plastic surgery to enhance the bodies of performers. For example, a comparison of centerfolds of the 1950s to millennium centerfolds reveals a dramatic change in breast size and shape. The resulting sexual imagery being viewed by boys and men shows artificially enhanced bodies of women being violently assaulted, sometimes by multiple men and often in multiple orifices (anal and vaginal penetration simultaneously), ending with ejaculation on the face, particularly the eyes of the female performer. While certainly the chapter devoted to bad boy behaviors as normative and celebrated focuses on this theme, other case study examples are also investigated in terms of hidden or cloaked misogyny as an underlying theme. A particular focus is the intersection of violence against women and porn chic, sometimes cloaked in humor and sometimes more blatantly and unapologetically articulated.

–2–

From James Bond to Tucker Max:
The Development of the Millennium
Unapologetic Bad Boy Pop Culture Icon

Fall is here, and campuses and surrounding communities are brimming with T-shirted college students lined up to eat, buy books, and move into dormitories. I am with my family on a last bike ride of summer, stopping in a favorite taco bar for lunch in the middle of the ride. Standing at the front of the line is a nice-looking young man out to eat with a group of friends, all gearing up for the start of the fall semester at the local college. Stamped on the back of this young man's T-shirt is the slogan "YOU LOOK LIKE I NEED ANOTHER DRINK," the now-popular slogan used to refer to the practice of putting on your beer goggles to have sex with women that you are too ashamed to have sex with sober. The question posed by this book in the most general sense is how a nice-looking young man in a small college town ends up out for a lunch in a family-friendly taco bar wearing a blatantly misogynistic shirt, without feelings of self-consciousness or shame.

A quick Google search on the phrase "You look like I need another drink" is revealing. The expression is linked to a particular popular song and has a devoted Facebook page with 65,312 members; I can buy the exact shirt worn by the young man for $9.99 online. Perhaps more disturbing is a website hot-linked to the Facebook website featuring a popular "You look like I need another drink" wine bottle hang-tag marketed toward women to be used for parties and weddings. The obvious social acceptance of this young man and his shirt in a small rural college milieu thus rests on a strong cultural foundation of social norms that are rooted in a widely disseminated media culture affecting not only men but also women and girls.

The headlines in the United Kingdom tell a similar story. In a story titled "Dirty Young Men" Janice Turner (2005) begins her commentary by underscoring the rising rates of normalized misogyny: "Pornographic poses, the going rate for sex, jokes about 'stupid tarts': the misogyny of the new breed of lads' mags is breathtaking." The article includes a description of a form found in a mainstream lad magazine that provides the reader with a method of calculating what the writer refers to as "pay for lay," with the writer dividing his number of shags per month by the average cost of a date. Male readership is also invited to participate in a "breast quest" by sending in pictures of their girlfriends' bodies to be rated by the rest of the magazine's readers.

The issue is at the top of the agenda in October 2011 when I travel to Washington, D.C., with the president of my institution and the director of our system's board of regents to attend a higher education summit on campus safety sponsored by the Department of Justice. Seated between these two powerful but relatively conventional men, I watch their expressions as Diane Rosenfeld, an expert on legal policy on violence against women, leads them through a PowerPoint listing the year's best examples of college misogyny. The year 2010–2011 was a particularly damaging one for Yale, where fraternity pledges were caught on a viral YouTube video chanting "No means yes, yes means anal!" outside dorms housing first-year female students.

Not close behind Yale in terms of public outcry, and also discussed by Rosenfeld (2011), was the widely publicized "Gullet Report" published by a fraternity from the University of Southern California. Again reinforcing nonconsensual sex (rape) as normative, the young male scribe refers to women as targets with "pies" and "gullets" to be penetrated, rated, and advertised to other bros. For those uninitiated in bro lingo, including, I might add, my university president, I have provided the blog writers' definitions of *target*, *pie*, and *gullet* here:

> I will refer to females as "targets". They aren't actual people like us men. Consequently, giving them a certain name or distinction is pointless.

> Pie: A target's vagina. Some of you may have heard phrases such as twat, cooter, muff, snatch, poontang, cock pocket, DNA dumpster, fun hatch, cock sock, the fish flap, spunkpot, whisker biscuit, or the rarely used, wizard's sleeve. All these terms are interchangeable and fine to use. However, for the use of this memo, I will refer to the target's vagina as pie.

> Gullet: Usually refers to a target's mouth and throat. Most often pertains to a target's throat capacity and its' ability to gobble cock. If a target is known to have a good gullet, it can deep-throat dick extremely well. My advice is to seek this target early in the night. Good Gullet Girls (GGG) are always scooped up well before last call.

To state again, the question must be asked: How did I end up in a room full of mostly male university presidents listening to Department of Justice–funded campus highlights of a season of misogyny committed by seemingly normal-looking young male students across the country? Worthy of note, these are acts of *public misogyny*. The bad boy stories recounted to the presidents were not the shenanigans of nasty boys hiding behind closed doors at not particularly well-regarded or well-funded institutions of higher education. Instead, the presidents were confronted with viral YouTube postings of male students from in some cases elite Ivy League institutions. These sons of privilege were marching in full view and chanting very loud words they would not write home to their mothers, their sisters, or their hometown girlfriends. Much to the chagrin of university presidents these front-page stories are talked about by everyone from the parents of a first-year female honor student to the mayor of the local community that borders the campus. The bad boys are out of the closet. How indeed did we get here?

Beginnings and Background: Exploring Millennium Masculinity

The examples of raunch eroticism that make up the next six chapters of this book are by and large performances for straight white males, with everyone else playing supporting roles—including men of color, gays, women, and girls. The outing of a roommate's sexual encounter with his male partner using webcam technology, discussed in chapter 8, is a vicious mode of policing male sexuality, keeping it between the lines defined by mainstream masculinity. The tween fashions created for younger and younger audiences of girls, described in chapter 4, are providing the duds for a commercially driven curtain call for a performance on the stage of male gaze and desire. Even hip-hop music, as talked about later in this chapter, is written to appeal most to a white male audience, with women treated like hos and blacks stereotyped as pimps and gangsters (Hurt, 2006). The proliferation of Internet pornography sites and the dissemination of related cultural products, which are the focus of chapter 6, are driven by a male white consumer who is getting younger and younger every day. Hooters Girls, Playboy Bunnies (see chapter 7), and *Girls Gone Wild* coeds (see chapter 5) are all servicing an entitled stable of guys who feel as if it is pretty damn normal to be at the center of the sexuality circus that is the world of porn chic. If

Figure 2.1 *Decadence.* Courtesy of Nicola Bockelmann.

you have any doubts that patriarchy defined by white male privilege is still alive and kicking, check out how sexuality is expressed and defined in American and British popular culture.

But as clear as it is that this book is about white male privilege and power, and the role of that privilege in constructing the popular culture that both surrounds and formulates our identities, a second major focus of this book is the reinterpretation of female empowerment as an expression of female sexuality by third-wave feminists and marketing teams targeting young female consumers. The emergence of what I refer to in chapter 3 as the sexy empowerment icon in American and British popular culture is posed in stylistic contrast to the stereotypical appearance styles associated with first-wave feminism in the 1960s and 1970s. The path to the porn chic circus we all now call home must be traveled by two routes, one leading from the moral public face of masculinity in the early 1950s, with its tightly controlled white button-down shirt and tie, to the emergence of the unapologetic bad boy of the millennium, and the other leading from the earth mother and radical feminism of my youth to the girlie-girl, prosex, vibrator-party culture of third-wave feminism. We start our journey by constructing the path to the male gaze that now holds so much of our popular culture in its grasp, the road to the cultural icon I refer to as the unapologetic bad boy, beginning first in the elegant digs of the international playboy icon of the post–World War II era.

Cultural Construction of the International Playboy Icon

The glorification of the man who is able to bed legions of beautiful women, and the idealization of the player who lands a continual stream of one-night stands, has to be traced back to Hugh Hefner and Ian Fleming and their creation of the quintessential ever-so-glamorous international playboy icon. This sexually adventurous male icon emerged simultaneously in American and British popular culture with the 1953 publication of the first *Playboy Magazine* and the 1952 publication of the first James Bond novel, *Casino Royale*. In stark contrast to the dominant moral tenor of the 1950s, which espoused a conservative family-based breadwinner role for men, Hefner's and Fleming's international playboy icon became branded almost overnight as the ideal role model for how a sophisticated man of the world navigates his way through romantic entanglements.

Using different literary genres, a monthly magazine and a series of novels soon moved to film, Hefner and Fleming both brought to life the latent fantasies of their 1950s male readership, drawing heavily on their own experiences. The two men came from markedly different family backgrounds. Fleming was the wayward youngest son of a revered war hero and Member of Parliament, and Hefner was the oldest son of a middle-class conservative Christian family. However, both men by their own self-reports grew up in sexually repressive households, with well-defined and narrow views of the proper male role within the family and the community. Fleming's father died a war hero when he was still a young boy. He grew up in the shadow of his father, a man remembered for his service contributions and moral rectitude, and that of his older brother, who, due to inherit both the Fleming fortune and the role of the proper patriarch, had excelled at Eton and Oxford. Hefner was the son of two Middle America schoolteachers with conservative outlooks on the world. Interviews of Hefner captured on film (Berman, 2010; Playbook Productions, 1992) describe a repressive middle-class childhood, including little physical affection from his parents and a strong socialization toward acceptance of the conventional definitions of male success in the 1950s—having a family, holding down a job, and being monogamous.

As young men both Hefner and Fleming experienced strong peer support for early manifestations of what would develop into the cool, debonair attitude of the international playboy icon. Fleming's school years in England were characterized by athletic success; however, it was not until a few years later, when he was enrolled in European private schools, that he really developed a personal style later known as the distinct "Fleming flair" and became recognized by his peers for his cool wit and easy ways with women. Hefner's biography also includes schoolyard accolades related to his early forays into producing comic books and publications and creating a magical social world around himself centered on creative performances, writing, and social interaction.

A second parallel in the lives of the two men was the rejection of predictable, stable work and home life at the stage when many of their peers were settling into careers and establishing families. Fleming accepted a banking position in his late twenties to ensure some degree of financial stability and freedom. During this period he continued to build his reputation as a connoisseur of fine living by hosting dinner parties for an exclusive circle, accompanied by a string of romantic entanglements not resulting in marriage. In contrast, Hefner, following the middle-class American script of the time, married and had children in his twenties, holding down a job with *Esquire*. Both men worked their way out of conventional definitions of manhood in their early thirties. Hefner ventured out of a traditional means of making a livelihood—working for someone else—and went out on his own to create *Playboy Magazine*. This was followed closely by his decision to go back to the bachelor life, resulting in a divorce from his first wife. Fleming rebelled by moving from his staid position in the banking industry to the British Naval Intelligence and delaying marriage until his late forties, and then marrying only due to pressure from his married mistress, who was carrying his child.

For both men the experiences of the next few years provided the defining characteristics of what would become the international playboy icon. Both men, in different parts of the world and in slightly different time periods, sought and indulged in the best wine, music, and food in the company of cultivated and educated men of the era. Fleming traveled with and worked for Admiral John Godfrey, a well-regarded and top-ranking British intelligence officer. During these formative years the future creator of the character of James Bond became well known internationally for his distinct Fleming flair in how he conducted his life and how he wrote his intelligence reports. Hefner courted and successfully recruited the most highly regarded writers and cartoonists for his new magazine, with many having well-established ties with time-honored national magazines such as the *New Yorker.* Both men also became well known as serial womanizers with style, connoisseurs of the opposite sex with extremely good track records of landing the babe.

Both men's lifestyle fantasies culminated in the literal creation of a fantasy world, an elegant hideaway governed by the needs and desires of the emerging international playboy icon. Fleming designed and constructed "Goldeneye," a tropical hideaway on the north coast of Jamaica that became a gathering spot for the worldly and connected male traveler. The intensive interviews included in Brigette Berman's (2010) film captured the late-night discussions among Hefner and his entertainment-industry friends that gave rise to the now-famous 1959 Chicago Stadium jazz festival and later the related creation of the first Playboy Club in downtown Chicago in 1960. Hefner's model of the modern urban male was suave, cultured, and a connoisseur of gourmet food, jazz, good writing, and beautiful women. In contrast to the working father of 1950s sitcoms, steadfastly loyal to his wife and family, this new international playboy icon was surrounded by a fabricated world that fed his sensual fantasies—from a mixed drink, to a saxophone solo, to a room full of beautiful women. Clubs opened not only in American cities but also in London and Paris.

The formal relationship between *Playboy Magazine* and Ian Fleming and his character James Bond opened with the publication of "The Hildebrand Rarity" in the March 1960 issue. This was followed by "The Property of a Lady" in 1964 and a serialized version of "Octopussy" in 1966. As the Bond films came out, *Playboy* was used as a style prop, with James Bond caught on film reading the February 1969 issue in the movie *On Her Majesty's Secret Service.* The culminating issue that firmly cemented the dual role of *Playboy* and James Bond in the creation of the international playboy icon was published in November 1965 and featured an interview with Sean Connery (the ultimate Bond) and a smorgasbord collection of Bond's girls, including Beth Hyatt on the cover.

The essential components of the international playboy icon were enmeshed in both the lifestyles and the creative output of Fleming and Hefner. All components of the icon in some way speak to the feelings of entrapment experienced by many men in the 1950s. In the post–World War II era many men returned home from abroad to small, insular communities after having lived wider lives as servicemen in Europe. They also returned home to full-time, in many cases monotonous employment followed by trips home in the car to their wives and children. Hefner's magazine and Fleming's books were widely popular with these men. The fantasy lives that both Hefner and Fleming created functioned to move these men out of their narrow communities and back into the wider world they experienced as servicemen. In terms of lifestyle, both men successfully transformed the drudgery of daily work into an exciting script, with Fleming living the life of a real James Bond and Hefner shooting photographs of female nudes and then, at least as fantasized by the readership, taking them off to bed. Finally, they presented a fantasy life of serial sexual relationships for men bound within conventional marriages.

At the same time that fathers were being affected by the fantasy worlds created by Fleming and Hefner, their baby boomer sons were having their sexuality sparked by the first easily accessible publications containing female nudes. "Regular dads" had *Playboys* stashed in their bottom drawers and out in the workbench in the garage, and their sons easily found and shared the publications with their friends. The James Bond films hit the screens just as these young men were coming of age, setting in place the transfer of this icon to the next generation of young men. It is this generation that formed the bridge between the fantasy world of the post–World War II veterans and the young men now affected by the millennium version of the international playboy icon, the unapologetic bad boy.

Key elements of this more elegant post–World War II male ideal are foundational to the later development of the more damaging unapologetic bad boy icon now operating full steam in the first decades of the millennium. First, and perhaps most formative, is the cultural norming of sexual objectification of the female body in both *Playboy* and the scripts of Fleming's James Bond novels. While certainly the focus on key sexually stimulating parts of the female nude body such as the breast or upper leg was not introduced by *Playboy* or the Bond films, together they moved this behavior into what was considered normal and acceptable within British and American popular culture. In addition, sexual attributes were presented as largely the full measure of the female character either posing for the magazine, working in the Playboy Club, or appearing on-screen in a James Bond film. A standard *Playboy* magazine in the 1950s included fiction, political writing, cartoons, and a centerfold. The fiction was there because it was written by a good writer, the cartoons were there because they were drawn by a well-regarded artist, the political commentary was there because it was insightful, and the centerfold was there because she had a rack, nice legs, and an inviting smile. The confining of females' assigned identity to sexual characteristics was perhaps most cleverly expressed by Fleming in the naming of Goldfinger's personal pilot, "Pussy Galore."

The second problematic aspect of this postwar male icon that made its way into the millennium is the transformation of serial uncommitted sexual encounters by men into a culturally accepted and idealized glamorous pursuit. The video footage of Hefner and other notable men in the Playboy Club and Mansion painted a cooler-than-cool picture of the man who is able to move from one uncommitted sexual encounter to the next at will, with no repercussions and no ill feelings on the part of any participants. Similarly, Bond moves through each film bedding female character after female character, with a few becoming victims of the evil forces but never of

Bond himself. The systematic nature of serial seduction as practiced by Fleming is noted by Hugo Williams (2002) in an article in the *Times Literary Supplement*:

> Ian Fleming had a tried-and-tested seduction ritual, we were told on a recent Channel Four documentary, *The Real James Bond.* He would ask girls round to his London house and serve them sausages in front of the fire. Pornography and nude playing-cards were also on the menu, as was a little light sadism. He was very good-looking and always dressed the same: dark-blue suit, bow-tie, short-sleeved light-blue shirt and loafers for speedy undressing. "All he had to do was press a button for whichever girl he wanted," said a friend.

The cultural acceptance of the male player, the man who can get any woman he wants at the drop of a hat, transmuted into a more manipulative and aggressive icon as these foundational elements were reworked in the rawer playing field at the end of the twentieth century.

Turn of the Century: The Entrance of the Unapologetic Bad Boy Icon

In 1974 *Hustler*, a rival, more sexually explicit men's magazine, made it onto the racks in the United States. The magazine's publisher, Larry Flynt, was a strip club owner expanding his empire to include publishing. Featuring not only more explicit photographs of women, *Hustler* also published some of the first blatantly misogynistic cartoons and features, including a monthly serial following the escapades of a pedophile named "Chester the Molester." With the publication and popularity of *Hustler*, sexuality spiced with high levels of misogynistic flavor makes its entrance into mass-marketed popular culture directed toward men and boys. *Hustler* magazine's full vulva shots, scratch-and-sniff centerfolds, and transgressions into child molestation upped the ante in terms of how women were being asked to perform for the male gaze, setting the stage for the full-scale development of the hard-core pornography industry and, more important in terms of this analysis, the mass appeal of misogynistic and clearly unapologetic bad boys.

Howard Stern

The crystallization of the pop culture unapologetic bad boy icon happened with the entrance of Howard Stern into the entertainment industry in the 1980s, with full-blown development in the 1990s. The personality he brought to the stage, characterized by self-deprecating humor, absolute obsession with all things sexual, and bullying under the guise of humor, would become the hallmark of the bad boys that followed in his wake. Stern made his start as a so-called shock jock on radio, and he is most well known for that role; however, he is self-described as the "King of All Media." This brag is based on his real success in multiple forms of entertainment. His off-radio successes are considerable and include late-night television, two best-selling "tell-all" autobiographies of sexual exploits, and pay-per-view and home video productions, as well as a movie made from his first autobiography that grossed $41 million in theaters in the United States.

The essential ingredients of the turn-of-the-millennium unapologetic bad boy are all established by Stern and reinterpreted by the boys who follow. First and foremost, Stern presents himself as absolutely and unapologetically obsessed with sex. In his best-selling books he opens with a salacious self-confession dating back to his childhood to establish his credentials with his audience: "I'm such a sex machine I could take a piece of wood and turn it into something erotic, something sensual, something perverse. Take puppeteering, for example. When I was seven years old my mother gave me puppets and within weeks I had puppet orgies in my basement for all my friends to see. And not just people puppets. There were horses, caterpillars, and clown puppets fucking and giving head. I have never changed" (1995, p. 3).

While Stern's level of reported sexual interest is intensely high, and the range of his charted sexual experience is self-reported as vast, the purpose of all this activity is very narrowly focused on achievement of male orgasm. Where you cum and when you cum and how many seconds you cum and what made you cum are all highlighted, with the bother of attempting to bring a partner to orgasm minimized and ridiculed as beside the point and a total waste of time. This focus on male orgasm, rather than sexual intercourse and relationship, allows Stern to present himself as married and faithful. Stern's myriad of trysts with other women are not presented as "affairs" but instead sexual conquests focused exclusively on achieving orgasm. He moves from bathtubs with babes (with his briefs still on), to live broadcasts with a titillating naked accomplice, to "hot" cyber chat rooms, achieving a string of orgasms without traditional intercourse. All acts are therefore classified by Stern as "not sex," and therefore he is "not unfaithful." This effectively allows him as a so-called regular faithful married man to live the life of a philanderer, with heaps of sexual experience falling outside the bounds of propriety.

Second, Stern takes on the guise of a self-deprecating loser. According to his own self-portrait, he is just an average Joe struggling to compete with much better-hung and -built studs and stuck with a series of powerful but idiotic bosses. Similar to his fixation on sex, Stern establishes his loser stud identity very early in *Miss America*, on the opening page. The tell-all memoir opens with Stern talking about doing phone sex with his friend Bill in high school, whom he describes as "the second biggest loser in my high school next to me—especially with women" (1995, p. 3). This loser identity is further reinforced on the second page of the memoir as he describes himself and his friend Bill and how they were perceived by others at their high school: "Our rap was that if girls could only look beyond the fact that we didn't have good looks and see that we had great personalities, they would fall in love with us.

THE TRUTH OF THE MATTER WAS WE HAD REALLY BAD PERSONALITIES IN ADDITION TO OUR UGLY FACES. Even the losers called us losers. And we were" (1995, p. 4). Stern also turns his self-deprecating humor onto his body, particularly his penis, which he over and over again classifies as undersize. He also bonds with the average Joe by complaining repeatedly about his boss, in so doing distancing himself from his role as celebrity and situating himself in the same power zone as his readers. In the case of Stern his most well-publicized battle with authority was with NBC executives, who once he was hired attempted to control his broadcasts and keep them within more acceptable limits.

Despite the admission that they are far from idealized models of male appearance, unapologetic bad boys expect only the most idealized porn-style appearances from women. Women are expected to get breast implants if they don't have large enough breasts, trim their bush to a nice, neat shape (or more ideally shave it clean), and have long, thin legs that go all the way up. This standard is policed with the decades-old version of the boy-ranking-girl system performed live on Stern's television show and, as Jackson Katz (2006, p. 174) points out, in high school cafeteria lunchrooms everywhere. The big difference is that on the *Howard Stern Show* female guests volunteer to go through this degrading ritual with the bad boy host and his ready sidekicks openly ridiculing them when their bodies don't live up to the porn star ideal.

The standard scripts of the unapologetic bad boy also include the construction of women as the enemy, the group to pull one over on—the nut cases who just don't understand how cool you really are. Following close on the heels of Stern's description of himself as a loser, he establishes the core conflict driving the lives of all unapologetic bad boys: how to get girls to fuck or blow you who really don't want to—or, short of that, how to compensate for your lack of real sex with phone sex, cybersex, and a range of other methods of getting to the climax: "On the weekends we couldn't get dates, so all we did was play cards, eat pizza, smoke cigars, and talk about how fucked up all girls were because they wouldn't go out with great guys like us" (Stern, 1995, p. 4). Methods of getting unwilling women to go along with your agenda espoused by bad boy guru Stern include hiding your real loser identity using online techniques and phone sex, and using drugs and alcohol to get the job done. The fantasy fucks Stern lists in *Miss America* are all rated 1–10 by his chance of actually scoring—a 1 is an impossible quest, and a 10 is practically already a done deal. Speaking about a fantasy fuck carrying a rating of 3, he comments that he might get his way "maybe if I drugged her" (1995, p. 147). Alcohol use is over the top in bad boy literature. Typical use patterns modeled by Stern include getting drunk in order to put up with less-than-ideal female partners and getting your partners drunk in order to get your way.

As put forward by Katz (2006) in his critique of Stern, a big part of Stern's appeal is that he says out loud and in a public venue what his male audience says in small, private male domains or doesn't have the nerve to say at all. Stern voices these forbidden messages loud, on as many channels and radio stations as possible, and in crowded rooms. At least one juicy forbidden message is typically used in the opening chapter of his memoirs, just to get the testosterone up and cooking. For example, in *Miss America*, page 9 takes you to the bondage farm, where the reader gets to enjoy watching bondage tapes with Stern. "I don't know why, but watching two chicks tied up, hanging from the fucking ceiling, with their legs spread, getting whipped…really drives me crazy" (Stern, 1995, p. 9). The story gets better, Stern reports, as the female reporter writing the story about the bondage farm, who is both cute and smart (and of course has "huge tits"), is tied up, has her pussy shaved, and ends up crying hysterically. The climax of the video is when the male lead actor "puts forty fucking clothespins on each tit, takes them off, ties her tits up with a rope, unties them, then takes two wooden clapboards, squeezes her tits together, and screws them tight" (p. 11). In Stern's big bold text it states, "I LOVE THIS TAPE. I pop it in and go to work on my cock like a jackrabbit and in two seconds, I explode" (p. 11).

In bad boy literature, humor is used to excuse all objectionable behaviors. Everything is accepted, everything can be said, and misogyny is allowed to reign supreme because in the end the performance is comedy. This is what allows Stern to say the forbidden. Critical responses to Stern then become self-serious rants that are easily dismissed, particularly if they have a feminist slant and come from a bright woman or from an articulate, just man, such as Jackson Katz.

Tucker Max

Tucker Max came up through a different route than Howard Stern, creating a following among his young audience using their medium of choice, the Internet. Max first made his name known for his "just after the sexual conquest" testimonial blogs, which according to him and as reported by the *New York Times* (St. John, 2006) were attracting 60,000 visits a day, even before he became a best-selling published author and celebrity. Max's track to fame started in 2003 with the publicity surrounding his posting of the details of his hookup with a former Miss Vermont on his website. She eventually sued, raising the notoriety of the encounter and boosting Max's website visits to a level where he began to have a national presence, resulting in the first television, movie, and book offers, all of which a very arrogant young Max turned down.

Dubbed "fratire" by *New York Times* reporter Warren St. John, Max's brand of male testimonial has linkages back to Howard Stern but also has a strong contemporary lens focused on hookup culture and speaks from the point of a view of a young, unmarried male. In the end Max's ability to read the contemporary male market won him a book offer from the man who might be named the patron of fratire, Jeremie Ruby-Strauss. Speaking of this male market for offensive literature, Ruby-Strauss explains the appeal of this millennium genre: "All of this is about over-socialization, or maybe an over-feminization of the culture. I think all of these books are about men searching for a model other than what they're being told to do, something more rebellious, less cautious and less concerned with external approval" (quoted in

St. John, 2006). In St. John's review of fratire he points out that Ruby-Strauss, unlike more traditional editors, had his finger on the pulse of the young male audience who spent much of their day online. Max and other trailblazers in the fratire genre cracked into publishing through the back door, with more traditional publishers scared off by the blatantly offensive attitude of the content. The Internet was the testing ground for these writers, with editors like Ruby-Strauss recognizing the value of studying the activity on a website to predict future sales.

At the question-and-answer and book-signing event I attended, part of Max's book tour for *Assholes Finish First* (2010), the young author fulfilled the basic components of the unapologetic bad boy icon as established first by Stern. First and foremost, of course, is absolute obsession with sex. Everything is centered on "It," and "It" is the sexual act focused on male orgasm. The very first question coming from the audience was "When did you do It last?" followed quickly on the heels by "How many total women?" Max is clever; remember, he graduated from a good law school. His fast glib response was not a number but rather "I always shower in between," and "Dudes that do it as much as I do don't have to count." This young bad boy entrepreneur also established his sex cred with the young audience by talking about the "Sexual To Do List" included in his newly published book. He was quick to correct an audience member who made the mistake of insinuating that the list was what Max "intended to do" rather than a list of completed sex acts. He clearly told the audience that he had successfully completed the whole list, throwing it to the other men in attendance to top that! Testimonials included on the list include him fucking a girl with a colostomy bag, titled "The Shittiest Hook-up Ever," and the even more degrading story of him fucking an amputee.

The absolute focus on male sexual orgasm was implied throughout the question-and-answer session but is strongly stated in the book within the sex stories. For example, in "Fucked-Up Pillow Talk" he ridicules a woman who has the audacity to bring up her own orgasm as a priority (148–149):

GIRL: Why don't you last longer during sex? Ten minutes is not long enough for me.

TUCKER: I don't understand. I lasted long enough for me to cum. Why would I go any longer?

GIRL: I want to cum too. What about me?

TUCKER: Who?

GIRL: Me.

TUCKER: Who are we talking about here?

GIRL: ME!

TUCKER: Who?

GIRL: I HATE YOU!

TUCKER: Who hates me?

In this brief interchange Max not only prioritizes his orgasm and dismisses his female partner's needs but also ridicules her for bringing up the question, and at the end of the quote he dismisses her entirely, essentially telling her that it really doesn't matter if she hates him, because she is no one.

Max, like Stern, uses self-deprecating humor to make the unapologetic bad boy connection with his audience: "I am just an average Joe, but I always win with women." In Max's case he uses his self-reported "average for a white guy" penis size and self-described "not the hottest looks" to connect with the average white male college student in the audience. His choice to stipulate that his penis is average for a "white guy" is not accidental, underscoring his appeal to his largely white male market with not particularly subtle racism.

At the book signing I attended a woman in the front row had brought along a blow-up sex doll that was significantly smaller than life size. Toward the beginning of the event Max walked up to the doll and put his fingers in the doll's mouth, commenting on the size saying it wasn't even big enough for him to get inside, and his penis wasn't all that large. Within his stories he makes a clear connection with what he refers to as the "average white guy," for example, in this excerpt from his tryst with a midget at a midget convention in Milwaukee, Wisconsin: "I got on bottom and had her ride me. Despite my best drunken attempts, I was unable to spin her like a top on my penis. It might have worked if my dick was longer, but alas, I am an average white guy" (2010, p. 130). Max also repeatedly stresses his average-Joe appearance to his audience. When someone at the book signing asked why he didn't play himself in the movie version of *I Hope They Serve Beer in Hell*, the young author responded with a self-deprecating laugh that he wanted someone good-looking to play the part.

Max's battle with authority is more widely defined as his disdain for what he terms "the proper path" of a college and law school graduate. This battle is expressed in terms of a lack of respect for authority work figures, such as internship supervisors, and more generally as a disdain for the drudge work that goes with most typical jobs. Similar to his mid-twentieth-century predecessors, Hugh Hefner and Ian Fleming, Max resonates with his male audience in part due to his disdain for and lack of engagement in a boring daily job. On his website, answering the question "Should I get a JD degree?" he writes:

> Do you want to waste three years of your life debating stupid and utterly irrelevant minutia? Then yes, get your JD. Do you want to get a degree that allows you work the rest of your life in a tedious, shitty, unrewarding job? Then yes, get your JD. Are you a boring, facile, socially retarded whore, desperate for the illusion of money and success, regardless of the cost to your life and the lives of those you love? Then yes, get your JD. Do you want to squander your existence sitting in a lifeless office, churning out ultimately meaningless paperwork? Then yes, get your JD. Listen to me people: There is a reason that lawyers have the LOWEST job satisfaction of any profession in America. THE JOB SUCKS. It is horrible. (Max, n.d.)

Max's professional life as captured on his website, like Hefner's and that of the international spy James Bond, appears ideal to the male voyeur. Unlike the work lives of most, Max has sex for a living and writes about it—the cruder the better, and the more it happens the more book contracts he is able to secure. Max also cements his relationship with young men from more lower- and middle-class backgrounds by poking fun at his Duke University law credentials—he becomes "one of the guys" by choosing a livelihood based on documenting his sex life over the status of a law practice condoned by a premier upper-class education at Duke.

The standardized scripts that make up Max's sex stories follow a slightly different story line than Howard Stern's but are still fundamentally driven by the sexual conquest theme. The stories often include friends playing the role of wing man (the person who entertains the friend while you go for the target) and buddies helping or sometimes hindering Max in his sexual pursuits. He thus brings in the bro and hookup culture found on college campuses, with both massive alcohol consumption and sex intertwined in the story lines.

In keeping with the parameters of the unapologetic bad boy icon, within Max's sex stories and on his website, he is wickedly cruel to women who do not measure up to male-gaze ideals. The young man wearing the T-shirt touting the slogan "YOU LOOK LIKE I NEED ANOTHER DRINK," discussed in the opening section of this chapter, is a clear indication of the popularity of the Tucker Max approach to alcohol use. In the Tucker Max world, men drink a lot, partly just to have fun but also to systematically mask the defects of their often less-than-ideal sexual partners. In one of the more famous Tucker Max sex stories in his first book, he recounts the night he met and had sex with the first woman he picked up from his then recently launched website. The first woman who filled out his form for requesting a date was immediately classified by Max as a fatty. Eager to get real results from his website he goes out on the date and follows through with bringing her home. Once the act is over, Max throws her clothing out the window to get her out of the house before his roommates can witness and attest to the fact that he fucked what they refer to as a "FatGirl" (2006, pp. 48–51).

Max's description of the overweight section of his female fan base is particularly callous on his website and in his published sex stories. The following description from *Assholes Finish First* is of a fan attending "Tuckerfest" in New Jersey in 2003: "I'm not sure I can convey in words how annoying this girl was. Sickeningly obese, covered in acne, at least three chins, with the loud obnoxious fat-girl voice that seems to carry for miles and never stops, she smoked, and had the stupidest sense of humor since…EVER" (2010, p. 176). Given these scathing descriptions written by Max about overweight fans, the first thirteen people in line for the book signing I attended surprised me. I arrived early to monitor the line of fans. An hour and a half before showtime ten of the thirteen in line were women, and of those women only two were what I would classify as traditionally attractive, and more than half were overweight. In fact, of the total audience of about 200, approximately 40 percent were women, and of that 40 percent a very small number were what Max would rate as top lookers.

Many were overweight and awkwardly proportioned. Max didn't tell any fat jokes at the book signing, and he put his arm around each one and had his picture taken, with the girls smiling widely and taking their photo with him home as a memento.

The photograph of Max on his first book standing with a woman with her face cut out and the words "Your Face Here" is read literally by his female fan base, with many standing in line to get their picture with him and many others propositioning him on his website. In a stark reversal of the typical boy-chase-girl script, in the Tucker Max narratives he is often passionately pursued by young women who feel it is a mark of status to be able to announce, "I was fucked by Tucker Max" or "I lost my virginity to Tucker Max." One young woman in his 2010 book tells him he should get T-shirts made announcing, "I was fucked by Tucker Max," then rescinds the idea, claiming that girls who hadn't done the deed would buy the shirts and make false claims. This particular young woman had "I was fucked by Tucker Max" tattooed just above her crotch with Max in tow all the way to the tattoo parlor. Pictures documenting that this "really happened" to this young woman are included in *Assholes Finish First*.

The peer status associated with being fucked by Max was joked about at the book signing, with him telling a story about a young woman who chased him down during his film promotion tour. After finishing the act in his hotel room she promptly grabbed her cell phone and sent out a mass text to everyone she knew, "probably even her parents," according to him, simply stating, "I just fucked Tucker Max." During the year that I was doing my Tucker Max fieldwork I visited a family in a large American city. The fifty-plus parents were clueless as to the identity of Tucker Max, but the twenty-year-old daughter reported that she knew a girl attending a local affluent suburban high school who had lost her virginity to Max. The story was that the young woman wrote an e-mail to Max recruiting him to speak at her high school. She was not able to book the speaking engagement, perhaps due to the school's wise intervention, but she was able to claim bragging rights for losing her virginity to him.

One way of understanding the courting of Max by a seeming legion of young women is to interpret the behavior as perhaps the ultimate act of self-objectification. On the back cover of Max's first book is a quote from a male fan who declares, "You are the coolest person I can even imagine existing. If you slept with my girlfriend it'd make me love her more." In some way, perhaps, young women are so socialized to the male gaze that they look at Max through the lens of their young male peers and boyfriends. Sleeping with Tucker Max, a simple hookup within college culture, in this context creates attention and perceived value for these young women. It is a popularly understood label of what Gail Dines (2011) refers to as "fuckability," perhaps mattering most to those young women who don't quite measure up to the popular culture ideal.

Similar to Howard Stern, Tucker Max says out loud what young white men are thinking but do not feel comfortable saying, at least not in a mixed public space. One of the clearest things his sex stories do for young men is to give them permission to use women as sex objects by clearly communicating to female partners within his sex narratives that they are being used:

> I was fucking a girl who lived in the same apartment building as her brother. One morning he saw us in the hallway leaving her place, said hi to her, then went into his apartment.

> GIRL: Sorry, he's not very social to guys I bring around.
> TUCKER: I wouldn't want to meet some guy who was using my sister as a cum dumpster either.
> GIRL: I'm not a cum dumpster!
> TUCKER: I didn't say you were. Clearly, you're a beautiful and unique flower. But I am *using you* as a cum dumpster. (Max, 2010, pp. 155–156)

The reality of hookup culture is that men have been given a free pass to use women, and many women are collaborating in their own abuse. This same message was clearly communicated by Max to his audience at the book signing. During the question-and-answer session he stated that he always tells women who he is and lets them know they may end up written up on his website or in his books, but they still show up and are still interested in having sex with him. The presentation of this high level of misogyny paired with women who are playing along, finding it funny, and lining up to participate and get on his website is similar to what Stern has been able to accomplish in terms of getting women to buy into participating in his shows in exchange for some level of celebrity status.

Max also steers outside of the comfort zone in terms of sexual fantasies tinged with racially motivated violence: "Before that day, I thought I was aggressive and dominant in bed. That was before a 5′3″ Vietnamese college girl tuned me out.... She wanted everything, and she wanted it hard.... I fucked in the ass with so much force it started to bleed. Not much blood but enough that I had to get new sheets. She didn't care, she just took my cock out, put a new condom on, and threw it in her pussy" (2006, p. 69). This same theme, that women like it really hard, is reinforced in sex stories where it isn't clear if the woman is enjoying the encounter or is in pain:

> 5:04: Drunk sex is great.
> 5:08: I decide that drunk sex in someone else's RV with a girl you don't know is even better.
> 5:10: I start hitting it hard. Every time I thrust in she yelps. It sounds like a yelp of enjoyment, and she isn't asking me to stop, so I hit it even harder.
> 5:14: I hit it harder. She yelps louder. (2006, p. 70)

This sex story ends in a humorous meltdown as the pepper spray in this poor young woman's purse is mistakenly released, spraying Max's package and leaving him stranded in a parking lot spraying his genitals with water trying to relieve the pain.

The issue of the young woman's yelps and what they were signaling (pleasure or pain) is left comfortably behind.

When I ask young women why they like Tucker Max, a typical response is "he is so funny." Following through on the unapologetic bad boy appeal of Howard Stern, Max tells his tales in a stylized tongue-in-cheek way that cloaks even the most callous misogyny behind a guise of humor. Sobering facts like the Vietnamese girl ending up in a student health clinic the day after her rousing tryst with Max, with both impacted bowels (from anal penetration) and a urinary tract infection, are glibly written off, blamed on the woman's own hypersexuality and Max's "amazing" performance. Certainly, exploring whether the "yelps" heard by Max are yelps of pleasure or pain is not invited for contemplation in his book. The walk-away message from these two sex stories is that women like it hard, even if they yelp and even if they bleed.

The real consequences of Tucker Max–style sexual behavior on college campuses, rather than "isn't this cool," were brought home to me as I overheard the discussion of several men who were in line in front of me at the book signing following Max's question-and-answer session. The clear peer leader of the group periodically vanishes from the line to check his laptop for hotels and the best routes to Florida for spring break, spending much of the time planning the spring break vacation for the group. The big problem facing the group seems to be who gets stuck driving, as everyone wants to get as drunk as possible to avoid enduring the long road trip to Florida. The peer leader steps up and agrees to drive, explaining that his decision is based in part on the fact that he is on a "somewhat permanent vacation." As the conversation among the four young men continues, I learn that he is suspended from the university due to a sexual misconduct violation, with no hope of return to any campus this year due to the violation's write-up on his official university transcripts. His suspension clearly gains him status in the group as the resident "bad boy." The fact that he has had to move away from campus into a condo and cannot even transfer to a different institution to complete his education isn't on the radar screen as an issue to these young men. When they get to the front of the line, Max calls them up as a group, "Hey dudes"; they get a group picture, and he signs condoms as well as one dog-eared copy of his book for the whole crew.

Stone Cold Steve Austin

Professional wrestling is the most popular form of entertainment among teenage boys in America. When I was a kid, wrestling was an amusing little outpost of culture. Today wrestling is sheer spectacle, a magnificently honed lure for the teenage male channel-surfer.... It's broadcast 15 hours a week on five different networks and is seen by 15 million people. Wrestling's violence doesn't scare me. Its ubiquity does. (Douglas Rushkoff, correspondent for *The Merchants of Cool* [Goodman and Dretzin, 2001])

Professional wrestling is the channel-surfing entertainment of choice for teenage boys. Once classified as a sideshow act watched by few, this spectacle of white masculinity became a mainstream and profitable entertainment industry during the same years as the buildup in the popularity of Howard Stern. The entrance of professional wrestling into the teenage/young adult MTV market in 2000 marked the formal recognition of the entertainment industry that professional wrestling was not a sideshow act but a dominating form of media for the young male audience. The seemingly overnight growth and profitability of this entertainment industry caught many inside professionals by surprise, who had grown up with professional wrestling as a marginalized and often ridiculed sport. For example, in an interview for the *Frontline* documentary *The Merchants of Cool*, Brian Graden, MTV's president of programming, commented, "It is huge with our audience at program levels that I could have never imagined. It is the hottest thing going among males 18-to-24 and, in fact, among teen boys" (Goodman and Dretzin, 2001).

Stone Cold Steve Austin emerged in the late 1990s as the first extremely popular unapologetic bad boy in professional wrestling. Prior to this time typical pro wrestling scripts had good and evil posed against each other, with the bad characters generally defeated by the good characters in the final round. Stone Cold's character changed the typical professional wrestling script as he became a top-billed wrestler with a nasty, bullying bad boy stage persona. Within the ring his character was famous for dominating everyone, including his boss and his stage wife, through a combination of intense verbal abuse and violence.

Stone Cold also follows the unapologetic bad boy formula laid out by Howard Stern. First of all, he presents himself and is perceived by his audience as an "average-Joe" guy. In the film *Wrestling with Manhood*, a young fan interviewed from the stands at a pro wrestling event says, "Austin is normal, goes to work, kicks some ass," clearly identifying with Stone Cold's long-standing and violent feud with his on-stage boss, Mr. McMahon (Jhally, 2003). This classic confrontation between a boss authority figure and the regular working stiff resonates with this mostly white young male crowd. For many of Stone Cold's young male fans, the wrestler acts out what they fantasize about, as he bullies the boss and has his way with the boss's daughter. These sentiments again echo Jackson Katz's (2006) key point that much of the appeal of unapologetic bad boys is that they perform and voice the forbidden thoughts and desires of their male audience.

The obsessive sexual interest of the unapologetic bad boy is fulfilled for Stone Cold by the very nature of contemporary professional wrestling performances, characterized by a steady stream of tantalizing presentations of barely clad female performers. While the presence of divas is pandemic in professional wrestling, Katz (2006) points out that the roles they are allowed to play are minimized to those serving male-driven sexual fantasy narratives, with many scripts pairing the sexual arousal of the audience with sexually degrading or violent treatment of women. Diva performances are often a disturbing mix of sexual objectification coupled with humiliation, often at the hands of the male wrestlers or McMahon himself. Some performances feature women humiliating other female wrestlers. For example, one skit featured women wrestling each other in whipped cream and gravy, with the winner being the wrestler who strips her partner faster. Audiences are given lots of opportunity to whoop and holler about the size of breasts and the wiggle of a G-string-clad bottom across the stage but also to experience sexual stimulation related to seeing a woman dressed like a child spanked by a male wrestler, or a simulated rape, with the woman responding that she is enjoying it. For those still not understanding the narrated link between sexual arousal and violence against women, some broadcast story lines go so far as to have male characters make a literal statement of the connection: "to see the pain in her eyes, the anguish in her eyes, it really turns me on" (Jhally, 2003).

The narratives that include male characters in the power roles of boyfriend, husband, or boss are even more disturbing. Men in these narratives are always in the controlling roles, with women who challenge their authority humiliated, typically using a combination of verbal taunts and physical violence. Typical scripts involve uppity wives or girlfriends who ask for too much and are then violently put back in line through a combination of physical force and verbal abuse. Young male audiences typically play the role of goading the action by chanting, "She had it coming!" mirroring the reality of domestic abuse, wherein the female victim is blamed for driving her man to do it. In a famous and popular boss narrative, Vince McMahon week after week threatened a popular female character with being fired to get her to engage in a range of humiliating behaviors including stripping, agreeing to sexual requests, and getting on her hands and knees in front of him and barking like a dog.

Like other venues dominated by the unapologetic bad boy icon, women are required to conform to narrow pornography-established ideals of appearance. When asked to rate female wrestlers, young men interviewed for *Wrestling with Manhood* (Jhally, 2003) literally cup their hands out in front of their chests and talk about the size of particular pro wrestling women's breasts. Female wrestlers struggling to both be strong-enough athletes to perform and yet have the curves required by the porn chic ideal often resort to breast implants to visually communicate both strength and bold sexuality. Jhally's video captures the transformation of the famous pro wrestler Chyna from a woman communicating the physical power of a real wrestler to a more standardized porn diva who posed nude for *Playboy* in 2000.

Like the other forms of mass entertainment driven by the unapologetic bad boy, blatant misogyny is cloaked behind a humorous facade within professional wrestling scripts. Audience members uniformly dismiss the seriousness of the misogyny by saying it is "just entertainment," and "none of it is real," without considering the damaging messages being communicated to both young men and women in the audiences. Katz's analysis points out that it is more complex than simply asking whether a young man watching this event is more likely to enact violence against another person. The bigger question, as articulated by Katz, is, "how realistic is it that boys who are immersed in pro wrestling's cartoonish world of brutish male thugs and compliant female sex objects can switch all of that off and relate to their female (and male) peers in a spirit of equality and mutual respect? It is clear that World Wrestling Entertainment sets up girls and women to be little more than compliant victims. But it also sets up boys and men to either be abusers and rapists—or to think like them" (2006, p. 172).

Eminem

Eminem rose to prominence as a white rapper in the late 1990s in the midst of the popular culture trend toward the unapologetic bad boy cultural ideals for young white males that I have been documenting throughout this chapter. Eminem entered the scene with an unapologetic stage presence characterized by Katz as a "clever [white] 'bad boy' act" (2006, p. 169). Adding to his appeal was a cool black-rapper attitude and the prerequisite set of misogynistic attitudes toward women, plus a monster dose of homophobia. His popularity with young white men and the women who jumped on board was based on his reputation as a rebel, the white guy who could really rap.

Similar to Tucker Max, Eminem fulfills the unapologetic bad boy ideal of having access to a ready supply of women by performing and writing music directed toward a primarily young male audience but nevertheless attracting the attention and high regard of a large fan base of women. Katz, who has also published cultural criticism focused on Eminem, expressed his dismay and puzzlement at this ability: "What are men to make of *New York Times* columnist Maureen Dowd when she writes, uncritically, that a 'gaggle' of her female baby-boomer friends are 'surreptitiously smitten' with a certain thirty-year old rapper whose lyrics literally drip with contempt for women? What are boys to think of an online poll in *CosmosGirl* magazine in 2001 that found him to be the 'sexiest musician'?" (2006, p. 165). Thus Eminem appears to young men to be a player, an underclass guy from Detroit who battled it up from the streets and got not only fame but dames. And, I would add, not only young naive girls, unaware of the world, but also a *New York Times* columnist with a highly educated and widely read audience.

Eminem's rebellion is waged largely on a gender battlefield, with his transgressions directed toward women and gay males. His rebel appeal rests almost solely on his bold willingness to describe violence against women and gays in very graphic terms and to get away it. Richard Goldstein, who wrote one of the most eye-opening early reviews of Eminem's music for *Village Voice* in 2002, argues that the supposed "rebelliousness" of Eminem is actually a "herd reflex," a massive embrace by a largely white male audience for the dude who is saying everything they want to say but feel they can't.

Stone Cold is as well known for his verbal put-downs as for his physical violence, with his audience often joining in with his misogynistic rants. In a similar way

Eminem lyrics are chanted by his fans both in live concerts and in school hallways and on playgrounds. Katz (2009) includes the following lyrics from Eminem's song "Stay Wide Awake" to highlight the level of misogyny found in the work of this popular rap artist:

Fe Fi Fo Fum
I think I smell the scent of a placenta
I enter central park, it's dark, it's winter in December
I see my target with my car, and park and approach her tender
Young girl by the name of Brenda and I pretend to befriend her
Sit down beside her like a spider, hi there girl you mighta
Heard of me before, see whore you're the kinda girl that I'da
Assault and rape and figure why not try to make your pussy wider
Fuck you with an umbrella then open it up while that shits inside ya

Embedded in the rants of Stone Cold and the lyrics of Eminem are what Goldstein calls "guilty pleasures." Under the guise of entertainment and art, both Stone Cold and Eminem allow male audiences to indulge in a form of misogyny that can be dismissed as art or entertainment but that still effectively protects white male privilege from the ravages of feminism and the growing power of the gay community:

Say what you will about redeeming social (or artistic) value: At its hard core, Eminem's poetics is pornography, and it's accorded the same privileges. Just as we've declared the XXX zone exempt from social thinking, we refuse to subject sexist rap to moral scrutiny. We crave a space free from the demands of equity, especially when it comes to women, whose rise has inspired much more ambivalence than most men are willing to admit. This is especially true in the middle class, where feminism has made its greatest impact. No wonder Eminem is so hot to suburban kids and Downtown *alter cockers*. He's as nasty as they wanna be. (Goldstein, 2002)

Porn Chic: The Embodiment of the Male Gaze and Desire

The turn of the millennium's cultural construction of the unapologetic bad boy icon and the media machine that grabbed hold of this guise as a means of charting out and outlining the male gaze and desire have created a persuasive and easily marketed version of masculinity. Certainly this icon doesn't influence or define all men, but its popular culture impact is extremely significant in terms of normalizing sexual scripts casting women in sexually objectified and degrading roles. This book takes an analytic approach focusing not only on how porn chic embodies male desire but also on when it plays roles in authentic expressions of female sexual agency. The method of exploring this often murky terrain of desire will be to follow the contours of raunch eroticism with systematic stops at the seven points of analysis outlined in the first chapter, discussed in regard to this particular chapter in the following.

Focus on the White Heterosexual Male Gaze

A widely heard criticism of contemporary popular culture is that it is hypersexualized. Every time we turn around we see exposed breasts, we hear sexually charged music lyrics, and we attend a university fashion show that includes a stripper pole on stage. What is typically not referenced emphatically enough is that the sexual world that surrounds us is constructed for a very particular audience, young white males. The fashions we create, the sexual imagery within films, the lyrics of the most popular musicians are created to titillate white male desire and as an afterthought are also sold to the rest of us so we can inhabit the white male's world.

The world as constructed by unapologetic bad boys is narrowly focused on the physical satisfaction of male desire through orgasm with as many women and in as many varieties of experience as possible. The running questions for Tucker Max at his book signings are: When was the last time? How many different women? How many different ways? All questions focus on his orgasms. The assumption in the unapologetic bad boy universe is that women are getting dressed to be consumed by men, resulting in the victim-blaming question that haunts rape prosecutions: "What did she have on?" If indeed it is assumed that what consumes the energy and dominates the motivations of girls and women is attracting the male gaze, then logic dictates that if she was dressed in a manner that attracted male attention, it was done purposefully to elicit a sexual response and therefore she is to blame for his behavior, the classic line being, "She brought it on herself."

The hard reality is that young girls are being socialized to dress to satisfy and court white male desire, even at very young ages. That is not to say that all girls and women purposefully get dressed to court an assault or that by dressing to fit these social norms women and girls deserve to be assaulted and raped. But let's be frank, without shadows hiding the facts. Within millennium popular culture what is prioritized, focused on, and continually reinforced is courting and satisfying white male desire. What needs to be pushed on and explored are the ways out of the cultural construct, working toward more expressions of healthy sexuality. This book explores both zones, the parts of popular culture where the prime and limited focus is on white male desire, and the zone where experimentation is occurring with regard to moving outside of the prescribed patriarchy into the worlds of a wider sexuality.

Sexual Objectification of Women

The dividing of women's bodies into parts and the rating of the parts by a single man or panel of men is part and parcel of the unapologetic bad boy universe. The now-normative acceptance of this strand of boy/man culture is rooted in the post–World War II opening of sexual mores by Hefner and Fleming, through creation of popular culture media (magazines, novels, and movies) that openly displayed women's bodies for viewing by a wide audience of men. This book explores not only men's sexual objectification of women but also the ways in which women and girls themselves have adopted the practice as "normal," leading to self-objectification.

Self-Objectification

In the unapologetic bad boy universe it is assumed that it is normal for women to self-objectify their own bodies. In the public judging venue created by the unapologetic bad boy universe and picked up by popular culture media directed toward women and girls, those who fail to measure their breasts, thighs, pubic zones, and underarms against the idealized standard are subject to public ridicule or a Facebook slam. Men's and boys' exposure to pornography sets the expectation that it is normal for women to shave their genital regions, get breast implants, and in more general terms set themselves up to conform to the standards set by the male gaze and desire. Acting outside of this normative behavior, choosing not to do a genital shave, for example, opens a woman to criticism and at times questioning of sexual orientation.

Sexual Attention and Sexualized Practice as Power

Working in tandem with the emergence of the international playboy icon was the power of the growing mass media to shower attention on those deemed deserving of the spotlight. Women who conformed to the *Playboy* and James Bond ideal achieved fast and broad celebrity attention, lifting "normal" girls next door into public positions of power. Quickly, women and girls learned that power was captured through good looks and male attention, setting in place the foundation for the development of the sexy empowerment icon in the late twentieth and early twenty-first centuries, as discussed in chapter 3.

Private Is Public

A cornerstone of unapologetic bad boy appeal is its roots in tell-all boy culture, the reporting back on sexual exploits to the guys the morning after, the points you get from your peers for getting her to do it. The online testimonials of Tucker Max, which eventually were strung together to make his first book, are a public version of that formerly private ritual talk back to the boys. Howard Stern plays with this public/private dichotomy in his dialogues and books as he strings along the audience with inside stories of how he runs to the computer for a cyber masturbation session as his wife and children head out the door to the park in the morning. Women willingly get pulled into the report-back mentality, with women text-messaging all their cell phone contacts on the morning after they fuck Tucker Max.

Extreme, Up the Ante

Media figures populating the unapologetic bad boy universe depend to a large extent on shock tactics to keep their audience engaged. The floods of gonzo and hard-core porn on the Internet have raised the ante for mainstream media. To capture the boy/man market, you need to show more and make it more violent. The integral role of the unapologetic bad boy, in both saying and doing the forbidden, forces the ante up for these entertainers and writers. In addition to porn-related sexual behaviors, the hard-porn focus on degradation of women has influenced the mainstream bad boys' entertainment strategies, with increasing amounts of humor based on bullying of and violence against women.

Misogyny

Goldstein in his music review of Eminem captured much of the appeal of the unapologetic bad boy when he argued in 2002 that what was drawing men to this openly misogynistic music was the desperate need "for a space free from the demands of equity, especially when it comes to women." Goldstein then goes on to explain Eminem's appeal to middle-class men and boys by arguing that it is among this group that feminism has been the most threatening. "He's as nasty as they wanna be," Goldstein argues. In other words, Eminem's lyrics and music give voice to the repressed rage, the anxiety about being marginalized by the growing competence being acted out by mothers, sisters, and female friends. With the increasing entrance of women and people of color into positions of leadership, the once-assumed primacy of the white male patriarchy is threatened, leaving open the door for misogynic discord.

–3–

The Birth of Pop Culture Porn Chic

The message is out in edited and single-author books, in articles in *Newsweek*, and on the *Oprah Show*. Porn chic is a key turn-of-the-millennium trend in the United States and Britain. Titles of academic articles and books on the topic include "Choke on It, Bitch" (Maddison, 2009, p. 37), *Pornland* (Dines, 2010), *The Porning of America* (Sarracino and Scott, 2008), and *Pop-Porn* (Hall and Bishop, 2007). Brian McNair (2002) has labeled the trend "striptease culture," Carmine Sarracino and Kevin M. Scott (2008, p. x) describe Paris Hilton performing "oral sex on a hamburger" in a fast-food television advertisement, and *Newsweek* declares that Halloween costumes sexualize children (Philips, 2007). Embodied in everything from centerfold images of female Olympic athletes, to college women flashing their breasts for *Girls Gone Wild* crews during spring break, to Hooters's well-endowed waitresses, the cultural presence of a new erotic ideal is undeniable. It tantalizes its audience with the blend of "real" women with pornography, and we are in its grip; in particular, young women are adopting its fashions and styles.

Valerie Steele (1985) has argued that style changes initiated by changing versions of feminine eroticism are posed in relationship to expressions of sexuality in the past. The flappers of the 1920s are thus posed in relationship to the nineteenth-century domestic–public dichotomy, wherein good women clothed in proper Victorian dress were the keepers of the home, and public "bad" women dressed in racy attire were the madams of the street. The flapper style was embraced in its time period in part due to its challenge to that division, a movement of the domestic into the public, and with it a more open regard for women's sexuality and eroticism. Similarly, the emergence of porn chic at the turn of the twenty-first century must be seen as posed in response to twentieth-century conceptions of female sexuality and empowerment. Given the key importance of celebrity culture to the transmission of current porn chic ideals, one must first grapple with the most visible celebrities of the twentieth century and what they exemplified.

Tracing the roots of this cultural shift leads us back to the opening of sexual mores in the 1960s and 1970s, and to the popularization of the centerfold led by *Playboy* in the 1960s, but perhaps most significantly to the launch of MTV as a New York City–based cable station in the late 1970s and early 1980s. Prior to the advent of MTV, popular culture, particularly as related to music and performance, was accessible to a select few who lived in cities hosting top acts and had the money and resources to get into the venues hosting the concerts. Leonard J. Beer, the current editor in chief of *Hits* magazine, was working as a young professional for *Record World* magazine based in New York City in the late 1960s and 1970s. In an interview for PBS's *Frontline*, he describes covering music pre-MTV:

> It was good then. It was. The music was great, it was exciting, it was new, it was fresh. There was mystery. Going to see a rock show was the first time you ever saw someone. You know, the artists were rarely on television. There was the "Ed Sullivan Show" when I was young and whatever, but there wasn't a lot of music on television. So you had to go to a concert to see someone. To pull the veil of mystery away and, you know, go see the Rolling Stones, or go see the Doors or go see David Bowie, or some of the incredibly exciting things—Pink Floyd—and when we were young, the amazing things that you would see for the first time when you went to a concert. (Beer, 2004)

Sheila Whitely (2000), citing Theodore Roszak (1970), traces the relegation of female recording artists to the fringes of the popular music scene in the 1960s and early 1970s, pointing toward the emergence of two male-dominated popular music genres: the school of cock rock, perhaps most vividly represented by the Rolling Stones, and the school of love (and, I would add, countercultural angst), as exemplified by Dylan, the Beatles, and Donavon. Female musicians of this era struggled to find a niche in the categories of music labeled to fit these two male-dominated music genres. The rock-world emphasis on raw sexual lyrics and bad boy "I am a player" lead singers set audience expectations that female lead singers would fill the same kind of bill. By 1979 the music industry was suffering. Sales of singles to teenagers, a mainstay of the 1960s and 1970s, had plummeted, and major record companies were suffering. Record companies began narrowing their artists to a few very salable, mostly male celebrity bands in order to stay competitive. This select list included Michael Jackson, Bruce Springsteen, Prince, and Lionel Ritchie (O'Brien, 2007, p. 78). The emergence of female rock-musician celebrity brands on MTV, most notably Madonna and Britney Spears, is a story that begins in the 1960s with Janis Joplin.

Janis Joplin: Ballsy Woman

Female artists' early attempts to find a legitimate position on the popular music stage in the last half of the twentieth century were fraught with identity issues. Janis Joplin, working out of a tradition of blues and rock, struggled to find an acceptable identity in a 1960s popular music subculture that largely expected entertainment from women, and music and ideas from men (Whitely, 2000). Joplin, as a strong musician, attempted to simply become one of the boys and participate fully in the production of her music. However, her position as a front singer and a woman was fraught with expectations for heightened sexual appeal and attractiveness, stereotypes that did not fit her physical type or bisexuality. Sheila Whitely, in her chapter on Joplin, quotes Country Joe McDonald, who links Joplin's early death of a drug overdose to this identity ambivalence: "Sexism killed her. Everybody wanted this sexy chick who sang really sexy and had a lot of energy…and people kept saying one of the things about her was that she was just 'one of the guys'…that's a real sexist bullshit trip, 'cause that was fuckin' her head around…she was one of the women. She was a strong, groovy woman" (2000, p. 59). This early expectation that a female star belonged up front in the band, and that her role was to be a sexy, energetic lead singer, would ultimately determine who made the short list in the compression of success to a select few in the 1980s.

The strength and dominance of the feminine/masculine dichotomy in the 1960s relegated Joplin to the margins of both masculinity and femininity. In the final analysis, Joplin just couldn't win. When compared to male performers, Joplin's raw musical style, on-stage bravado, and off-stage aggressiveness were interpreted by many as an attempt to overperform all the men "in an attempt to prove herself" (Whitely, 2000, p. 66). These same behaviors made her stand out from more traditional female performers, causing some to label her as "degenerate" (p. 66). Joplin, reading the tenor of the time, did not openly reveal her bisexuality, a fact that would have even further distanced her from acceptance by the mainstream music culture of the time period.

Madonna

The successful launch of the first rock music female brand by Madonna is rooted in women's experimentation with front-singer identity in the British, New York, and Los Angeles punk scenes of the mid- to late 1970s. Similar to Joplin, the female punk lead singers understood that to successfully compete with male musicians they needed to step away from stereotypical female sexuality and attractiveness. However, that is where the easy comparison with Joplin ends. While Joplin in many ways felt compelled to compete on the same playing field with men, to one-up their sexual prowess and aggressiveness, punk women turned feminine sexuality on end, demanding a reinterpretation of female power and identity.

Madonna entered the music and dance scene in New York during the height of the disco and punk era in the late 1970s. She moved to New York with a strong dance background but limited singing credibility. Madonna's songwriting and stage persona was literally formulated experientially as she worked her way through the club scene in New York. She was particularly drawn to the female punk bands of the era, and the stage guise she put together for her first live performances and MTV videos is an amalgamation of what she observed on New York club stages.

Punk Influences in Madonna

British punk style, with its juxtaposition of bondage fetish references, underwear as outerwear, and edgy schoolgirl attitude, was picked up by Madonna from the Brit band The Slits, whom she went to see perform in the clubs in New York. The lead singer Ari Up, interviewed by rock historian Lucy O'Brien, remembers Madonna in the front row at those performances and is quick to take some credit for the guise of the early pop icon:

"I'm pissed off she's never worn a T-shirt with THE SLITS written in sequins. She owes us. She ripped off her early fashion ideas from Viv," Ari said in 2005. "Viv would wind rags in her hair and don lingerie as outerwear. We'd be dressed half in bondage fetish gear, half in Doc Martens, with our hair all out there, scowling at everybody.... People wouldn't know if we were a pin up or what." (O'Brien, 2007, p. 34)

According to Madonna, another significant role model was the New York–based lead singer for Blondie, Debbie Harry (O'Brien, 2007, p. 45). Like Ari Up, Harry fought through many obstacles, including an unofficial radio boycott in the United States in the mid-1970s, to become the aggressive lead singer of an otherwise all-male band. In an interview with O'Brien (2007, p. 45), Harry talks about this break-through: "An aggressive female front person had never really been done in pop," she said. "It was very difficult to be in that position at that time—it's hard to be a groundbreaker." Even more so than Ari Up, who sang with a girl band, Harry had to command front-stage lead attention from the audience, as she had a backup band of strong-willed and intense male musicians, including her partner, Chris Stein.

Perhaps more significant, in terms of Madonna's many later reincarnations, was Harry's deconstruction and reinvention of the Hollywood platinum blonde stereotype. A traditional "looker," Harry crossed over into the porn chic world early with a career stint as a Playboy Bunny. The band name, Blondie, came out of catcalls Harry had received from truck drivers based on her stereotypical "blonde bomb" appeal. O'Brien captures the look cultivated by Harry and makes the connection to the pop culture reinterpretations of Andy Warhol: "With her bee-stung lips and cartoon peroxide style, Harry's image was an ironic comment that celebrated the tradition of the glamorous blonde while sending it up. She was the first Warhol-style pop-art blonde in pop music" (2007, p. 45).

The Los Angeles punk scene, with its focus on the remaking of a housedress from a Goodwill store, cheap layers of costume jewelry, and overdone eye makeup, also impacted the look that Madonna crafted for herself. In particular, Maria Raha points to the influence of the singer Cervenka: "While thrift store dresses, boots, piles of jewelry, and dark eyeliner may have been popularized by Madonna in 1985, it was arguably first donned by Exene Cervenka in the mid-'70s" (2005, p. 46). Madonna also picked up on the confidence and swagger of these earlier female punk lead singers. Similar to Madonna's exodus from the Midwestern United States to New York, Cervenka left Chicago at the age of twenty and went to Los Angeles, where she invented herself as a performer by infiltrating a male band and becoming the lead singer. Raha tells Cervenka's story this way:

Born Christine Cervenka in Chicago, Illinois in 1956 and raised in Tallahassee, Florida, Exene hopped the first ride to Los Angeles she was offered in 1976. She met Doe in 1977 and he asked to use her poem "I'm Coming Over", in his new band. Much to Zoom's dismay, Cervenka wanted to sing her own words rather than turn them over to Doe. "I admit it" Zoom has said. "I was originally horrified that John was bringing his girlfriend into the band." Cervenka ended up providing the perfect complement to Doe's voice, conveying the sadness of the lyrics, often sounding like a weeping woman against Doe's unfazed steadiness. (Raha, 2005, p. 43)

The stark power of Cervenka's lyrics and stage presence, and her ability to command center stage with an all-male band, is captured in this quote from her collaborating band partner Doe:

She had poems that were obviously songs, plus she was cut from classic lead singer cloth. She was such a badass! I pretended to be, but Exene was the real thing. She had an ax to grind, the sadness of her mother's death, and the unusual wiring that made it possible for her to throw a drink in someone's face and still be right. She totally delivered as a lead singer. (Raha, 2005, p. 44)

Madonna would carry this same cocksure confidence into the sessions with her early bands. Like Exene she had an axe to grind, but she chose the axe that her young female audience most identified with, a desire to take control, to be the center of attention, to challenge the passive "good girl" gender constructions they felt were holding them back. O'Brien's analysis of Madonna's power focuses on her ability to capture this moment for young women and girls:

To be twenty years old in the late 70s was to be at a cultural shifting point, when a binary world of black/white, male/female, good/bad, virgin/whore was beginning to break down. With her unfailing instinct, Madonna tuned in to this change and embodied it, turning herself into a cultural force. She combined elements of punk style with underground dance and Europop disco to come up with the concept of Madonna. (2007, p. 35)

Thus through a combination of edgy ties to porn and girl culture (British punk), defiance of American rules of femininity (LA punk), and taking "50s Hollywood-blonde schlock one step further and welding it [all] to a self-driven 80s global marketing [machine]" (O'Brien, 2007, p. 45), Madonna moved to the middle of the stage and became the best-selling female artist of all time.

Girl-to-Girl Bonding and Marketing

There is a black-and-white photo from 1985 where I'm sitting on my grandma's back porch steps. I'm wearing endless bangle and black jelly bracelets, multiple strands of pearls, and far too much makeup. My hair is ratted high, with a black ribbon headband tied in a floppy bow to hold back my messy curls. All I needed was a pair of lace cut-off gloves, and my Madonna look would have been complete. Even at age five, MTV had seeped into my life. (Maisano, 2006)

This quotation is from a little girl who grew up with Madonna and even at age five was copying her idol's image in the hopes of attracting attention and power. While it likely took MTV to downsize the look to age five, Madonna's appeal to female adolescents was immediate, beginning with her earliest live performances in New York and on the college circuit. In her biography of Madonna, O'Brien describes her early appeal to young girls: "Madonna's appeal lay in...the sense that she was a normal pretty girl. Even though she had her hip New York devotees, when she started out, Madonna attracted a mainly teeny bop crowd of enthusiastic girls. The early 80s fans were responding to 'honest-to-goodness blood, sweat, and lip gloss' rather than some remote goddess" (2007, p. 48).

Cyndi Lauper had some of the same appeal to female audience members as Madonna and also crafted a dyed-hair, thrift-store, post-punk "girlie girl" identity that had audience appeal with adolescent girls. In an interview with O'Brien, Lauper describes her reaction to her early concert audiences: "I was shocked at the [audience] reaction. I'd go out on stage and the audience would be filled with girls screaming, ripping at my clothes. I'd never heard girls screaming over a woman before, and at first I thought, they think I'm gay. The only bad thing is I wasn't!" (quoted in O'Brien, 2007, p. 79). O'Brien correctly analyzes the audience reaction to Lauper's performance as an early symptom of the transformation of female adolescent audiences from groupies chasing after the cutest Beatle to a group of young girls hungering for role models who were desired objects by men. Lauper's assumption that they were screaming and tearing off her clothes as an expression of *their own desire* is false; instead, they are passionately identifying with her as an example of a powerful young woman, in control of male desire through her celebrity and sexual-icon status.

While Lauper had much of the same appeal to live audiences, and actually beat Madonna to the punch with top-ten singles and her 4.5 million–selling debut album, Madonna managed her image much more successfully than Lauper through a series of provocative and well-staged early MTV performances. Dating back to her 1984 hypersexualized performance of "Like a Virgin" at the MTV Awards, Madonna was read by her audience of most often adolescent girls/young women as a maverick, an attitudy girl/woman who is overcoming gender-imposed barriers through owning her own sexuality. David Tetzlaff points out that in her early film roles Madonna was unapologetically seeking fame, attention, and money, without regard for being bound within traditional notions of relationship: "From the beginning, Madonna's self-representation in promotion and publicity material portrayed her defiantly independent, a woman who challenged and overcame gender restrictions. This representation was greatly bolstered by Madonna's role in the popular Hollywood feminist film *Desperately Seeking Susan*. In contrast with the image of woman as nurturer...she clearly articulated that she was out only for herself, the stardom and its perks of money, power, and respect" (1993, p. 245).

The route to power, as vividly portrayed by Madonna, involved the creative remaking of the performance of femininity to be self-serving, self-aggrandizing, and overtly sexual, resulting in a heightened degree of attention and hedonic power. Madonna's appropriation of powerful symbols of control, such as crucifixes and corsets, communicated quickly and effectively with her young audience that she wasn't afraid of or intimidated by the traditional confines of Western morality. The disturbing walk-away message for a young woman attending a Madonna performance, or watching a music video, is that the sleaze you own pays, and pays big. Madonna went far in creating a misguided message to young girls and women that the traditional penalties for what was once called slutty behavior no longer applied: "You, my darling, are in charge of your own sexuality, use it to go places, and don't let THEM hold you back." A second important message of Madonna as an icon is that the route to power is through representation—that you need to get your image out, it needs to be provocative, it needs to grab attention—and if you do that, success will follow.

The Sexy Empowerment Icon: A Marketing Brand

There is much debate about the importance or relevance of Madonna in terms of cultural analysis and artistic impact. To focus clearly on where she fits and how important she is, it is important to return to Valerie Steele's (1985) style theory, with its emphasis on the linkage between what is emerging and the past. Madonna came of age during the early women's liberation movement, with its emphasis on earthy definitions of female sexuality coupled with the idea of gaining power in the political sphere and workplace. She early on experienced some of the impatience with the older women's feminist agenda that would be expressed later by self-labeled "prosex" feminists such as Debbie Stollar (1999), who felt the movement was "antisex" and vindictive. She picked up the deconstructionist messaging of the punk movement, with its concept of reinventing female sexuality as power, and turned this message of sexy empowerment into a defined and salable commodity. Madonna's version of power—sexy and image based—and part of the rock/pop scene created an immediately cool and liberating message.

The launch of the "Material Girl" as an exclusive clothing line at Macy's in fall 2010 by Madonna and her daughter in some ways draws a definitive outline around Madonna as a brand. The juniors/tween clothing line features studs, layers and lace, fingerless gloves, and the layers of jewelry that put together the challenging sexy look of Madonna as she emerged in the early 1980s as a pop icon. The launch of the exclusive brand at Macy's flagship store in New York in August, just in time for back-to-school shopping, caused lines around the block, with reports of high sales figures. John Mitchell (2010), writing on the *Popeater* news site, interviewed a Macy's shopper buying the brand, who described the Material Girl consumer as "a fearless girl that's not afraid to be bold and try things." Madonna herself told Mitchell that "a Material Girl is a girl that is interested in fashion and interested in a sense of humor. [She] is an adventurous human being."

In many regards, what Madonna did in the 1980s, and continues to do with her brand in the millennium, is to create an icon, a branded image that captures the beginning of the co-opting of the 1960s and 1970s feminist struggle for empowerment by commercial interests at the end of the twentieth century. She was not the first to pick up the appeal of superficial messages of empowerment, particularly to young female adolescents. The early tobacco-industry slogan "You've come a long way, baby," from the Virginia Slims advertising campaign in the 1960s, was directed toward young women and used a sexy form of empowerment to very effectively sell cigarettes to underage women. Madonna's construction of pop cultural appeal was more intuitive than that of the tobacco-marketing team and was based largely on her own personal struggle to reach stardom. The result of Madonna's efforts was the construction of a female celebrity brand that has worked extremely effectively in selling music and product to very large numbers of female consumers for over two decades.

The sexy empowerment icon, Madonna's concept of success based on using provocative, attention-getting versions of sexuality to become a recognized, photographed, and profitable brand, is used over and over again in the case studies in the following chapters. What Madonna essentially put together into a salable package are the four key ingredients that Rosalind Gill (2008) stresses are integral to postfeminist media culture directed toward a largely young and female audience. First and foremost, the emphasis is on the sexual body, often but not always surgically enhanced. Second, the body is self-objectified, posed for view, purposefully soliciting the male gaze. Third, the presentation includes imagery, text, or actions indicating that the woman displaying herself is doing it because she wants to, that it is her choice. Finally, there is an empowerment theme, a "go girl" power message that communicates that this is the route to success: "This is the way to make it, so come along and be like me."

Britney Spears: "You Want a Piece of Me!"

The basic message that resonated with the young female audience and that was communicated so well by Madonna—that you are powerful, babe; use that image, use that sexuality—continued to work well for those following in her wake, coming out of both the music and the soft-porn industries. The now-famous kiss between Madonna and Britney Spears at the 2003 MTV Video Awards ceremony signaled not just a turning over of the baton but a lowering of the acceptable age of advertised sexuality. *Rolling Stone* magazine's first cover story on Spears had a cover headline reading "Britney Spears: Inside the Heart, Mind and Bedroom of a Teen Dream." The now-famous cover featured a young but busty Spears splayed open for view like an innocent and partially clad *Playboy* centerfold. If the cover was too subtle, the photograph inside the magazine of Spears in her bedroom surrounded by dolls clearly links childhood to sexuality and common forms of child pornography. *Rolling Stone* is

Figure 3.1 *New York, New York.* Courtesy of Nicola Bockelmann.

self-aware of its complicity. A writer for the magazine credited Spears with cultivating "a mixture of innocence and experience that broke the bank" (Daly, 1999).

Spears, unlike Madonna, entered the business as a child, propelled by a mother who eventually landed her in her opening role as a member of the Mickey Mouse Club, at the very young age of ten. However, very similar to Madonna's career trajectory, Spears was propelled forward by a record label and the images of her projected by the mass media. The early *Rolling Stone* cover and article were preceded by her very publicized and successful debut album, "Baby One More Time," which became the best-selling album ever recorded by a teenage artist. The MTV video promoting the title track was a "must be viewed" success, bringing together hot schoolgirl sexiness, a bare midriff, and the now-accepted Madonna brand of young female empowerment. In the United States the title track sold 500,000 copies on its first day and later was nominated for a Grammy Award for Best Female Pop Vocal Performance. In the United Kingdom the track was equally well received and later became the twenty-fifth most successful song of all time in British chart history.

Also in sync with her mentor Madonna, in 2010 Spears transitioned from being simply the front face of the exclusive Kohl's Candies line of junior and tween (age 7–16) fashions to having a Candies, Designed by Britney Spears Limited Edition

Collection. The marketing campaign for her limited-edition collection features Spears in hot schoolgirl styles with headlines directly targeted to her teenage girl consumers—"love this skirt, for dancing, fun and flirting!"—and ripe with explicit sexual innuendo—"you want a piece of me." Outdoing her mentor Madonna, Spears made it to number one on the Forbes Top 100 Celebrity list in 2002.

Miley Cyrus

The influence of the sexy empowerment icon is apparent as one reviews the career path of Miley Cyrus from a young Disney star to the controversy surrounding a well-publicized performance that included a pole-dancing section at the 2009 Teen Choice Awards. The trend throughout the celebrity stories of these three iconic American teenage girls is toward corporate invention of the sexy empowerment icon. Madonna, through her stubborn wit and ingenuity, made her way through the music and dance world, networking and making connections that ultimately got her onto MTV and into the limelight. She entered into the business as a young adult and fashioned her own success largely on her own terms.

Spears's route to celebrity status was launched by early intervention from executives at Jive Records responding to a voice-over tape she submitted of her singing over a Whitney Houston song. Spears herself wanted to enter the music scene as a more mature voice, directed toward an older audience. She was groomed by the record company for the young pop music market, and her young pop brand is largely their invention, although Spears herself made the critical decision to perform her first MTV show as a Catholic schoolgirl. Her later personal challenges and professional collapse, in contrast with the successful management of Madonna's career, could perhaps be explained by Spears's early entrance into celebrity status and the degree of corporate control that was asserted over her development at a young age.

Miley Cyrus, in the guise of Hannah Montana, is a Disney-brand invention, put together carefully to sell product to the young-girl marketplace. In part, the Disney influence was mitigated by her father's involvement in the country music and film industry and the creation of her public identity, but the influence of the Disney mass media and marketing machine in her dramatic rise to success is indisputable. Disney is one of only five extremely large companies that target youth culture. These five companies own a majority of the film and music studios, commercial cable stations, and major television networks. Disney's decision to launch Cyrus to the young-girl market through the Disney brand Hannah Montana moved her image into pop icon status almost overnight when contrasted with Madonna's struggle to get in the right place at the right time to be noticed and promoted.

The original Hannah Montana brand was purposefully crafted by Disney to be wholesome and directed toward young girls and their mothers. Cyrus was presented as a good role model, with her Christian upbringing stressed in media appearances.

As she matured and began performing more music engagements, she and her appearance-management team quickly learned the tricks of using staged moments to flaunt sexuality while still holding on to that "young girl" appeal. Similar to both Madonna and Spears, the Hannah Montana brand staged a well-televised and -covered moment of sexual transgression, thus pulling Cyrus out to the forefront in terms of coverage and attention. For Cyrus it was the now-infamous ice cream cart pole-dancing section of her performance at the 2009 Sunday's Teen Choice Awards, followed by a series of highly sexualized media opportunities.

Spears posed for the controversial *Rolling Stone* cover when she was seventeen and with that launched herself as a young sexy empowerment icon. Cyrus moved the age down to sixteen and did it on a Sunday evening for the Fox Teen Choice Awards—the now-infamous strip-pole debut. Cyrus's performance, costuming, and song lyrics together captured the four key components of the sexy empowerment icon script as outlined by Gill. The performance is clearly focused on the expression of sexuality, with short leather shorts, a cutaway shirt revealing Cyrus's bra, and body moves emphasizing the sexual features of her body. If there is any doubt as to the priority given to male attention, the strip-pole section of the show clearly makes the connection for the viewer and draws dramatic attention to the performer's body and sexuality. In terms of demonstrated choice and autonomy, the entire stage is catering to Cyrus, with a supporting cast of characters acting on her whim. She is at the center of decision-making power. The story within the lyrics captures the theme of empowerment. It is the story of a Nashville girl who moves to Hollywood and makes it big time on the radio. As Cyrus shimmies and shakes her way down the runway and on the pole of the ice cream cart, the message is clear: The way to get here is through an empowered version of sexy.

Lady Gaga: Transcending the Sexy Empowerment Icon

I purposefully didn't read reviews of Lady Gaga's music in advance of sitting down to watch her videos as I was attempting to get a raw understanding of her work. I knew from being a mother of an eleven-year-old and working as a university professor that her lyrics and music videos were well known to be sexually explicit and a topic of conversation among young people from grade school children through the college students in my classes. Her lewd repeating chorus "I want to ride on your disco stick" had become a schoolyard anthem of sorts at the local grade school where my eleven-year-old was enrolled, much to the dismay and chagrin of both parents and teachers. Simulated sex gestures and movements from Lady Gaga's most popular videos had also taken off on the playground, started by the kids who had managed to jump through the parental hoops to gain access to her videos online, and copied by the rest.

I was both surprised and disturbed by the videos, in their clear manipulation of themes that have haunted the work I have done as an activist to decrease gender violence on college campuses in the United States. Lady Gaga is clearly not the standard sexy empowerment icon script that we have seen repeated since its early invention by Madonna. As a performer onstage and in videos Lady Gaga challenges the more reflective members of her audience, unfortunately not the elementary school set, to consider the destructive power of the male gaze, the commoditization of female sexuality, the damaging control of the mass media over our identities. *Los Angeles Times* journalist Ann Powers (2009) captured the difference between Madonna's work in the 1980s and Lady Gaga's in the millennium: "In the 1980s, Madonna employed bondage imagery, and it felt sexual. Gaga does it, and it looks like it hurts." As Powers articulates, this is the leap that Gaga makes, that makes her work significant, and is the reason why it has the potential to move discourse beyond the confines of the male gaze. Despite the challenges Madonna posed to audiences to consider women's sexuality as self-chosen and empowering, she remained within the comfortable zone of "sexy." Lady Gaga pushes past sexy to disturbing.

In her interview with Powers (2009), Lady Gaga comes closest to expressing this intention. Early in the interview she talks about what she refers to as "celebrity life and media culture," which she felt were "overbearing pop-cultural conditions" for her generation. Later in the interview she says what she is "trying to do is take the monster and turn it into a fairy tale," making reference to the disturbing mass media and pop culture themes that emerge in her videos. She is self-reflective regarding her position within her videos as a hypersexualized female. In the interview with Powers, Lady Gaga explains that, within the video, "me embodying the position that I'm analyzing is the very thing that makes it so powerful." In some regards the "me" she is referring to is a woman, but she is also challenging the entertainment industries' treatment of female pop icons as commodities, as a method of creating a brand. She explores these themes most vividly in her music video for "Bad Romance." Coupled with the messages of her videos are the public appearances and statements she has made supporting gay rights, again aligning herself with an activist stance.

In some ways Lady Gaga, like other female pop singers following in the wake of Madonna, has utilized the proven success of becoming another version of the sexy empowerment icon. However, in significant ways she steers off the predictable track and disturbs the customary response. Lady Gaga, similar to others working with this pop culture identity, emphasizes the sexual body. This is the first, and I would argue most visible and significant, component of the sexy empowerment icon as articulated by Gill's framework. The impact of Lady Gaga's embrace of this first step toward the now-standardized hypersexualized message of the sexy empowerment icon cannot be too heavily stressed. Many viewers stop here. Lady Gaga's name is recognized by the eleven-year-old in the playground, and the vast majority of her audience, because of her over-the-top sexuality, her mimicking of masturbation onstage, and the graphic repeatability of her sexually charged lyrics. In this way she is conforming to the now-established norm for female pop music performers.

Lady Gaga veers seriously off the customary construction of the sexy empowerment icon track when she begins to add in the second and third ingredients of Gill's postfeminist girl-empowerment model. The second key ingredient, according to the Madonna script and Gill's mass media model, is a focus on the male gaze and desire. As Powers points out in her commentary, Lady Gaga's bondage appears to really hurt, in contrast to Madonna's. Lady Gaga's performances often cross a line where the sexy moves into the disturbing. This edgier exploration contrasts vividly with the more typical hypersexualized pop music icons who follow Madonna's lead and stay within the parameters of a performance directed toward and courting the male gaze and desire. Lady Gaga also paints a more disturbing picture of Gill's third ingredient, the girl-empowerment emphasis on choice. In simple language, "this is my sexuality and I can do with it what I please!" Underlying much of Lady Gaga's performance art is a deep questioning of whether the woman displaying herself is doing so by choice or by coercion or force. Explored areas of force or coercion include the underlying constant pressure on women to dress and act to satisfy the male gaze and desire, the pressure on female performers to fulfill the sexuality-related expectations of the marketing/entertainment machine, and, at the level of the consuming female audience, the power of mass media images of female sexuality to control and influence girls and women.

Perhaps the most succinct and well-known examples of these challenges can be found in her "Bad Romance" video, which in April 2010 became the all-time most watched YouTube video with 184 million hits. Released on both Lady Gaga's website and YouTube, the opening hours of "Bad Romance" were compared by Francis Lawrence, who directed the video, to his early years making videos for MTV. In talking with Powers about the meaning of this popular video, Lady Gaga said she intended the video to probe "how the entertainment industry can, in a metaphorical way, simulate human trafficking—products being sold, the woman perceived as a commodity" (quoted in Powers, 2009). As a part of the buying and selling of female sexuality captured within the video, the power of the male gaze over female appearance and sexuality is deliberately deconstructed and at times brutally analyzed. The video takes place in a futuristic spa populated by women who kidnap Lady Gaga, dress her, and haul her off to perform for a sexy but scary audience of men. The preparation of Lady Gaga for auction to this ominous large circle of men takes the viewer through the process of preparing for the male gaze. She is sold to one of the men, whom she kills. The final scene of the video is a still of her in bed with her once-upon-a-time captor's burned corpse lying beside her. The lady is in complete control, with the hot bullets from her breasts still firing and burning the corpse.

The final vignette of "Bad Romance," with the triumph of Lady Gaga over the male villain, puts her back in control and power. She is no longer being forced to dress and perform for a male audience; she is no longer a captive. Lady Gaga's famous shooting breasts captured in the final scene of "Bad Romance" are the embodiment of the fourth component of the sexy empowerment icon, as brought to life by Madonna and theoretically outlined by Gill. In the final analysis, even if you are sold off as a sexual commodity, sexualizing yourself will lead to power (and in this case very sexy bullet bras!). Thus, despite the challenges to the branding and selling of female sexuality found in "Bad Romance," in the end the superficial walk-away meaning is the same as with every other sexy empowerment icon, that being sexy is a fast means of gaining power.

Lady Gaga's live performance in New York in January 2010 as reviewed by Jason Zinoman (2010) captures many of the same themes as the music video for "Bad Romance." In Zinoman's review he points out that Lady Gaga casts herself as a victim in a string of confining but fashionable guises as she performs a series of her major hits: "[Lady Gaga] casts fame (and her audience) as the looming threat in this story and herself as the scream queen, the perpetual victim. Her elaborate set pieces make a show of helplessness and vulnerability, boxing her slight blond figure inside a glass cube in her propulsive hit 'Just Dance'; encasing it in a rotating series of orbs during the brooding 'Bad Romance'; and in her most twisted image, chaining her hair to a black pole controlled by two men in 'Paparazzi'" (Zinoman, 2010). As in the "Bad Romance" music video Lady Gaga explores the control and commoditization of female sexuality by the entertainment industry and the male gaze and desire, in this case onstage live in front of a New York City audience. In one instance she is encased inside glass, perpetually on view, with no place to hide. In the final guise she is literally chained to a pole controlled by men, and not just random men, paparazzi—the ultimate expression of fame and celebrity as threat.

The socialization of young women to rely on their sexiness for attention and power is emotionally carried forward in a monologue Lady Gaga delivers to the audience, captured in Zinoman's review: "Midway through the show, the emotional narrative shifts when this flamboyant star, alone onstage, pauses to deliver a short monologue. Skillfully transforming into an insecure teenager racked with angst, she bashfully flops on the ground and, in the plaintive voice of a performer hooked on applause, asks the audience if she looks sexy. Quickly shifting to her superstar persona, she underlines the artifice of this plea, adding self-consciously, 'I hate the truth'" (Zinoman, 2010). Similar to the dramatic climax of the "Bad Romance" music video, in the finale of this stage performance, she takes the power back through the symbolic use of a gun that she hoists out of the piano and uses to spray the audience with bullets.

The ultimate question becomes whether the messages Lady Gaga codes into her performances and music videos are the messages communicated to a significant number of members of the audience. Nancy Bauer, in her 2010 opinion piece for the *New York Times* online, asks this very question:

> Gaga wants us to understand her self-presentation as a kind of deconstruction of femininity, not to mention celebrity. As she told Ann Powers [also quoted earlier in this chapter], "Me embodying the position that I'm analyzing is the very thing that makes it so powerful."

Of course, the more successful the embodiment, the less obvious the analytic part is. And since Gaga herself literally embodies the norms that she claims to be putting pressure on (she's pretty, she's thin, she's well-proportioned), the message, even when it comes through, is not exactly stable. It's easy to construe Gaga as suggesting that frank self-objectification is a form of real power.

Bauer's point is that it is easy to read Lady Gaga's performances as communicating the simple message that the road to power is through self-objectification, making yourself hot so you can attract the right guys at the bar Friday night. It takes more thought and a more mature intellect to deconstruct her message as a reflective analysis. This might happen in a media literacy course, but it doesn't happen on the playground as one eleven-year-old shows another eleven-year-old how to move to express the meaning of "riding on your disco stick"!

The movement of Lady Gaga's influence onto the playground and then onto the web in a YouTube video of a grade school fan is captured in an anecdote in Emily Herbert's biography of the star, wherein she tells a story of the celebrity hearing about a six-year-old in her thrall: "Lady Gaga's subject matter was adult-oriented, to put it mildly, but she was creating very catchy music and so it was inevitable that the younger generation would listen in—and then try to do it for themselves. A video was posted online of a young girl [six years old] singing Lady Gaga's songs, and the Lady herself was more than a little taken aback" (2010, p. 124). Thus, despite her attempts to create active discourse on the commodification of female sexuality, the fast pick-up message of Lady Gaga's body of work, for a wide majority of her audience, is that the clear route to power for girls and women is indirect and runs through internalizing the male gaze and desire, followed up by constructing an identity that meets and feeds those expectations.

Exploring the Contours of Raunch Eroticism

Focus on the White Heterosexual Male Gaze

In an attempt to compete successfully in the male-dominated rock-and-roll industry, female performers shifted and played with appearance in an attempt to both express some degree of power and yet also be marketable within the growing media culture of the late twentieth century. Early on, Janis Joplin discovered that competing on a level playing field by just playing good music, simply attempting to be one of the guys, was self-destructive for a female performer. The female performers who followed quickly learned that directing their appearance toward the male gaze through the creation of a sexy but powerful stage presence won both the acceptance of the male rock establishment and also the attention of female fans, eager to copy the performer's style and dress to also pull in male attention and therefore achieve some level of social power.

Sexual Objectification of Women

The rock-and-roll world of the 1960s and 1970s was a male establishment quick to minimize and marginalize the serious work of women, particularly those who in some way threatened the status quo. Women were pressured to succumb to using sexual attractiveness as a method of gaining attention, acceptance, and ultimately power. This led first to the use of sexuality as a survival and entrance strategy by performers like Madonna and then later to its use as a corporate branding strategy for performers like Britney Spears and Miley Cyrus. Lady Gaga's recent attempts to create reflection on the sexual objectification of women through her music, videos, and performances are stopped fast in their tracks by the public's socialized reaction to the sexual objectification of women. What is noticed first, and what continues to resonate, is the hypersexuality of Lady Gaga, thus reinforcing the sexy = power pattern so dominant in American and British popular culture depictions of women and girls.

Self-Objectification

With the entry onto the celebrity stage of female pop singers openly courting the male gaze through their dress styles, lyrics, and stage performances, sexual objectification ceases to be passive and becomes something that women are doing to themselves. Sexy dress styles and movements are often combined with blatantly sexual lyrics moving women from objects being manipulated to active pursuers of male sexual attention. The change in the age of these performers, down into their teenage years, and their rampant popularity with teenage (and younger) girls, creates a socialization pattern directed toward self-objectification, which is explored in chapter 5. Lady Gaga's attempt to create discourse about the damage inflicted by self-objectification in her stage performances and videos is drowned out by her audience's patterned response to sexualized female stage performers, which in effect dismisses this discourse in favor of the now-common equation of empowerment with female sexuality.

Sexual Attention and Sexualized Practice as Power

Madonna's pop culture identity quickly became that of a sexy empowerment icon with the ability to be used as a brand directed toward young women experimenting with their burgeoning sexuality. Madonna's successful use of this strategy was then picked up by the music industry to use as a means of linking empowerment and, more important, consumer products to young, sexy female performers such as Britney Spears and Miley Cyrus. Though she is not consciously courting this response, Lady Gaga's popularity and financial success are largely bound up in a slightly (but not too) deviant version of the sexy empowerment icon. In many ways, Lady Gaga, like Madonna, uses her slight deviance to court the interest of the public, but it is her hypersexualized appearances and lyrics that command broad attention.

Private Is Public

The lack of separation between a performer's public life and private life due to the intense scrutiny of the mass media pulls the intimate stories of performers into the tabloids and into the lives of the young people who follow the performers. The up-the-ante cultural norms encourage the mass media to follow stories with racy story lines, thus exposing young audiences to the sexual lives of celebrities, adding to the connection between sex and power in the minds of young consumers.

Extreme, Up the Ante

The increasing use of the sexy empowerment icon to sell product and also as a means of launching oneself as a performer has resulted in a media marketplace in which getting attention is becoming more and more difficult. As a result "off-the-chart" sexuality stunts are performed in highly visible contexts to brand the performer and ensure continued interest from her fan base. One of the best examples of this was the inclusion of the stripper pole in Miley Cyrus's Teen Choice Awards performance, the provocative *Rolling Stone* magazine cover shots of Britney Spears, and the high level of sexual content in Lady Gaga's videos, which pull the young audience to the table eager for more.

Misogyny

The story of the emergence of the pop sexy empowerment icon from the rock-and-roll wreckage of early female performers such as Janis Joplin is underwritten by misogynistic attitudes toward female musicians who didn't play by men's rules: that is, that women need to be sexy to succeed. Female performers who didn't conform to that ideal, or who pushed too hard to challenge it, were thrown to the side first by the music industry but then also by male and female audiences socialized to expect sexualized power onstage.

–4–

Midriff Marketing:
Teaching Girls the Power of Sexy

Mary Pipher (1994) brought the words and experiences of adolescent girls and their parents into living rooms and libraries throughout the United States and Britain with her still-groundbreaking study of the breakdown of self-confidence that frequently signals departure from childhood for girls growing up in the millennium. A paragraph from the introduction of her book, *Reviving Ophelia: Saving the Selves of Adolescent Girls*, captured the psychological effects of adolescence on many young women:

> Something dramatic happens to girls in early adolescence. Just as planes and ships disappear mysteriously in the Bermuda Triangle, so do the selves of girls go down in droves. They crash and burn in a social and developmental Bermuda Triangle. In early adolescence, studies show that girls' IQ scores drop and their math and science scores plummet. They lose their resiliency and optimism and become less curious and inclined to take risks. They lose their assertive, energetic, and "tomboyish" personalities and become more deferential, self-critical and depressed. They report great unhappiness with their bodies. (1994, p. 19)

This summary of effects is perhaps more vividly illustrated using the real experiences of girls that Pipher captured in her book. In the following case study Pipher captures the transitional moment of a particular girl as she experiences the transformational impact of being evaluated on her appearance by a male classmate:

> Geena was a chubby clarinet player who liked to read and play chess. She was more interested in computers than makeup and in stuffed animals than designer clothes. She walked to her first day of junior high with her pencils sharpened and her notebooks neatly labeled. She was ready to learn Spanish and algebra and to audition for school orchestra. She came home sullen and shaken. The boy who had his locker next to hers had smashed into her with his locker door and sneered, "Move your fat ass." (1994, p. 55)

What has happened to Geena is that she has been reduced to being measured by what Gail Dines refers to as "fuckability." Speaking to a mostly female college audience, Dines (2011) drew the crowd to a painful version of laughter as she recounted the narrowing of girls' aspirations during their tween years from sports, academics, and the arts to one narrow focus: "Am I fuckable." One of the key points of this chapter is to illustrate that this transitional moment is unfortunately happening at a younger and younger age, with many girls yet in upper elementary school already experiencing the effects of sexual objectification and self-evaluation based on the male gaze.

The theoretical underpinnings of Pipher's analysis rest in a variety of disciplines that have examined gendered differences in how men's and women's bodies are analyzed and assigned meaning. John Berger's now-classic analysis of the female nude within Western art history is a foundational cornerstone. Berger was one of the first to articulate the dominance of the male gaze and male desire in the depiction of women within visual imagery in the West. Key to understanding Berger's line of logic is the contrast in meaning between being naked and being nude. The female nude, according to Berger, is a woman purposefully posed to be "seen naked by others and yet not recognized" (1972, p. 54); in other words, the distinct humanity of the naked woman is sacrificed as she becomes an object created for the male gaze. Berger goes on to argue that seeing the female body as an object stimulates the "use of it as an object" (p. 54), thus setting the stage for men's often casual use of women for sexual pleasure, a theme that resonates throughout Western history.

Berger's most classic line, "Men act and women appear," is widely quoted in books such as this one and captures the fundamental difference in how males and females are socialized to interact as sexual and thinking human beings. Perhaps more important, however, is his contribution toward understanding how women begin to look at their own bodies through the eyes of a male audience, the process of self-objectification: "*Men act* and *women appear.* Men look at women. Women watch themselves being looked at. This determines not only most relations between men and women but also the relation of women to themselves. The surveyor of woman in herself is male: the surveyed female. Thus she turns herself into an object—and most particularly, an object of vision: a sight" (1972, p. 47). Thus, girls and women are surrounded by imagery that not only sexually objectifies their bodies but further trains them to look at themselves through the eyes of a male audience and assign value based on the male gaze.

A range of scholars (Freedman, 1986; Kaiser, 1989, 1997; Lips, 1981; Morgan, 1972) have detected significant differences in how men and women are socialized to express and experience power. Males are socialized to an agonic ideal focused on attaining direct physical or decision-making power over others. As this is acted out in the images and appearances that comprise popular culture, males are depicted as "players" in a range of domains including sports, sexuality, Wall Street, and politics. In contrast, women are socialized to attain power indirectly by attracting the attention of those in direct power. As acted out in popular culture scripts women are most often assigned roles in which they are pursued by men as a result of their physical attractiveness. Popular scripts include story lines focusing on the power of a beautiful woman to positively influence male actions by functioning as an attractive beacon of goodness, the classic "quest" scenario, beautiful women falling from grace as a result of attractive power gone astray, the classic "deserving slut" scenario, and ugly

Table 4.1 Coding of Gender Ideology: "Doing" versus "Being"

Doing	*Being*
Emphasis on achievement and action	Emphasis on appearance and attractiveness
Physical effectiveness	Physical attractiveness
Adventure script in popular media	Romance script in popular media
Agonic (aggressive and active) power	Hedonic (indirect and attracting) power
Ideology of building character	Ideology of maintaining character

Source: Kaiser (1997).

ducklings (often with tomboy spit) transformed at adolescence into beautiful women who then find their rescuing Prince Charming and live happily ever after!

The contrast between popular culture ideologies underlying male and female gender constructions and the clear linkage to gender-based differing modes of attaining and measuring power is articulated by Susan Kaiser's (1997) gender-role dichotomy (see Table 4.1). This model charts the clear differences in how males and females are socialized to attain and measure power, with men placed in action roles and women playing the passive roles and attaining power through indirect attractiveness. As girls enter middle school, they directly experience having their methods of attaining feelings of accomplishment dramatically limited by the shift from the "doing" side of the dichotomy to the "being" side of the model. The young woman who went to school eager to try out for orchestra (a "doing" role) is quickly put in her place when the locker door slams and she is labeled "fat" by a male peer. On the "being" side of the model, she has lost all her power, and the ability to go back over to the other side is not presented to her as a viable alternative.

Pipher published her book in 1994 with what she refers to as a "hurricane warning" at the end of the introductory chapter, informing us that as a culture we are in a dangerous storm situation regarding how we are socializing and responding to female adolescents (p. 28). To our credit, a body of good scholarship has emerged since then further documenting and discussing the problem and offering some solutions (see, for example, Durham, 2008; Lamb and Brown, 2006; Opplinger, 2008; Sarracino and Scott, 2008). More significant, however, is the development of a marketing machine that has taken advantage of the precarious psychological state of young women by creating advertising and products reinforcing the strength of Kaiser's dichotomy. Premised on the idea that the way a girl gains power is through attracting the sexual attention of a male audience, the advertising industry made a marked millennium shift from passive shots of beautiful women to more active displays of women and girls purposefully courting male sexual attention. Often paired with empowerment language such as "girl power," the model's sexual attractiveness that is being "sold" is purposefully presented to the young female consumer as empowering, equating with being "hot," with being the "it girl," with being in control and powerful.

As a response to growing public concerns focused on the apparent increase in the sexualization of girls in American culture, the American Psychological Association (APA) formed the APA Task Force on the Sexualization of Girls. According to the report issued by this task force in 2007, sexualization occurs when any of the following takes place:

- a person's value comes only from his or her sexual appeal or behavior, to the exclusion of other characteristics;
- a person is held to a standard that equates physical attractiveness (narrowly defined) with being sexy;
- a person is sexually objectified—that is, made into a thing for others' sexual use; rather than seen as a person with the capacity for independent action and decision making; and/or
- sexuality is inappropriately imposed upon a person. (American Psychological Association, Task Force on the Sexualization of Girls, 2007, p. 1)

This chapter examines a range of examples of porn chic products and trends directed toward preteen and teenage girls, ending with an exploration of the seven themes and how they are manifested within this particular age group.

Figure 4.1 *Baby.* Courtesy of Nicola Bockelmann.

Midriff Marketing: You Need to Be Hot

The *New York Times* headline was direct and to the point; it was just a few weeks before the Fall 2010 Fashion Week, and the question was "What Do Girls Want?" (Horyn, 2010). The article goes on to chart out the online websites that have been created to click into and project the buying habits of girls and young women. *AD-WEEK*'s fall 2009 headline was even more to the point: "Probing the Minds of Teenage Consumers" (Straczynski, 2009). The article goes on to quote the CEO of a youth and teen marketing trend service: "Brand marketers that target teens have so many variables to consider, including their interests, brand loyalties, shopping behaviors and internet usage. This segmentation breaks down not only what teens are interested in, but where and how they shop, and how they respond to direct mail, digital advertising and in-store marketing. It also shows how teens use different forms of traditional and new media" (Straczynski, 2009). The marketing industry's intense focus on teenagers was first brought to the attention of a wide public audience with PBS's 2001 broadcast of a program entitled *The Merchants of Cool* (Goodman and Dretzin, 2001). Featuring the commentary of media critic Douglas Rushkoff, the program outlined the scope of the marketing industries' influence over teenagers and coined the term *midriff marketing* to capture the millennium packaging of sexy girlhood.

The advertising industry's focus on teenagers, according to Rushkoff, began in the 1980s as their disposable income surpassed that of their parents: "At 32 million strong, this is the largest generation of teenagers ever, even larger than Baby Boomer parents. Last year teens spent more than $100 billion themselves and pushed their parents to spend another $50 billion on top of that. They have more money and more say over how they'll spend it than ever before" (Goodman and Dretzin, 2001). Coupled with this increasing ability to buy have been escalating rates of media exposure among children and teenagers due to the increasing media venues available to young people. The average exposure of American children and teenagers to combined mass media has reached 6 hours, 32 minutes per day (American Psychological Association, Task Force on the Sexualization of Girls, 2007, p. 5), with Rushkoff estimating in 2001 that an average teenager processed "over 3,000 discrete advertisements in a single day" (Goodman and Dretzin, 2001). This massive amount of advertising directed toward the teenage market is owned and controlled by a small number of very large companies. Of these entertainment and marketing giants, Viacom with its MTV commercial network is the "coolest" and the most influential in this market (Goodman and Dretzin, 2001), with teens watching this network an average of six hours a day (Durham, 2008, p. 31).

Alissa Quart (2003), in her book focused on the importance of branding to the teenage market, infiltrated the world of teenage trendspotters, working for such teen retailers as Delia's, an entrepreneurial direct-mail start-up that became successful at the turn of the millennium in delivering just-on-time trends to teenage girls. Delia's was started in 1996 by two male Yale roommates who hired female college students and recent graduates from the Fashion Institute of Technology and New York University to advise their product-development team. These young trendspotters were the influential "it" girls who had a strong history of holding the attention of their peers and had a history of both spotting and starting trends in their social groups. Using the language of fashion-diffusion theory (see Lynch and Strauss, 2007, pp. 130–131) these two young entrepreneurs recruited innovators and early adopters to trend-spot and at the same time influence their peers toward the emerging Delia's brand. What they were going after was fast-moving trends that were easy to design and to produce and that could be marketed nationally through direct mail. Who they were going after was the 34 percent of the female teenage market that adopts fashion trends early, following their also-trendy peers.

The success of companies like Delia's testifies to the effectiveness of using the teenage girl insider, a practice that became an industry standard. Beginning in the late 1990s an industry emerged to meet the need for trend research on this lucrative marketing segment. Look Look, a trend research firm founded in 1999 by Baysie Wightman and DeeDee Gordon, is one of the best-known services specifically focused on understanding global youth culture. A *New Yorker* magazine profile titled "The Coolhunt" in 1997 captures the early years of this now extremely successful trend analysis company. In that early profile Malcolm Gladwell accurately predicted that "what they have is what everybody seems to want" (1997, p. 78), which was a way into the world of street youth culture throughout the world. Now commanding extremely lucrative fees for access to trend information online, Look Look is an international player in the hunt for the next way to sell a brand or look to a teenage consumer.

One of the key millennium methods of marketing to teenage girls was to repackage femininity, pulling from the language of feminism yet linking to the socialization of young women toward the male gaze and desire. The result was the development of the midriff advertising archetype, a girl dolled up in the sexy tools of adulthood, selling product that promised to make the teenage consumer hot and give her power. In the words of Rushkoff: "I am midriff, hear me roar. I am a sexual object, but I am proud of it" (Goodman and Dretzin, 2001). Inspired by the midriff-baring celebrity Britney Spears, the advertising stereotype launched a marketing bonanza that is still working on the female teenage consumer worldwide.

The midriff is technically the part of the female body also referred to as the abdomen, and it became sexualized beginning in the late 1980s, headlined by Madonna's pierced belly button broadcast worldwide in music videos. Fashion trends of the late 1990s and the turn of the millennium completed the look with low-slung hip-hugging styles, raised shirts, and exposed thongs, often combined with lower-back tattoos and pierced navels. Spears connected the look to a sensibility when she skyrocketed to popularity at age sixteen as a self-proclaimed virgin dressed to flaunt in sexy Catholic schoolgirl fashions.

Rosalind Gill (2008) points out the four defining themes that characterize midriff advertising. In slightly modified language they are (1) an emphasis on the female body; (2) a shift from sexual objectification of the body by others to self-objectification (what Gill refers to as *sexual subjectification*); (3) presentation of female models as sexually assertive, in charge of their own eroticism; and (4) an emphasis on gaining power through sexual attractiveness. This type of advertising is in marked contrast to the more straightforward use of women's bodies to sell product that underwent serious critique by Jean Kilbourne in the 1970s. With the release of the first version of *Killing Us Softly* in the late 1970s to the updated 2010 release Kilbourne focused on the turning of women's bodies into objects to sell products. Some of her more recent examples are drawn from the alcohol industry's predilection for overlaying product labels onto women's midriffs. She also uses alcohol advertising to illustrate the dividing of women's bodies into sexually charged parts that are used over and over again to sell a range of products from fishing line to sandwiches:

> In recent years, women's bodies in alcohol ads are often turned into bottles of alcohol, as in a Tanqueray gin ad in which the label is branded on the woman's stomach. (Kilbourne, 1999, p. 246)

> "The best little can in Texas" pictures a close-up of a woman's derriere with a beer can held up against it. (Kilbourne, 1999, p. 247)

In both cases the advertising, directed primarily toward a male audience, depends heavily on sexual objectification of women's bodies to attract men's attention and therefore move product.

In contrast, midriff advertising, directed toward young female consumers, focuses on the empowering potential of the model's, and by implication the female consumer's, body. The girl seeing the advertisement is led to feel that if she can get herself to look like the model she will be empowered, be cool, be hot. The female teenager has already been socialized to objectify her own body, imagining how it appears to others. She has also been socialized to divide her body into parts, comparing her breasts, legs, and midriff to those found in advertising. What the girl looking at the ad swallows whole, unless she is slowed down by lessons in media literacy, is that the most important and perhaps only road to power and success open to her is through her body. She is told over and over again, by every image she sees, that being hot matters, and it matters a lot.

From Disney Raunch, to Limited Too "Hot," to American Apparel Porn

The socialization of young girls to the porn chic ideal starts early. The pressure on parents to purchase provocative clothing for young girls often begins with T-shirt slogans linked to midriff sensibility but also creeps into the design of underwear and pajama styles for girls. Sexually linked slogans are also frequently found on the rear-seat section of shorts and pants, mimicking the style trend that started in young adult female exercise fashions. A commentary in the British newspaper *The Guardian* in 2007, titled "The High Street Porn Brokers," brought this trend into public discussion in Britain: "Earlier this year Asda was condemned for stocking lacy black underwear aimed at girls as young as nine, although perhaps we shouldn't be too surprised at this move, when their parent company Wal-Mart is busy selling US teens a T-shirt bearing the hilarious slogan 'Some call it stalking—I call it love.' The clothing store Next also got in on the game with their T-shirt for 5–6 year olds, emblazoned with the immortal line: 'So many boys, so little time'" (Elliott, 2007).

In the United States Diane Levin and Jean Kilbourne appeared on the popular *Today Show* in 2008 as a publicity launch for the release of their book *So Sexy So Soon*, mainstreaming the discussion of the selling of sexually charged product to children. The list of products easily available to purchase to doll young girls up as little Lolitas is outlined in their book:

- Mainstream national chains such as Target and J.C. Penney are selling padded bras and thong panties for young girls that feature cherries and slogans such as "Wink Wink" and "Eye Candy," slang terms referring to sexual appearance and sex.
- "So Many Boys, So Little Time" is the slogan on one fitted T-shirt sold in a size made for six-year-old girls.
- A T-shirt for a four-year-old girl says "Scratch and Sniff" across the chest.
- Gym shorts for ten-year-old girls have two handprints on the back—one on each cheek—zeroing in on the spot supposedly waiting to be grabbed, patted, or pinched. (Levin and Kilbourne, 2008, p. 42)

There have been isolated consumer protests against the trend. In 2002 Abercrombie Kids released a line of thong underwear for preteen girls that included sexual innuendos, resulting in storefront protests and the eventual removal of the underwear from the racks. Consumers again protested Abercrombie Kids in April 2011 when they offered a swimsuit with a fully padded push-up bra on their children's website.

Not mentioned on the list but a clear leader of the pack in terms of media impact is the Disney marketing machine. The 2010 headlines in the United States included "Disney Child Star's Clothing Line Deemed Too Racy by Some," with a follow-up discussion of the launch of a children's wear line by the eight-year-old Disney star Emily Grace Reaves. Criticism of the line included the sexual poses used in the promotional materials, the inclusion of what appeared to be a stripper pole in the photo shoots, and the use of a combination of tutu styles, lace stockings, leopard prints, and boots to create styles that bordered on and mimicked the sexy lingerie found on soft-porn sites.

The line between little girls' and older girls' fashions began to blur in the late 1980s as marketers moved fashion sizing designations to fit the demands of the industry and consumers. Stores like The Limited, Gap, and Abercrombie & Fitch began to create children's apparel, with some lines and shirt and underwear slogans crossing over between sizing categories. As this industry trend gained steam, it was formally named with the acronym KAGOY, standing for "kids are getting older younger" (Schor, 2004, p. 56). It became increasingly common to find sizing for girls' fashion lines that stretched between size 4 and size 16, lumping very young girls with the much older and more physically developed tween market. Tweens were originally defined by the advertising industry as a market segment of eight-to twelve-year-olds, called *tweens* because of this highly profitable group's placement between children and teenagers. Once named, the tween market began steadily working its way down into the younger sizes, with some retailers even moving things like adult-style thongs into the toddler racks.

As the tween market segment stabilized in the late 1990s, many retailers designated ages seven to fourteen as the consumer market for their apparel, carefully focusing on girls old enough to begin applying pressure on parents, particularly mothers, to purchase the new trendy items, most often referred to as the "hot" looks. The story of the evolution of this market segment is probably most accurately told by examining the extremely successful evolution of the tween spin-off of the Limited Brand, Limited Too. Limited Too was launched in 1987 as a companion store to The Limited, offering birth-to-teen clothing for girls. In the late 1990s the Limited Too brand focused its attention on the age-seven-to-fourteen market, designing a store and logo distinctly targeting this newly defined demographic, and later creating the more budget-friendly Justice label, also marketed to this age bracket and their mothers. In 2008 the two brands combined under the Justice name and logo; they now have 900 stores and are market leaders serving the tween consumer.

The Justice website is careful to link empowering messages with hot new fashions. The company introduces itself by stating that it has hot fashions that give girls self-confidence: "Our creative teams lead the industry providing the hottest fashions for tween girls, ages 7 to 14—fashions that help girls express their individuality and self-confidence. The result of this creative firepower is legend with tween girls— and we wouldn't have it any other way" (Justice, 2010). This message is repeated in the mission statement for the company, which directly addresses the mother as the consumer of product for her daughter: "At Justice, we enhance a tween girl's self-esteem by providing her the hottest fashion and lifestyle products, in a unique, fun, interactive environment...all at a great value for mom." The message of "hot fashions" again pops up on the company website in the description of the typical girl who purchases and shops at Justice stores: "It's her voice, her smile, and the delight she expresses with every visit to our store, that keeps us focused on delivering the hottest fashions in an everything-for-her destination."

As one explores the fall 2010 website, selling the "hot" message is central to the marketing of apparel. The opening page is set up to look like a catalog cover and includes the headline "Layer up with Hottest fall fashions." The first listed section of the website is labeled "hot shops" and includes an even hotter section, labeled "hottest looks!" A review of the actual clothing in many ways does not live up to the "hot, hottest" promises, so in many ways the hot terminology is more marketing than substance. What the marketing accomplishes, however, is to socialize the young tween to her role as the sex object in the unapologetic bad boy script. It helps to narrow the expressions of empowerment and self-confidence applied to girls by themselves and by others to being hot and dressing sexy in these early formative years. Thus, as girls enter their teenage years they have been socialized to consider that the route to power is through sexual attractiveness.

Sharon Lamb and Lyn Brown's (2006) interviews with teenage girls illustrate that this message is registering. These girls definitely get it; they know their job is to be hot:

> "The way I dress says that I have a nice shape." "It says I'm fine." "It says that I want guys' attention." One acknowledged, "I wear makeup so boys can see the good side of me." Another said she wore both "preppy and slutty clothes [which say that] I'm tough but still sexy and a girly girl." (2006, pp. 34–35)

They have also absorbed the complex messages of "pink" that they were exposed to as young girls—that it is an innocent "girly" color but, when combined with a silver or black edge, can move into "sexy" and "hot," especially when combined with a label on the rear of the short shorts saying "Pink."

> Girls know that looking sexy is cool: "It makes me look hot and cool." With help from Victoria's Secret Pink line, which reaches down to middle schoolers via their stuffed toy giveaway with every purchase, they also associate pink, sexy, girly and cool: "I like to wear pink because it shows that I'm girly." "They say I am a fashion princess, and I love to look good." "I wear sexy little shirts that say to everyone that I am outgoing." (2006, pp. 34–35)

According to a survey also conducted by Lamb and Brown, teenage girls are attracted to two distinct looks, both highly influenced by porn chic messaging and style details. The first look is more mainstream and "cute," with an emphasis on creating self-confident styles that closely follow the tween look of mainstream marketers such as Justice, discussed earlier. The cute "hot" fashions for this age market are slightly edgier in style (more body-revealing) and are often combined with humor to create sexual allusions. Pajamas, for example, may include a clear sexual slogan such as "Hello My Name is Hottie" (Lamb and Brown, 2006, p. 36).

The second look is an alternative style attracting girls who are interested in projecting a more individual and less mainstream fashion look. Hot Topic is a store favorite. Lamb and Brown cite an *Elle Girl* story advising this edgier girl: "Take two parts frilly. Add a dash of denim and a pinch of metal. Mix well" (2006, p. 40). The net result of this slightly edgier look is still a Lolita mix of innocence and sexuality served up for a male audience. Lamb and Brown describe the photo shoot capturing this Lolita with Hot Topic's alternative fashion edge:

> And so the fourteen-year-old model wears a satin pink shirt with flower embroidery, extremely short denim shorts studded with metal, barely hiding a white lace garter belt holding up thigh-high white stockings. "Isn't it fun to be a girl?" We're asked at the beginning of the photo layout. The same girl poses next to this question wearing a metal chain necklace and a string of pearls, a white lacy top, the same lacy garter belt holding up transparent thigh-highs with stars on them, finished off with big work boots. We have to add that she is standing pigeon-toed to emphasize that little-girl-gone-sexy bad look. (2006, p. 40)

Interviews conducted by Lamb and Brown (2006) with the young sales associates helped to sort out the buying habits and preferences of the young female teenagers shopping at Hot Topic. A big draw for the middle school girls, described by the Hot Topic sales associates as "little sluts," was merchandise with the Playboy insignia, particularly found on accessories. The quick labeling and stereotyping of the middle school girls attracted to Playboy logo merchandise by the older sales associates is telling in terms of the judgmental responses of female peers to porn chic worn by others.

Older high school–age and young college-age women are more directly marketed apparel using porn chic references, with at times blatant borrowing of stereotypical pornography photo setups and scripts. Calvin Klein was one of the first designers cited for pushing the envelope in terms of underage models and sexuality with his 1980 jeans advertisements featuring a fifteen-year-old Brooke Shields and the headline "Nothing comes between me and my Calvins." His 1995 campaign using models as young as fifteen years old in short porn-style narratives in which an off-camera voice smoothly cajoled models into removing their clothes was extremely controversial for its clear linkages in format and style to 1960s vintage "picture-set" pornography. Eventually, under legal challenge from the U.S. Department of Justice, Klein pulled the ads out of circulation, but their work had been done and the jeans were a big hit that season.

Abercrombie & Fitch has also taken the heat in the older-girl market for pushing the envelope in terms of using sexuality to move product. In 2005 the Women and Girls Foundation of Southwest Pennsylvania organized and got national attention for what they referred to as a "girlcott" protesting the selling of what they considered degrading T-shirts at Abercrombie & Fitch. Slogans on the shirts included "Who Needs Brains When You Have These." After the story was picked up by Katie Couric on the popular *Today Show*, as well as a broad range of other popular American media giants, Abercrombie & Fitch pulled the shirts from the shelves and eventually produced a line of shirts designed by the protesters with more positive messages. The impact, however, seems to have been fleeting, as the fall 2009 back-to-school college men's collection cashed in on the *Girls Gone Wild* trend, including T-shirts imprinted with the slogan "Show the Twins," with an image below of a woman flashing two college males. The men's T-shirt collection also included the following two slogans: "Female Streaking Encouraged" and "Female Students Wanted for Sexual Research." The trend toward these shirts is directly linked to the now-popular and accepted unapologetic bad boy icon, discussed in chapter 2.

American Apparel, the Los Angeles–based American urban trend company, has most clearly and directly tied itself to soft-porn marketing strategies, even to the point of gaining praise for its website from a porn-industry trade magazine (Wolf, 2006). Dov Charney, the young, hip CEO, has selected what he refers to as "young metropolitan adults" as his market segment, and his audience is clearly comfortable with the sexually aggressive and subversive aesthetic he brings into his advertising and fashion shots. Wolf (2006), writing in the *New York Times* on the American Apparel advertising aesthetic, describes the ads in this way:

> The ads are also highly suggestive, and not just because they are showcasing underwear or clingy knits. They depict young men and women in bed or in the shower; if they are casually lounging on a sofa or sitting on the floor, then their legs happen to be spread, frequently they are wearing a single item of clothing but are otherwise undressed; a couple of the young women appear to be in a heightened state of pleasure. The pictures have a flash-bulb-lighted, lo-fi sultriness to them; they look less like ads than photos you'd see posted on someone's Myspace page.

Patrice Opplinger's (2008) analysis of the American Apparel fashion shoots in a spring 2006 catalog described the models and poses as "skanky," a word likely to fit Charney's commitment to selling product using what he terms "pervie" marketing strategies (Wolf, 2006).

Pigeon-Toed Lolitas: Halloween Gets Hot

Halloween masquerading over the course of the past fifteen years has become a significant fall event on college campuses across the United States. The State Street Halloween Party in Madison, Wisconsin, one of the largest university campus events in the country, started in 1979 and gradually built up a national reputation for being "the place to be on Halloween" for college students and young adults from throughout the region. Rates of participation in the festival were estimated at between 60,000 and 70,000 from 2001 to 2003, growing to about 80,000 in 2004 and peaking at 100,000 in 2005. In 2006 the city of Madison took over the planning of the event from university student government due to rioting problems among student participants, many of whom had traveled in from outside the city; this led to lower participation rates (from 32,000 in 2006 to 44,000 in 2009).

During this same time period the development and marketing of "adult" Halloween costumes has become a major business in the United States. As Halloween college events have become increasingly popular at large as well as small campuses, temporary Halloween costume stores have opened in the local malls to serve the college student shopper. The contents of these stores differ from those of other local retailers in that the costumes are directed primarily at older consumers, with sizes and thematic content matching the college shopper's needs and preferences. Online sales of adult costumes began in the late 1990s. Some more traditional costume websites have expanded to include what the industry classifies as adult costumes; in other cases, new websites emerged specializing in the young adult market. Currently, mainstream children's retailers such as Toys R Us include lines of what are termed "sexy adult costumes," featuring a sexy Goldilocks, a sexy Girl Scout selling cookies, and a black vinyl nursing uniform (very short, very hot). Male adult costumes, while available, are not as intensely marketed online as "adult costumes." More typically, pictures of women's costumes are featured as examples of adult merchandise. As an illustration, the site wondercostumes.com speaks directly to the female consumer in their description of their adult costume inventory: "Wanna spice it up! Look for a sexy costume for this Halloween Costume party and be the center of attraction! Explore for a wide selection of Adult Costumes. You will also find wigs, masks, wings, hats and other costume jewelry to complete the makeup. Disguise yourself in the magical world of costumes, have fun" (www.wondercostumes.com). Note the promise that the wearer will be the "center of attraction," a direct play into the socialization of women toward hedonic methods of achieving power, as discussed earlier in this chapter. A survey of offerings of men's adult costumes results in several categories of action-figure costumes including traditional superheroes, bad guys, space fantasy characters, pirates, and slashers (Macmillan, Lynch, and Bradley, 2011).

Female teen, tween, and children's costuming has followed in rapid pursuit with, in many cases, very slight differences between the costumes designated as "adult" on the costume websites and catalogs and those sold to the younger female market. The reaction of scholars and activists to this trend is captured in Gigi Durham's opening paragraph in the introduction of her book on media sexualization of girls: "Last Halloween, a five-year-old girl showed up at my doorstep decked out in a tube top, a gauzy miniskirt, platform shoes, and glittering eye shadow. The outfit projected a rather tawdry adult sexuality. 'I'm a Bratz!' a tot piped up proudly, brandishing a look-alike doll clutched in her chubby fist. I had an instant, dizzying flashback to an image of a child prostitute I had seen in Cambodia, dressed in a disturbingly similar outfit" (2008, p. 21).

The costume on Durham's doorstep, in a wide range of variations, is showing up on doorsteps and in school hallways throughout the country. A survey of a children's costume-supply direct-mail catalog delivered to my door in fall 2010 revealed a preponderance of sexually suggestive costuming for the little-girl and tween and teenage markets. In the little girls' sizes (3/4 to 7/8), approximately 62 percent of the costumes included sexually suggestive poses, makeup, and details, 24 percent fell into the classic princess category in terms of poses and theme, 3 percent were gender-neutral costumes (presented on girls), and 11 percent were what I would term cute costumes designed for girls, without princess or sexual references. In total, 86 percent of the little-girl costumes dressed America's daughters to attract the male gaze, with a vast majority of those costumes already courting sexual attention.

The survey of costumes sized to fit the tween and teenage market revealed an even more pronounced bias toward "sexy girl" imagery, with 96 percent of the costumes evoking a sexual response from the viewer and directed explicitly toward a male audience. With such names as "Voodie Sweetie" and "Angelicious," and promises that the wearer will "melt their hearts," the catalog copy accompanying the costumes underscored the centrality of sexuality to the costumes' appeal to young female consumers. The small number of outliers from this trend included in the catalog included a fashion costume linked to the 1960s and a rather fashionable mummy.

This Halloween sexy girls' trend has been covered by the news media, with the mainstream American magazine *Newsweek* devoting a 2007 story to the topic. The article's title directly links the sexy costumes for little girls to the raunch term *eye candy* and "kiddie porn." The familiar argument that sexy dressing enhances girls' self-esteem is also included, with the costume buyer for the Lillian Vernon direct-mail company dismissing the seriousness of the charge by saying, "Girls today seem to like a little pizzazz. The same old princesses aren't where it's at anymore. We don't want to say they're sexier, just more confident" (quoted in Philips, 2007). The *Newsweek* article highlighted the now-familiar but nevertheless disturbing trends toward the reported onset of eating disorders among girls at younger and younger ages, coupled with low self-esteem and depression. Three years later, however, the disturbing trend is still full-blown in the catalog delivered to my mailbox. The message was crystal clear to my eleven-year-old son, such that he easily mimicked (without me prodding or tutoring him) the pigeon-toed, index-finger-in-the-mouth pose of the sexy girls selling costumes to their peers in the fall 2010 catalog.

Barbara Dolls to Bratz to Madame Alexander

A page in doll history was written in fall 2010 with the redesigning of the classic Madame Alexander Cissy doll by Jason Wu, the young designer of Michelle Obama's inauguration gown. The combination of a storied and elite doll manufacturer and a young designer spotlighted by the Obama White House was a winning marketing decision. Dolled up in porn chic style, Wu's debut collection of dolls including "Vice," "Lust," "Envy," and "L'enfant Terrible" hit websites and stores in 2010 and transformed the classic Cissy doll first introduced by Madame Alexander in the 1950s into the millennium porn chic doll "Neo-Cissy." Wu's stylization of the classic doll in black undies, attached garters, and fishnet hose in 2010 was followed up in 2011 with nude bodices, thigh-high stockings, and dyed and mussed hair, all in the spirit of the new porn chic Neo-Cissy.

My examination of an original 1950 Cissy doll revealed modestly developed rounded teenage breasts, an unpronounced waistline, and childlike and child-proportioned legs and arms. As has been argued well by Robin Gerber (2009), the original Cissy, when first marketed by Madame Alexander as a fashion doll, was no competition for Mattel's overtly sexy Barbie. A style review of Cissy's original wardrobe revealed conservative 1950s styles of modest length, fabric, and cut.

The Jason Wu trend seems to have taken solid hold at Madame Alexander: Not only is he designing for Cissy, but he has launched his own line of new "Alex" dolls, including "Graphic Content Paris," described as follows on the Madame Alexander website:

> 16 inch Graphic Content Paris has dark, olive green eyes and waist length black hair worn under a sweet nothing of a hat. It, a confection of black eyelet that wraps around her head and is finished with a bow on top, accentuates the seductive shimmer of her make-up and looks smashing with her flirty black dress. The sleeveless, full-skirted dress of twisted tulle is enhanced by a fuchsia satin bodice overlaid with a sheer, black velvet windowpane fabric that's threaded with silver. A fuchsia satin sash at the waist, black lace panties, pink pearl teardrop, with gold studs, earrings, a black clutch detailed with an over-sized bow and flocked turquoise, "wrapped to the ankles" stilettos that are finished with a bow at the heel, add the last bits of panache to Graphic Content Paris' enticing look. (http://www.mfd.net/product/graphic-content-paris-doll-2026.cfm)

For those who have followed recent doll trends, and the controversy surrounding the hypersexualized Bratz dolls, the new Jason Wu trend might be labeled "Bratz meets Madame Alexander." This could perhaps be compared to the Queen adopting a "pervie" London street trend. While Madame Alexander dolls are collector's items and not widely affordable to a mass market, the introduction of porn chic doll making into this exclusive and storied company signals a high level of acceptability for the hypersexualization of the female fashion doll, a story that really begins with Barbie.

The Barbie doll was introduced by Mattel in February 1959 at the national Toy Fair in New York by her creator, Ruth Handler. Ruth was forty-three years old and the executive vice president of Mattel. She was a proven entrepreneur who had played a fundamental role in launching her toy company as a national leader. To date Mattel had depended on two things: (1) the creative genius of Ruth's husband to invent toys that resonated with 1950s popular culture and (2) Ruth's ability to market and move her husband's merchandise. The Barbie doll was Ruth's baby, and while she had the superficial support of her husband and the other men at Mattel, they were dubious of the doll's ability to appeal to the American market.

The original Barbie doll was a remake of a German doll that Ruth had purchased on vacation and given to her two daughters as a gift. The "Bild-Lilli" German doll was a sex toy gag gift inspired by a female character named Lilli in a German comic strip published in a tabloid newspaper called *Bild-Zeitung.* Lilli was a provocative, sexy character who got her way with men using her sexual charms and a limited degree of cleverness. Like the original Barbie, Lilli's hair was pulled back in a bouncy ponytail, her lips were pursed and ready, her eyelids were heavily lined with mascara, and she had long legs that went all the way up, and a bosom to match. She was a dame to be reckoned with, and unapologetically sexy. The Lilli doll was put together by the comic strip's cartoonist and was originally sold in establishments frequented by men, such as bars, adult sex shops, and tobacco stores. At the point when Ruth purchased it, the doll was making its way into some children's hands in Germany, but it was still primarily marketed to men.

Gerber (2009) points out that the sexiness of the new Barbie contrasted vividly with the other American dolls and paper dolls of the 1950s, which tended toward childlike, or at most prepubescent, bodies and cute chubby faces. Like the original Madame Alexander Cissy doll discussed earlier, Barbie's fashion doll competitors carefully steered clear of blatant sexuality and modeled their dolls closer to the look of the well-established baby doll market. Way ahead of its time, Barbie was the first adult-proportioned and stylized doll marketed to girls. The first response of toy-industry leaders, including Ruth's husband, Elliot, was guarded. Gerber's book on the launch of Barbie includes a classic quote from Elliot to his wife: "Ruth, no mother is going to buy her daughter a doll with breasts" (2009, pp. 7–8). The results of the 1959 launch appeared to support Elliot's claim, with the major names in toy retailing passing up the Barbie as unsalable.

Ruth didn't give up. Despite the reception at the Toy Fair in February, Barbie was introduced in a series of television ads in March. The television advertising, as well as the design of the final doll, was strongly influenced by the marketing advice of Ernest Dichter. Dichter was one of the first well-known motivational advertising researchers and was hired by Mattel to work on the marketing of not only Barbie but also other controversial toys, including guns for boys. Not afraid to use sex to sell product, "he pronounced that phallic-looking lipstick packaging was more attractive to women, and that necktie manufacturers should contrast an old, limp tie on an older man with a 'smooth, colorful, erect and manly' tie on a younger man" (Gerber, 2009, p. 106).

Unlike the other men Ruth was working with in the toy industry, Dichter was not put off by Barbie's sexiness; in fact, he directed Ruth to make her breasts even larger. Working with interview data he gathered from a fairly limited number of girls and mothers, Dichter concluded that girls liked the dolls because they were glamorous and looked how they hoped to look when they were older. However, mothers, as predicted by the mostly male toy-industry leaders, were put off by the blatant sexuality of the doll. Since mothers had the power to purchase, Dichter advised Ruth to downplay the sexuality of Barbie in the television advertisements. Instead, the advertisements presented Barbie as a teen fashion model that girls could play with to learn to dress and accessorize. The response to the television advertising was delayed, but by early summer orders for Barbie were higher than the supply available from Mattel's Japanese manufacturers. The "It" toy for little girls in the early summer of 1959 was Barbie.

Way ahead of its time, Barbie was a harbinger of the porn chic dolls to come. What was different about playing with Barbie was that little girls identified with Barbie as a grown-up version of themselves. Gerber points out a pivotal point made in 1963 by a writer for the *New York Times*, who clearly articulated the paradigm shift marked by the entrance of Barbie into the doll market: "Ruth predicted that Barbie would be a kind of Rorschach test for little girls' imaginations, and she was right. By 1963 the *New York Times* wrote of the 'revolutionary idea that little girls today are viewing the girl dolls increasingly as themselves and not as their babies'" (2009, pp. 110–111). Girls' identification with Barbie became the marketing entry point for using advertising to affect and narrow how girls envision themselves and their future roles and aspirations. A second critical point articulated by Gerber about the Barbie doll is that it was modeled after a doll originally created to attract male sexual attention. What Barbie's marketing managed to do, almost single-handedly, was to focus the attention of toy advertising directed toward girls on toys that helped them imagine the power they could get through growing up pretty and, in the millennium, being a little bit sexy.

Bratz dolls were revolutionary not in their sexual suggestiveness so much as in the fact that their sexual explicitness was specifically designed from the get-go to appeal to a little girl's imagination and play habits. The original sexy look of Barbie was co-opted for the little-girl market by a shrewd entrepreneur who slightly modified the doll for the new consumer. In contrast, the designer of the Bratz doll ratcheted up the sexual appeal and the dating-script marketing to appeal to the little girl being influenced by our culture to see herself through a lens of sexual objectification, sexual fantasy scripts, and social power derived through attracting the right boys. When she or her parents buy the Bratz doll, they also buy the dating scripts, the marketing scheme that the road to empowerment is through sexuality, and the "girls need to be hot" messaging of the brand.

Cultural model theory holds that children learn models of how to conduct their lives from the marketing schemes used to sell them products. Particularly in dimensions of their lives in which children lack experience, researchers have shown that these marketing-driven models have an impact on the socialization patterns of children and adolescents (Bachen and Illouz, 1996; Duveen and Lloyd, 1990). Using this stream of logic, marketing hypersexualized dolls that are scripted into sexually objectified but seemingly powerful roles to sexually inexperienced girls has the potential to affect how they envision themselves sexually and how they enter into relationships with others.

Exploring the Contours of Raunch Eroticism

The lessons girls are learning as they watch television commercials, read ad copy, and play branded video games result in patterns of self-objectification. In the millennium girls literally learn to see themselves through the lens of the male gaze and desire by absorbing the marketing that surrounds them. The marketing machine is in full gear and headed in the wrong direction in terms of offering young girls scripts that lead to empowerment and authentic sexual agency. It is clear that some girls are able to synthesize rather than succumb to the barrage of hypersexualized messaging and enter into young adulthood empowered and thoughtful. What needs to be asked, however, particularly given the analysis of the following seven symptoms, is what individual power outliers, small numbers of girls and women, have to transform cultural trends and behaviors?

Focus on the White Heterosexual Male Gaze

The marketing scripts and design details that chart the meaning of products for young female consumers are dominated by an assumption that these young girls are preparing themselves to perform gender for a male, predominantly white, heterosexual audience. From the poses and characters offered to girls by the Halloween costume industry, to Bratz dolls wearing sexually provocative dress and sold with accompanying dating kits, to a tween fashion T-shirt imprinted with "Who Needs Brains When You Have These," the clear message to young girls is to measure their worth and value based on their ability to attract male attention and regard. Underlying but not as obvious is a bias toward white males as the norm. For example, the Bratz marketers, careful to give the appearance of cultural diversity in the creation of the female dolls, offer two white male dolls to support (and view) the rest of the female cast.

Sexual Objectification of Women

The most damaging impact of the case study examples reviewed in this chapter is the normalization of the sexual objectification of the female body that occurs as girls and young women are bombarded with imagery and scripts dominated by scantily clad images. Research indicates growing levels of visual display of fully or partially nude female bodies in advertising (Sullivan and O'Connor, 1988; Busby and Leichty, 1993; Reichert and Carpenter, 2004), with the practice so common that its presence is no longer a point of surprise for children, both boys and girls. The era of going downstairs at a relative's house to look through the pile of *National Geographic* or even *Playboy* to find the few pictures of bare breasts buried in the pile of magazines is clearly over, replaced with a media "pile of breasts" often disconnected from real people, real situations, and real children's lives.

Perhaps more disturbing is the trend toward sexual objectification of not only adult women's bodies in advertising but girls' bodies as well. The American Psychological Association's 2007 study of the sexualization of girls cites research pointing toward this growing trend in advertising, with girls often posed seductively with adult women wearing matching clothing (American Psychological Association, Task Force on the Sexualization of Girls, 2007, p. 13). Dating back to the series of Calvin Klein Jeans ads featuring a fifteen-year-old Brooke Shields, the use of girls, or models dressed to look like young girls, in advertising is increasing and, with that, girls' tendency to identify with the advertising.

Finally, the sexual objectification messages carried into dolls marketed to young girls enter into their consciousness at a key developmental stage where they are formulating roles and scripts to follow later in life. The difference between the background noise of sexuality surrounding girls in our culture and particular products designed and marketed to fit into the play habits and imagination of young girls is noted by the American Psychological Association's report: "Although these dolls may present no more sexualization of girls or women than is seen in MTV videos, it is worrisome when dolls designed specifically for 4- to 8-year-olds are associated with an objectified adult sexuality. The objectified sexuality presented by these dolls, as opposed to the healthy sexuality that develops as a normal part of adolescence, is limiting for adolescent girls, and even more so for the very young girls who represent the market for these dolls" (2007, p. 14).

Self-Objectification

The scripts embedded in advertising, coupled with the imagery girls confront as they shop online for clothes or fantasize about a new Bratz doll, continually remind and teach girls that their one big job is to look good and attract the boys. When a little girl shops for a Halloween costume, she is bombarded with choices and poses that flirt with and attract sexual attention, teaching her to self-objectify and court the male gaze in advance of the blossoming of her own sexuality. Again, what is most damaging is the normalization of this patterned response, with girls taught to shop, dress, and behave while imagining the response of a male audience. As they are caught before they have formulated set patterned responses, these messages become ingrained and natural to these girls, who then carry the patterns into adulthood.

Sexual Attention and Sexualized Practice as Power

Clearly, throughout all the examples discussed in this chapter, girls are being taught that getting sexual attention will give them power and influence. Halloween costume advertising copy is filled with links between flaunting one's sexuality and being noticed, popular, and cool, and being a fashion trendsetter. The opening lines of costume descriptions from a fall 2010 catalog include "Cast your heavenly glow!" (in your Angelicious Light-Up Costume), "You could start a new fashion trend in this cute kimono-style costume," and "You are destined to steal hearts, dress in this royal costume." The Justice tween girls' website declares that "at Justice, we enhance a tween girl's self-esteem by providing her the hottest fashion" and further that Justice fashions "help girls express their individuality and self-confidence" (Justice, 2010).

In marked contradiction to the marketing messages of empowerment are the disturbing results from social historians studying current teen sexuality that indicate that while girls report feelings of empowerment when they provide oral sex and other sexual acts for men, they do not report experiencing any pleasure or fulfillment themselves (Durham, 2008, p. 55). So even in the narrow realm of sexuality, the message is not ringing true in terms of giving these girls authentic sexual agency. In broader terms, the underlying message that what really matters is your physical appearance, over and above physical and mental accomplishments, sets girls up to have lowered achievement levels in other important areas, such as academics and sports.

Private Is Public

While boys' Internet usage has been in the spotlight as a research topic, comparative usage rates based on gender indicate that girls and boys are online in about equal numbers (Lenhart, Rainie, and Lewis, 2001; Roberts, Foehr, and Rideout, 2005), with girls out in front of their male peers in early middle school (Lenhart, Madden, and Hitlin, 2005). Research I conducted during the early years of Facebook found extremely high rates of raunch-inspired cyber-identities among first-year female college students, indicating that young women had been groomed while still in high school to visualize themselves in sexually objectified terms. Online marketers to girls such as Bratz have hot links to Facebook sites, encouraging girls to create profiles and offering sexy role models in the line of dolls for the current season.

Extreme, Up the Ante

The merging of the advertising and entertainment industries, and the small number of very large companies controlling the media, results in a ruthless spirit of competitiveness and no-paths-barred mentality in terms of selling product to girls. Using the argument that the consumer needs to be continually stimulated with newness, the trend is toward shock value. Advertising teams are focused on how to move porn chic into a younger and younger market, and product developers are focused on how to make it as skanky as the public will tolerate. "Sexiness" or "hotness" is the button that keeps getting pushed, a little harder every time, to ensure the product being sold will be noticed by an increasingly oversaturated market of raunch.

At the same time that the product is getting a little raunchier, the girls are being socialized to feel that the best and fastest route to power is to be the one in the hallway who gets the most attention from boys. The pressure to push the envelope and wear their skirts a little shorter, to have the most risqué Halloween costume so that—in words drawn directly from Halloween ad copy—they can be the "center of attention," is intense for girls. The convergence of both of these up-the-ante trends results in advertising, product, and behavior all pushing the sexuality barometer up for younger and younger girls.

Misogyny

The clearest link to misogynistic attitudes used within products and marketing for girls can be found in the slogans and images on T-shirts, underwear, and the posterior area of girls' pants. Often relying on humor as a mode of acceptance, these slogans condone a range of misogynistic behaviors. Examples I found available for sale online included a girls' tight-fitting T-shirt imprinted with the image of a video game controller on the breast front with the words "Grab Here and Rotate" and a pair of work-out pants with a pair of hands printed on the rear, visibly inviting an ass grab. Within all these examples misogyny is hidden beneath a veneer of humor. All the examples are both designed and marketed to be purchased and worn by young women and girls, who then neatly fit within a cultural world dominated by the male gaze and male desire.

–5–

Girls Gone Wild: College Coeds Flash
Their Goods

Female flashing of the breasts in party or bar contexts became a part of American college and spring break culture beginning in the late 1990s. Joe Francis, the founder of *Girls Gone Wild* (*GGW*), a company specializing in capturing the behavior on film and selling it on videos and online, does $40 million a year in sales. Francis has become a major porn-industry player by marketing the "girl next door" as cross-over porn star (Dines, 2010; Levy, 2005). Using flashing of the breasts as a lead-in, Francis has carefully constructed a franchise focused on soft porn performed by "real" college girls. While understood and publicly marketed as primarily showing breast exposure, *GGW* videos include explicit sexual acts ranging from footage featuring girl-on-girl sex in the shower to young female coeds with carefully waxed pubic areas inserting dildos into their vaginas.

The *GGW* brand was carefully constructed by Francis to give the appearance of fitting into mainstream American popular culture. The fact that Francis successfully took advantage of a trend already occurring within American college culture made it easier for him to promote *GGW* as a branded product carrying lifestyle messages of "fun," "party time," and "girl-next-door co-eds ready for action." Despite these overtures to mainstream popular culture, Francis is working directly with others in the hard-core porn industry. To underscore this argument Gail Dines (2010) points out his ties to WebQuest, an interactive service for firms linked to hard-core porn distributors, and the presence of *GGW* at the national porn trade conventions. Conceived by others in the porn industry as functioning as a form of bridge between hard-core porn and popular culture (Dines, 2010), Francis has found a niche that is making his company a lot of money.

The roots of *GGW*'s marketing success can be found in behaviors happening on college campuses and at spring break locations beginning in the late 1990s. Young women were voluntarily flashing their breasts, and at times being pressured to flash their breasts, to a growing audience of male peers, often armed with cameras and camera phones. The widespread acceptability and prevalence of flashing behavior is testified to by a ten-year study of the behavior that I conducted at a small state-supported rural campus in the central United States, characterized by a homogeneous undergraduate student body of approximately 13,500, with 95 percent coming from within a fifty-mile radius of this farm belt university. As this book is being published (2012), the *GGW* buses are still visiting the campus, but at the beginning of the research the flashing behavior was native to the campus, and videos and photographs distributed on the web were contributed by male college students attending the event, not *GGW*'s trained crews.

Female flashing[1] on the campus where this research was conducted first began to occur on the Saturday night following the annual homecoming football game in a two- to three-block area in front of a set of six bars in a commercial district adjoining campus, commonly referred to by students as "the Hill." Due to a riot in 1996, in 1997 the street in front of the bars was closed to traffic during this celebration, in an effort to confine the student crowd to a controlled area that was closely monitored by both campus and community police. High concentrations of students who had been drinking prompted the police to address the celebration as a potential riot situation, with police present both in uniform and undercover throughout the crowd. Police staffing for homecoming was done at potential riot level. The local police chief estimated that on a typical Friday or Saturday night about three to four officers were assigned to the Hill area, with others available if needed. On homecoming, the staffing was increased to over forty officers in the two- to three-block Hill area, including state patrol officers, city officers, and reserves.

Flashing of the breasts emerged as a street behavior in 1997 after the street was blocked off to traffic due to the riot in 1996. Female flashing started as an isolated behavior occurring as the bars closed and students crowded into the barricaded street area. Flashing behavior increased steadily from 1997 to 2003. By the time I got out into the street in the fall of 2000 flashing had become a central focus of the university homecoming celebration, with flashing happening as early as 8:30 in the evening in 2002. Due to police actions and campus interventions discussed later in this chapter, flashing moved from spontaneous student-initiated behavior to a *GGW* promotional tour event after 2005. The *GGW* tour events were staged in particular bars, with the *GGW* camera crews moving from one bar to the next taking footage of breast and bootie exposures, with limited flashing activity happening in the public streets in front of the bars. Great anticipation for the event was created by having the bus parked in front of the bar district for the day preceding the *GGW* tour event inside the bars.

During the early homecoming-celebration years, a majority of the flashing occurred in the public space in the streets in front of the bars, which is where I concentrated my fieldwork. I also witnessed a limited amount of flashing on balconies off of student apartments and on the streets surrounding the bar district. Female flashers within the large crowd were typically carried on men's shoulders, in order to be seen by a larger audience. Most early flashing behavior was confined to breast baring, with isolated incidents observed in both 2001 and 2002 of female flashing of the pubic area and buttocks, combined with flashing of the breasts. In 2011, at the close of the research for this book, "bootie flashing" of the buttocks was very common within the bars.

Young men often attended homecoming street events in groups, partnering with friends in the early years to bring video equipment. In the later years most men showed up with their own cell phones with imaging capability. Mardi Gras–style beads were sold at the local bookstore and were worn around the necks of male students as they went down to campus and were given away to flashers throughout the night. Informal interviews of numerous student participants while I was doing fieldwork, as well as documentation in the form of e-mail attachments shown to the author by students, indicated the widespread sharing of images of flashers from homecoming through websites and e-mail. Female students also attended the celebration in groups, with small numbers attending with male dates. Couples generally stayed on the fringe of the crowd. Men with female dates typically did not participate in the flashing audience behavior, such as pressuring women to flash, taking cell phone pictures of the action, or chanting at flashers.

Over the course of the homecoming-celebration research, police interviews and field observations documented a trend toward a more male-dominated crowd, with small numbers of women mostly staying out of the center of the crowd or walking through quickly. Police and field observations also detected a trend toward larger numbers of participants traveling from other colleges both in and out of the state,[2] drawn to the event by computer chat rooms and radio commentary focused on the flashing behavior. Police arrest patterns clearly indicated that outside visitors, rather than local college students, constituted the largest percentage of problem crowd members, with over 75 percent of citations given to people outside of the campus community.

Beginning in 2002, recognizing that flashing behavior was the principal draw for male crowd members traveling to the campus for the celebration, and in order to decrease groping and other gender-related violent behaviors in the crowd, police began to systematically take young women down off men's shoulders and lead them out of the crowd. This effort showed some success in decreasing flashing, as young women did not want to be approached by officers. In 2003 crowds were so dense that it was difficult for police to reach flashers in the hub, so the strategy did not work as effectively. In 2004 a system dividing the Hill into two sections with a barricaded police tunnel through the middle allowed officers access to the dense hub at the center of the crowd. This access in combination with the installation of surveillance cameras decreased flashing behavior significantly, eventually virtually ending the street flashing, moving the behavior inside bars and restricting it to tour events staged by *GGW* in cooperation with the local bar owners.

Flashing as Discourse: Understanding the Meaning

My research on flashing advanced the understanding of flashing behavior on two fronts. The first major contribution of my research is the use of flashing behavior to expand Duncan Kennedy's (1993) definition of provocative dress to include sexually revealing behaviors when enacted by dressed participants in a social rather than a performance setting such as a strip club. Kennedy (1993, pp. 163–164) used a semiotic approach to define provocative dress as female appearance styles that deviate from the accepted norm in a specific social situation, toward sexual suggestiveness and/or body exposure.

Second, the theoretical focus of my analysis considered flashing behavior within the body of recent feminist scholarship focused on the role of dress and appearance in the expression of female sexual agency and/or sexual objectification. In particular, I was interested in approaching the problem from the vantage point of a Foucauldian feminist, focusing on the exercise of power within a microenvironment and its effect on the constitution of female and male identity and sexuality. As a related component, I sought to understand the behavior in relationship to dominant cultural discourses about male sexuality.

Flashing as a Form of Provocative Dress

Consistency regarding how a label of "provocative" or "sexual" dress is assigned within the academic literature is problematic. Researchers typically have devised their own methods for differentiating what is commonly called "provocative" or "sexual" dress for women from more conservative styles, but conscious and deliberate attempts to build research around a commonly held definition are not apparent in the literature.

Many of the quantitative studies exploring the concept of provocative dress have used attribution theory to analyze participant responses to different dress and appearance styles. These studies utilized carefully constructed pictures depicting models in what researchers select as sexually provocative clothing; these are then contrasted with another slide (or other slides) that the researcher determined to be more conservative clothing (Cahoon and Edmonds, 1987; Edmonds and Cahoon, 1984; Johnson, 1995; Workman and Orr, 1996). Researchers using this technique held certain variables constant, such as model and context, so that what is measured is the impact of the changing dress style on the viewer's perceptions. A related study (Alexander, 1980) used fictionalized vignettes in which the dress styles of a rape victim, as well as other variables, were purposefully manipulated. In other quantitative studies the researchers relied on the participants to make their own judgments regarding what constitutes "seductive" dress or a "sexy" personality. For example, in Fiore and De-Long's study of apparel cues and personality, participants were asked to match a "romantic, sexy, alluring" personality to distinct sweater types (1984, p. 269).

As put forward by Alinor Sterling (1995, p. 98), Kennedy's definition is unique in offering "the beginnings of a theory of how provocative dress is signified." Kennedy's definitional separation of exposure and context when looking at provocative dress is a substantive contribution to research focused on the relationship between dress and sexuality. Early stages of my fieldwork focused on student perceptions of flashing, especially regarding whether to situate or understand the behavior in the context of research on strippers (see Egan, 2000) or attempt to examine it as a form of provocative dress (Kennedy, 1993; Sterling, 1995). Interview data I gathered from students clearly indicated that students differentiated the breast-baring behavior they witnessed or participated in at homecoming from paid work done within a club or bar setting.

First, a great majority of students interviewed viewed flashing as a spontaneous, unplanned behavior, in an environment very different from a club or strip bar:

> The environments are totally different. A topless dancer goes into work expecting to take all of her clothes off, or whatever. And someone that goes to the Hill on homecoming does not necessarily expect to [plan to] flash.

Many students differentiated flashing from club stripping behavior based on the context in which the behavior occurs. In some cases the fact that it was a public setting, in which anyone could see the behavior, including underage audience members, made it clearly different from stripping:

> A topless dancer is in a private club where you have to be a certain age to see it, on the Hill it is right out in the open so the public can view it.

The public context was central to many of the students' responses, with many echoing the idea that the behavior's occurrence in an open context, where audience members were not paying to enter for a staged performance, made flashing very different from stripping.

Students also brought up the increased risk to flashers, when compared to the protected zones surrounding a paid stripper in a club:

> Well, a topless dancer is in a place where there is security. The place is closed in. Whereas on the Hill, I've seen guys just practically tackle the girls.

Finally, repeated interviews made reference to the professional paid status of a stripper, compared to a flasher, with some students assigning greater agency to the paid dancer:

> A dancer at *Flirts* [local strip bar] does it for a living, they don't have any problems with it, and I don't think they regret it.... I think compared to a girl on the Hill, like doing that, she wakes up the next day feeling retarded or stupid. A stripper knows exactly what she's doing and even if she's drunk she knows she is at work, and that is what she has to do ... rather than [in contrast with] a girl on getting drunk and waking up the next morning and saying, "what the hell did I do."

Students' tendency to assign strippers a greater degree of personal agency is typical throughout the interviews, with one first-year female student even stating that strippers had more "dignity."

Supporting the research decision to classify flashing as a form of provocative dress are associations that student interview participants made between flashing behavior and other forms of revealing dress worn in the bar context. For example, in discussing women who might be more likely to flash, or who have flashed, students often brought up examples of women who might dress in more provocative styles in a more general bar setting. Dress styles like "skirts and tank tops in December" were linked to flashing behavior and to crowds and bars frequented by first-year students, in which "dirty, groping, grabbing" behaviors were common. A female student, when asked about expectations regarding women's behavior during homecoming, stated that "a girl was expected to dress in as little as possible, and not really be modest at all, and probably be drunk and hook up with some guy," a statement that stressed the prevalence of provocative dress at homecoming and the association of flashing with those other forms of body-revealing female appearance found at the event.

Fieldwork as well as related earlier research (Lynch, 1999b) reinforced the categorization of flashing as a club/bar provocative dress style that students clearly differentiated from what they often referred to as "casual dress." The term *casual dress* was used by students to describe a more conservative dress style that easily fit within the normative range of dress expected in the college bar setting. First-year female students, in particular, were often stereotyped for appearing in what older students classified as provocative dress styles that clearly marked that they were young, on campus for the first time, and out for a good time.

Constitution of Gender through Exercise of Power

As articulated in the opening chapter of this book, Marxist and Foucauldian feminists both offer bodies of research and theory relevant to the analysis of flashing behavior. Marxist feminists use Karl Marx's theory of alienation to argue that women are socialized to objectify their own bodies, experiencing their own sexuality as a form of indirect pleasure as they imagine a male audience's response to their bodies (Bartky, 1990; Johnston, 1997; Fredrickson and Roberts, 1997; Calogero, 2004; MacKinnon, 1982). In contrast, Foucauldian feminists view power as productive, with women's as well as men's identities in flux, formulated over and over again in local social contexts through the exercise of power. This theoretical position leaves open possibilities for liberation as well as domination within a given social context. Feminist scholarship influenced by Michel Foucault, supporting the idea that appearance can be subversive, stresses that women "create individual identities by putting together [their] own self-representations" and further that "mainstream fashion...continuously changes its own definitions of masculinity and femininity and plays with gender all the time" (Wilson, 1990, p. 69). Thus feminist scholar Jana

Sawicki (1991) argues that careful study of particular instances and individual experiences is necessary to understand the multidimensional and pluralistic nature of power as expressed within a specific context.

Duncan Kennedy (1993) elaborated on this work in his semiotic definition of provocative dress, discussing what he refers to as "sexy dress subculture," a culture within which women's sexuality is celebrated through defiant and blatantly sexual dress styles, an experimentation that he argues can result in agency and transformation of gender. Similarly, Linda Scott interpreted power and agency in beauty and sexy dress culture. In discussing cosmetic culture she argued that "advertisements call up competing ideas of beauty for readers to consider and negotiate" (1993, p. 132). Molly Hite, in analyzing Madonna's enactment of flamboyant female desire, argued that the performance is subversive and turns the passive object of desire into "a producer of meanings" (1988, pp. 121–122).

Caution is advised, however, in determining the degree of agency expressed by sexy dress styles that have become popular fashion trends. Many feminist scholars (Sterling, 1995; Bordo, 1991; Haug, 1987) have questioned the degree of free choice women and girls have within the imposed patriarchal system of modesty and objectification dominating popularly practiced fashion culture. As reviewed in the opening chapter, Ellen Riordan's (2001) analysis of the Riot Grrrls, the young feminist movement emanating out of the West Coast girl music culture of the 1990s, traced the transformative power of the early movement to its eventual commodification in the form of the Spice Girls. However, in the end Riordan found that later, more popularly embraced celebrity fashion icons such as the Spice Girls diluted the original subversive meaning of the Riot Grrrls' dress and appearance, moving the message they communicated to fit much more easily within existing patriarchal patterns focused on attracting the male gaze and desire.

As a microenvironment the homecoming celebration offers the opportunity to observe and analyze the constitution of male and female genders through the exercise of power, offering what Sawicki articulates as "a hierarchal context of power relations at the micro level of society" (1991, p. 8). My participant observation and fieldwork at homecoming celebrations revealed very clear gender differences in how flashing and the more general homecoming celebration were perceived and experienced by male and female members of the crowd. Sizable numbers of both male and female participants were drawn to the event because it was simply the thing to do on homecoming weekend, and "everyone is there." Interview data as well as fieldwork observations revealed that female students were warier of crowd behavior and expressed more reservations than their male counterparts:

Female Perceptions

The guys really bother me, how they will yell at people for not flashing and if a girl gets picked up that doesn't want to be picked up and even if she starts crying the guys start screaming at her.

Male Perceptions

> Personally, I like the idea of homecoming. I like the idea of, you know, going on the Hill, and then the girls flashing, and alcohol, and the friends, and having a good time.

The contrast in how male and female students experienced the Hill was aptly captured in one interview where a male student contrasted going to homecoming with his friends in the past to attending the event with his girlfriend two months prior to the interview:

> I have had the experience of going to homecoming with my buddies, and that was pretty laid back, I guess. A fun time, you know, we just watched the scenery [interview participant begins to laugh, with "scenery" referring to flashing]. But I had the experience a couple of months ago, taking my girlfriend on the Hill for homecoming, and I was a lot more aware of the situation. I was a little more uptight. I was concerned if you will, I didn't want anybody grabbing my girlfriend, so it was a lot more stressful.

Female flashers described the decision to flash as spontaneous, influenced by alcohol, and most often a result of being pressured or in one case "forced" to flash by male friends or crowd members. A typical description of being physically pressured to flash is captured in an interview with a female junior who had attended the celebration for three years and flashed many times:

> It was my freshman year, I was just standing there and I wasn't even doing anything to make a person wander up to me, but some guy just came up and put me on his shoulders, and, like in front of the crowd, or whatever, and just started chanting, "show your tits," and that was totally not my choice to do.

As I observed in the field, once the female students were lifted onto the shoulders, it was very difficult for them to get down, as the crowd swelled around the potential flasher, often grabbing for her breasts or other body parts until she gave in and flashed.

Flashers explain the motivation for flashing as alcohol induced and as a way of getting attention. One student stated that alcohol was the "100 percent motivator" and that no one "would do it sober." In explaining their own behavior all nine of the flashers interviewed claimed they had been drinking, with many describing excess drinking. When asked whether she was drunk, one flasher answered in one word: "bombed." All flashers I interviewed used the word *attention* to describe why female students flash. One interview with a flasher included a more in-depth analysis of why women succumb to male pressure to flash:

> I mean a lot of times girls do what guys want them to do just to feel like they are "in" or just to feel like they "are" something, and maybe they feel that if a guy wants them to flash then you know it makes them feel more popular and secure about themselves.

Young women admitted to me that they felt badly about the behavior later, with one flasher stating that she felt that flashers "look like sluts." Many were very anxious about the possibility of their images appearing on the Internet or of being seen flashing by someone they knew on campus. Descriptions of the Hill environment during homecoming captured feelings of insecurity based on aggressive male behaviors. In describing male behavior, terms used included "violent and rough," "grabbed forcefully," "forced," and "tackle." Despite these largely negative feelings about the behavior, a majority of flashers had repeated the behavior at more than one homecoming celebration.

Motivations that female students who had not flashed assigned to the flashers typically fell easily within the pattern of women's socialization toward the male gaze that was captured in the flasher interviews and articulated by Sterling (1995), Bordo (1991), and Butler (1999). A sampling of responses falling into that pattern is listed here:

I guess there is something on their minds, like they are being accepted by these guys. All these guys at that second want them, scream for them. They [the guys] like what they see and that is really nice...so many girls are looking for a guy in their life to accept them, and stuff like that.

They do it for attention...to make them feel better about themselves, that somebody actually wants them.

Lack of self-esteem among flashers, as made evident in the second quote, is a constant theme throughout the interviews. Many students assumed or claimed to know that the self-esteem of flashers is lower than normal and that the behavior is a means of getting male attention for a woman who doesn't have high regard for herself.

The semiotic playfulness discussed by Kennedy (1993), wherein women enact provocative styles of dress in order to test or change existing gender roles and expectations surrounding sexuality, did not emerge as a theme in my interviews. From a male perspective, "often the girls are not very attractive, so unless they are pressured to do it, they won't get attention. I feel that they want to get the attention, whether they are intoxicated or not." Thus, although the potential for flashing to be an exercise of female power and sexuality within the microenvironment of the Hill existed, what was in fact constituted were male and female identities reinforcing patterns of females serving as objects of the male gaze and desire.

These documented gender differences in how the celebration was experienced indicate that the exercise of power during the homecoming celebration produced at a microlevel a pattern of domination in which men felt empowered through relationships with other male crowd members to coerce and pressure women to fulfill sexually objectified roles. In addition, female students who succumbed to the pressure to flash consistently followed a pattern of seeking male attention that they and other interviewed female students presented as understandable and normal. Other women watching the flashers justified and/or explained the behavior with phrases like "I guess there is something on their minds, like they are being accepted by these guys... so many girls are looking for a guy in their life to accept them, and stuff like that."

Reinforcement of Hegemonic Masculinity

A limited amount of quantitative research supports the idea that women construct provocative (i.e., body-revealing) appearances for an intended male audience. Ed Edmonds and Delwin Cahoon's 1984 study concluded that women are aware of the impact of sexually provocative dress on men, with women who perceived themselves as sexually attractive preferring dress styles that would fall into the more provocative category. The response of the male audience also has been established as significant and measurable, with male respondents rating women as more sexual and seductive when wearing provocative dress (Abbey et al., 1987).

Complicating factors related to interpreting the results of these studies have been pointed out by Sharon Lennon, Kim Johnson, and Theresa Schultz (1999), who cite research indicating that males are more apt than females to read sexual intent into dress and other forms of communicative behavior (Abbey et al., 1987; Goodchilds and Zellman, 1984). These researchers argue that a range of motivations, including desire to conform to popular fashions, lead women to dress provocatively and that miscommunication can occur when men read these messages as a form of sexual interest. The seriousness of this miscommunication is testified to by the often large and inappropriate role of a victim's appearance and dress in discussions of blame for a sexual assault.

Research on male sexuality supports the preceding research stressing gender differences in how sexuality is experienced. Bruce Ellis and Donald Symons (1990, p. 529) found that "men are more likely to view *others* as the objects of their sexual desires, whereas women are more likely to view *themselves* as the objects of sexual desire." The fundamental tie between the cultural construction of American masculinity and sexual objectification has been identified by multiple researchers. Gary Brooks (1997) and Jack Litewka (1974) identified primary elements of male sexuality, including sexual objectification of women, voyeurism, and a tendency toward fixation on certain portions of female anatomy, including the breasts.

Men's view of sexuality as a contest has resulted in terminology and attitudes toward male sexuality that differ dramatically from those applied to women. Leah Adams-Curtis and Gordon Forbes (2004) found that men with histories of multiple sexual partners tend to be labeled as "players" or "studs," marking the influence of the late 1950s and 1960s international playboy icon in the construction of normative masculinity in the new millennium. In contrast, women with the same histories are labeled with negative terms such as "slut" and "whore." Further, some versions of sexual coercion of women by men are viewed as within the parameters of normal behavior by both college-age men and women, due in large part to the notion that men are "on the make" and in adversarial roles with their female partners (Adams-Curtis and Forbes, 2004), again reinforcing the influence of the behavior of the international playboy icon with his focus on serial conquest.

The misreading by men of the intentions of female dress and/or behavior, as found in the reviewed literature (Abbey et al., 1987; Goodchilds and Zellman, 1984), was visibly evident in observations made during fieldwork, as well as the content of many of the interviews. Male audience members often read a woman's presence on the Hill or in the midst of the crowd as evidence of her willingness to flash. For example, the male respondent who made the following comment assumed that half the women on the Hill during homecoming were there planning to flash, a figure that does not fit with fieldwork notes or interviews of female participants, in which not one woman indicated that flashing was a premeditated decision:

I think people stay on the Hill for one reason. The people that are there want to see it [flashing]. Definitely I think it causes more ruckus or violence like rape and arrests. Compared to any other night on campus, it is like you go out and "do anything." I think it is mostly social but flashing is why many people go there. Probably 50 percent of the girls want to go out there and flash.

In addition to assuming female students were at the celebration because they were planning to flash, male crowd members also more generally misread female intentions, assuming that if a woman was on the Hill during homecoming, she was open to groping behaviors, actions that would not be acceptable in another context. Thus, in multiple ways, women's decision to attend the event was often read by men as a form of provocative behavior, particularly when combined with either flashing behavior or body-revealing dress styles.

Numerous women interviewed described being grabbed by male crowd members as they tried to make their way through the homecoming crowds. The following excerpt from a female student captures the experiences of many college women, who walked down to the Hill "just to say we did it" but ended up being treated as potential flashers by the men in the crowd:

Oh, homecoming, it was horrible on the Hill. It was one of the most traumatic experiences of my life. Probably about 11:30 or so we just walked down to the Hill just to be able to say that we had done it, and when we got there.... I mean not even two minutes after we got down there, we just got swarmed into the mess of things, and like guys were grabbing. One of my friends slapped a guy because he had grabbed her, so she slapped him, and there was one time there was four of us all holding hands so we wouldn't get separated. We just got mobbed. Guys just swarmed at us. My friend from out of town was crying because she was real scared, and it is just really messed up, tormenting, very horrible, the most horrible experience in my life.

The idea that men view sexuality as a form of conquest was also a theme found in interviews and observed during fieldwork. Male students' pressuring of female students to flash, including acquaintances and friends, was observed during all attended homecoming celebrations. A typical form of coercion witnessed in the crowd was the lifting of sometimes willing, sometimes unwilling, female students up on the shoulders of male crowd members. Once the young women were up on the shoulders, the crowd noticed them and started to chant in unison, "Show your tits," often successfully pressuring young women to flash. Students also captured the process in their interviews:

> Last year the weather was nice, so it was okay to be outside compared to the year before. We ran into people that we knew, and we kind of hung out with them, but I hate getting close to the crowd because they grab you and try to lift you up. It is kind of scary...especially this year. My friend was trying to get through the crowd, because a friend of hers was supposed to meet us, and these guys grabbed our feet trying to lift us up. I just kicked them away...we just got away from them and just kept pushing. The people that did that were from her home town, and they knew her so they just thought it was okay.

As discussed in the previous section, while both flashing and nonflashing women often explained flashing as motivated by a desire to attract male sexual attention, other students place greater emphasis on the role of male pressure in initiating the behavior. Some interviews very simply stated that the principal reason women flash is that they are pressured by men. A typical short response to a question asking about the motivation for female flashing is "I think they just get drunk, and are pressured by men to do it." Other students gave a more graphic picture of how the pressure feels, and how much the body was violated by male crowd members, as they coerced women to flash:

> The guys would just come up at us at the Hill and try to get us to flash, and [they were] yanking on our shirts and touching, touching, hands everywhere...so we just like all held hands and tried to be together, so me and my friends are like throwing elbows, telling people to stop, and eventually we made it back out [of the crowd], you definitely need to stay outside on the edges and not get into the center of the crowd.

Some students directly attributed flashing to male chanting behaviors, observed during fieldwork, in which large groups of men focused on individual women and used hand gestures to point as they chanted, "Show your tits." A male fraternity member described the situation as follows:

> I think that some of them do it out of fear. Ya know, you hear the chants, use whatever chant you want, but guys get to the point where they are angry if they don't see what they came to see at homecoming.

In fieldwork observations, I witnessed over and over incidents where male and sometimes female friends pressured young women to get up on a male's shoulders, resulting in the potential flasher being surrounded by large crowds chanting, "Show your tits!" Young women unwilling to succumb to the pressure of the crowd were rudely booed and at times assaulted by thrown beer cans and bottles. A student described the crowd response to flashing, or the possibility of flashing, as "one big wave toward the girl." Fieldwork observations in crowds as large as 2,000 and interviews of female students documented that within this large crowd male behavior was often frightening and/or intimidating to the young women who were being targeted. In addition to field observations of women being coerced to flash by men, the interviews I conducted with campus police yielded similar results:

> Flashing seems to be socially accepted, people don't comprehend the danger to the flashers, and it sends the wrong signal to men. When asked why they did it, women usually say that they were frightened, drunk, or coerced. I think flashing is demeaning to women, and definitely a starting point for other activity [gender violence].

In summary, on the street and in the middle of the crowd, the homecoming celebration is experienced as a male-driven event, with women playing sexually objectified roles assigned by the audience, with little agency given to women to experiment with or express their own sexuality. The clear sense that males view the event as oriented toward their own desire and needs is captured in this quote, in which an interviewer asks a male student for any closing comments or additions to the interview:

Interviewer:	What would you like to add to this interview?
Male participant:	Stop the meatheads.
Interviewer:	What does that mean?
Male participant:	It's a male mentality. I'm a male, and you are a female, and you are mine.

Two of the fundamental aspects of hegemonic masculinity as defined in the millennium, reinforced by this research, are the tendency to accept as normal the sexual objectification of women and the tendency of many men to view sexuality as conquest. Both of these behaviors are the direct legacy of the international playboy icon that emerged as an idealized masculine standard in post–World War II America and Britain. The focus on the breast as a site of sexual objectification supports Litewka's (1974) findings that men tend to fixate on particular parts of female anatomy. It was also a conscious choice by Joe Francis to link his mainstream porn enterprise to the early breast-baring layouts of *Playboy*, now accepted as part of American popular culture, rather than to make a connection to the still somewhat marginalized world of hard porn.

Summary and Discussion

Kennedy's contribution to the understanding of how a label of "provocative" or "sexually alluring" gets placed on a dress style worn by a woman is an extremely useful conceptual tool. The major contribution of Kennedy's definition is the inclusion of context and normative standards as a means of determining what is considered provocative dress. Rather than relying on the degree of body exposure, fabrication, and drape of the dress style, or the judgment of a varied group of survey participants, Kennedy considers paramount the context in which the dress is worn and the normative standards for that context. If the dress style does not fit the context due to increased body exposure or suggestiveness, the dress style is labeled provocative in his system. This definition is particularly relevant in the contemporary situation, where public dress standards vary considerably from one context to another.

What is missing from Kennedy's analysis is the impact of a woman's behavior on the meaning assigned to her dress style. A dress style that might be considered acceptable and normal becomes provocative when a woman's behavior deviates toward sexual suggestiveness. Female behavior on the Hill during homecoming included many incidents in which women wearing conventional bar attire were temporarily labeled provocative, due to flashing behavior or simply the willingness to participate in the celebration where flashing was occurring.

The application of a Foucauldian analysis to this microenvironment reveals that although a potential for challenge to male-centered sexual experience exists on the Hill through flashing behaviors, the experiences of students indicate that flashing in this context is serving to reproduce the cultural pattern in which women are sexually objectified in the service of the male gaze and sexual desire. The exercise of power on the Hill produces a male-dominated spectator-driven event, with women at times forcefully coerced into flashing behaviors. Explanations for the behavior provided by both flashing and nonflashing female participants most often focused on women's need for sexual attention from men, supporting the theoretical argument that women are socialized to self-objectify, seeing themselves as objects of the male gaze (Sterling, 1995).

Patterns of hegemonic male sexuality were reinforced at the microlevel by this event. The tendency of dominant versions of male sexuality to sexually objectify women, fixate on specific parts of female anatomy such as the breasts, and view sexuality as conquest are reinforced powerfully through this microevent on a single small college campus. The use of violence and force to coerce women to fulfill male sexual needs that was detected in the female interviews, coupled with the depiction of homecoming by most men interviewed as a fun bonding time with friends, presents a disturbing picture of this slice of college life and the ways in which these patterns may be connected to the current high rates of gender violence on college campuses.

Exploring the Contours of Raunch Eroticism

Focus on the White Heterosexual Male Gaze

The audience being served by the flashers on the Hill during the homecoming celebration was clearly white, heterosexual, and male. All the flashers I observed during my four years of homecoming street fieldwork were white, even though the research was happening in an urban area with a significant African American population. The male crowd that dominated the street was by and large made up of whites between sixteen and twenty-five, with some white males traveling from as far away as Texas. I noted that as the event moved inside the bars as a *GGW* bus tour event, the crowd expanded to include a slightly more diverse ethnic mix, but white males still dominated the bar audiences as well.

This same audience is targeted by the *GGW* franchise, and a "10" within a typical *GGW* script, according to Dines (2010, p. 31), is "young, white, blonde, blue-eyed" and, of course, big breasted. To make her point regarding the exclusion of racially diverse women from *GGW* scripts, Dines describes a scene from *GGW Sex-Starved College Girls 3*: "The camera hones in on three girls, two white and one black. All three look excited to be on *GGW*, but it is the white women who get all the attention. As they begin to kiss, the camera focuses on the white women. The black woman stands perfectly still, not knowing what to do with herself as her two friends get into a heavy make-out session. As the scene continues, the camera blocks out the black woman completely" (2010, p. 31). The appropriation of girl-on-girl sex acts to serve male desire is symptomatic of the position of privilege the white male holds in this game, with no room afforded to women, lesbians, or gay males.

Both male and female students were drawn down to the Hill to celebrate homecoming, particularly first-year students, who felt it was a rite of passage to participate in the annual event. The contrast between how one male student described the event, as "and then the girls flashing, and alcohol, and the friends and having a good time," and how one young women remembers the event, as the "most horrible experience of my life," reflects clearly that the event developed as a cultural performance to please a male audience, often at the expense of participating women.

Sexual Objectification of Women

The *GGW* focus on breast flashing as an entry point to the soft-porn exploitation of college-age women points to the foundation of sexual objectification underlying the Joe Francis enterprise. While it can certainly be argued that the *GGW* products contain explicit sexual content and offer more than a naked breast, it must also be recognized that the brand most exploits the long history of male fixation on the exposed female breast as a marketing device. The in many ways superficial separation of *GGW* from the porn industry, and *GGW*'s resulting close affiliation with popular culture, in large part rests on its reputation for being a "tit show," not a company that produces sexually explicit videos. The fact that sexual objectification of women's breasts is interpreted by much of the viewing public as "a bit of fairly innocent fun," in contrast with other forms of marketed porn, tells volumes about how internalized and normalized sexual objectification of women has become in the United States and Britain. Francis and his ingenious marketing team have correctly gambled on the assumption that a vast majority of the media audience will not connect the dots leading from objectifying the breast to treating individual women as disposable sexual objects. In the world of "this is just a fun peep show," *GGW* can operate on campuses and across culture more generally as an entertainment company, not a purveyor of pornography.

The strong contrast between how male and female students experienced the homecoming celebration on the Hill, with men reporting that it was fun and that "probably 50 percent of the women flash," and women describing being groped and coerced to flash by male members of the crowd, points toward the active sexual objectification of women by men at this event. Young men attending the homecoming street celebration assumed that if a woman was on the Hill, particularly if she was not with a male escort or date, she was there to flash. Young women attending the event therefore became sexual objects to be viewed by the crowd, simply by choosing to go to the Hill for homecoming. In marked contrast, the female students attending the event as observers felt used and at risk, and they created strategies to stay safe and away from the heart of the crowd.

Self-Objectification

The interviews with women who went to the event planning to flash revealed that it was most often a repeat performance; in other words, the woman had flashed the year before and was doing it again. Female flashers indicated they were seeking attention from male crowd members, and while they described being pressured to flash, most admitted to self-objectification, having made the choice to flash rather than being explicitly forced to flash. All expressed that they felt badly about the behavior later, that they felt pressured to do it, that it was alcohol induced, and that it made them feel like what many referred to as "sluts."

The role of alcohol and crowd coercion in the decision to flash makes it difficult to argue that this is a clear example of self-objectification. With some women describing their condition as "bombed" at the point when they decided to flash, the question needs to be asked of the male-dominated crowd, or more significantly of a professional team like *GGW*, whether they are taking advantage of a sometimes underage inebriated girl, socialized to self-objectify to gain the attention of men. The fact that the women had returned to the event and flashed again demonstrates the strong power of socialization toward self-objectification in this age group.

Dines stresses the role of prior socialization in grooming young women to succumb to the overtures of the *GGW* crews: "After speaking with young women who appeared on *GGW*, what has become clear to me is that Francis and his team are experts in manipulating these women into becoming the raw material of his product. The important point is that these women have already been seasoned by the culture to see themselves as sex objects, and Francis and his team build on this by overwhelming them with compliments about how hot and beautiful they are and what beautiful bodies they have" (2010, p. 30). Thus *GGW* paints a picture in the young woman's mind of how she will appear to a male audience, thereby helping her construct an image of her sexual power so that she then flashes in order to embody it.

Sexual Attention and Sexualized Practice as Power

Fieldwork observations as well as the results from the student interviews indicate that the young women who flashed at homecoming were seeking sexual attention and felt that the sexualized practice of flashing had the potential to give them a certain degree of power. Both male and female students, however, were quick to recognize that the flashing performance did not result in the young woman feeling powerful but instead often led to classification as a "slut" and feelings of shame. This was particularly true if the flasher found or heard about images of her breasts being circulated online. Similarly, Dines's (2010) interviews with women whose images had been captured and subsequently circulated by *GGW* video crews indicated some extreme and detrimental life changes, including dropping out of college.

Private Is Public

My four years of initial street fieldwork coincided with the development of cell phone photography technology. During the first two years of fieldwork I observed male students carrying video equipment and cameras to the event in order to capture foot-age and photographs of the flashing. The invention and spread of cell phones with imaging capability dramatically affected male crowd members' ability to widely disseminate images of women over the Internet.

The first flashing on the Hill occurred in 1997, preceding by one year the first release of a *GGW* video, in 1998. With the growth of the *GGW* national brand, the activity on the Hill became part of a national trend, with Internet blogs following the event and men traveling from out of state to attend. The transformation of what was originally a public, one-time-only, limited crowd performance by a college girl into a widely disseminated, and in the case of *GGW* marketed, image caught the women captured on film by surprise. I personally witnessed the traumatized reactions of women who experienced having images of themselves sent by mass e-mail by male students photographing the event with cell phones. The reaction of women captured by the *GGW* video crews and later seeing themselves in marketed videos resulted in a number of largely unsuccessful lawsuits and criminal complaints.

Dines's (2010) analysis points out that traditionally spring break was a time pe-riod when young people escaped the confines of "normal expectations" and let loose for a weekend of fun. As the spring break locations were on beaches a long way from home, there was a sense of escape and a feeling of freedom to experiment.

Thus spring break was a liminal zone, a temporary escape for young college students. The photographing and taping of these experiences by *GGW* video crews violated the private spaces of these young students and made their experiments in some cases permanent and lasting within their private, academic, and professional histories.

Extreme, Up the Ante

In many ways what Francis managed to do was capitalize on an already-existing spring break trend. MTV crews and other filmmakers such as Chip Olson (Mead, 2002) had been filming spring break culture for the college audience for a number of years preceding the breakout videos of *GGW* in the late 1990s. What Francis did was push the porn envelope on this trend to make it more marketable. While the late-night television advertisements featured flashing women, hidden inside the videos was much more explicit girl-on-girl pornography. In essence, he "upped the ante," made the already-existing street trend a little raunchier, and cashed in on the big prize, a multibillion-dollar franchise featuring "real coeds" in soft-porn videos. This in turn pushed the envelope on college campuses as well. The homecoming celebration I researched grew out of its early roots as a local event drawing crowds from the surrounding community and campus to a national event drawing men from as far away as Texas to see young Midwestern coeds flash for the crowd and their cell phone cameras.

Within the *GGW* video footage itself, there is the staging of what Dines (2010, p. 30) refers to as a "voyeuristic thrill" game, wherein the audience of men is invited in to watch the *GGW* crew attempt to talk young "good girls" into flashing for the camera. The crews up the ante quickly after the girls agree to flash, with attempts to convince the young and often very drunk young women to follow them to hotel rooms to film more explicit sexual footage. Part of the excitement, argues Dines, is derived from seeing a "real" girl perform on camera for the first time, innocence removed, all on tape, and all for sale.

Misogyny

The combination of alcohol and an intense focus on the male gaze and male desire created a field day for misogyny on the Hill during homecoming. Young men threw empty and full beer cans and bottles at both women who refused to flash and also women they felt "just didn't quite measure up" to their expectations. Women's bodies were openly groped as they tried to make their way through the crowd, and women without friends and/or escorts were at risk of being hoisted on a man's shoulders and pressured to flash. The assumption that if a woman was on the Hill she was there to flash dominated the male ethos, with some men traveling across three states to get to the event and wanting to make sure the drive was worth it. Commentary on posted photographs and videos after the event continued the misogynistic dialogue, with male viewers posting often less-than-complimentary comments about flashers' bodies.

In comparison to the fieldwork I conducted, the footage and images captured by *GGW* crews are purposefully cleaned up to present a fun party-like atmosphere. Blatantly coercive behavior on the part of surrounding peers or the actual *GGW* camera crew is not included in the marketed tapes, so while the cameras capture the "thrill of the game" in terms of convincing "real" girls to flash, they do not capture any of the darker footage of girls breaking down under the pressure or expressing anger, or of crowds degrading a hesitant young woman. Within the more sexually explicit *GGW* footage, the raw hard-porn footage of women being violently penetrated and degraded by men is replaced by softer girl-on-girl action or masturbation scenes that skirt on the border of popular culture and allow *GGW* to ride the profitable border between the pornography industry and popular culture.

–6–

Creating, Molding, and Performing
Mainstream Porn Identity

Polaroid sex emerged as a form of amateur pornography in the late 1970s and early 1980s with the invention of the first instant camera. The ability for any individual to instantly produce pornography without going through a darkroom opened the door for amateur photographers to produce work and compete to get into venues like "Hustler Beaver Hunt," a repeating section of *Hustler* magazine devoted to publishing the salacious photographs of its readership (Waskul, 2004). As Dennis Waskul points out in his overview of the use of technology to create amateur pornography, the Polaroid was followed by a string of inventions including, most significantly, camcorders and the World Wide Web, which moved the ability to create and disseminate pornography into the hands of virtually anyone willing to devote a limited amount of time to grasping fairly simple technology.

At the same time that the ability to produce home pornography was dramatically accelerating, the level of access to pornography was also gradually increasing. The astronomical increase in access occurred, however, with the establishment of the World Wide Web in 1991. The instant and easy access by literally everyone to explicit sexual materials through the Internet is having the largest impact on how sexuality is experienced in the millennium. Yes, we have new ways of producing pornographic images. And yes, this process is more democratic in that it allows amateurs to produce their own images. But what truly changed our everyday experience of sexuality was the ability of literally anyone to transmit images to vast audiences instantly. In Waskul's words:

> At its core, what is most new about Internet sex is its unprecedented access. Never before have so many people had such easy access to so much sexually explicit material. Previous technologies made sexually explicit materials available, but adult movie theaters, pornographic bookstores, the dank and dimly lit back room of neighborhood video rental shops, the embarrassment of purchasing a nudie magazine at a local gas station, and similar controls have always kept the availability of these materials somewhat limited and rather tightly confined. The Internet has significantly changed that. From the comfort of one's own home and under a dense veil of anonymity, an enormous range of sex is ready available at one's fingertips. (2004, p. 4)

Figure 6.1 *Porn Chic VII.* Courtesy of Nicola Bockelmann.

An additional relevant point is that the Internet moved easy access to pornography into the hands of young audiences still in the formative stages of developing their sexual identities and expectations. While I was visiting the United Kingdom working on this book, the *Sunday Times Magazine* carried a front-page story on the impact of Internet pornography on teenagers. The story opened with a case study example of a boy first exposed to online pornography at age nine: "Tom was nine when he first looked at porn on the internet. At first it was a little secret, something he did every month or so. But by the time he was 12 and away at boarding school, he was surfing porn sites on his laptop under the bed covers every night. To camouflage what he was doing, he hid his favorite pictures inside Word documents" (Mills, 2010, p. 17). The article goes on to recount that by the time Tom reached the age of sexual activity he had been trained and educated in what he described as "a pretty inappropriate mixed bag of fantasies and scenarios" (Mills, 2010, p. 18), which didn't work in or fit very well with a real relationship.

While women and girls are not typically directly viewing pornography at nearly the same rates as boys and men, the hypersexualized norms of the porn industry have worked their way into the mainstream and are significantly affecting what women accept as normal in terms of how they present their bodies in public and private spaces. In a nutshell the expectations the boys glean from pornography sites become transferred onto the women and girls who surround them. The young men enter into relationships with women with expectations set by the women they have watched in porn videos.

Young women learn early that the more closely they conform to porn chic ideals, the more attention they will get from their peers. For young women in particular, appearing sexy is increasingly seen as a daily regimen, not something put on for a night out. Gail Dines (2011) points out that "teachers, including elementary school teachers, often complain that their female students look more like they are going to a party than coming to school," and two chapters of a recent book titled *Pop-Porn*, one focused on elementary school (Bishop, 2007) and one on college fashions (Harvey and Robinson, 2007), examine the wearing of sleaze fashion on a daily basis by girls and young women in America. The exposure of a wider audience to porn has also had the effect of moving porn standards of appearance into the mainstream, with increasing numbers of women opting for breast implants and a shaved or waxed pubic region.

Molding the Mainstream Porn Body: Transformation of the Normative Ideal

Shifting ideals of beauty, such as the dramatic movement from the more voluptuous ideals of feminine beauty of the Victorian era to the late twentieth-century thin and more athletic ideal, bring with them dramatic changes in how women's bodies are shaped through the use of undergarments and in some cases plastic surgery. According to Anne Hollander (1975), these changes are often inspired by images of the body, pictures that inspire a new look, a new interpretation of beauty. While Hollander focused her analysis primarily on the depiction of women in painting, the pictorial images of beauty that we are now commonly exposed to are most often popular culture photographic images found online, in print, and in films or videos. Contemporary photographic images often utilize touch-up techniques such as airbrushing to achieve ideal body shapes and looks. Plastic surgery enhancement of the breasts and other parts of the body to mirror pornography ideals has become increasingly common among celebrity figures, thus changing the popular culture images of women.

Breast Implants: The Millennium Solution to a Bustier Ideal of Beauty

Evidence is now clear that that the century-long commitment to the thin, more athletic ideal of beauty that emerged in the early 1900s has been replaced in the millennium by a bustier, more voluptuous ideal. Breast implants, while not yet normative in all parts of the country, are becoming more widely accepted. Even in the rural farm belt of the United States, the trend is taking off, with a student in my class reporting to me that both her roommates arrived on campus in fall with completed breast implants. Health concerns related to the silicone implants that caused a decline in surgeries in the early 1990s appear to be quelled, with wide adoption of the trend in saline implants, particularly in southern California, Texas, and Florida:

> Surgery for breast enlargement (including breast lifts) has grown by 257 percent since 1997, reaching 432,403 patients last year [2004], according to the American Society

Figure 6.2 *Asylum.* Courtesy of Nicola Bockelmann.

for Aesthetic Plastic Surgery. Saline implants, filled with water, have largely replaced silicone in the United States. In total surgeons have performed about 1.3 million augmentations in the last decade, not enough to have a broad impact on the American clothing market in a population of 149 million women. But the implant trend has affected the styles sold in designer boutiques in certain cities and regions where surgeries are most popular. (Wilson, 2005)

Fashions on store racks in regions strongly affected by this trend are beginning to reflect the new ideal, with larger sizes being offered:

In regions where breast augmentation is most popular the wave of implants is skewing the selection of designer clothes sold at some stores, favoring sizes and styles more ample on top and creating a new market for alterations. With many plastic surgeons saying that Los Angeles is the country's implant capital, the Beverly Hills branch of Neiman Marcus sells more dresses in Size 12 than any other, while Sizes 8 and 10 are the most popular for designer evening wear at other Neiman branches, said a buyer for the chain, who linked the phenomenon to customers who had surgically increased their busts. (Wilson, 2005)

However, changes in dimensions of dress forms are considered more significant. In addition, designers are exploring potential style changes related to the aesthetic of dressing a body that is busty but slim. The current mismatch between runway styles and this new millennium ideal is captured by Brian Bolke, a high-end Dallas boutique owner:

> For women who love fashion, breast enlargements and designer dresses do not go together. These women have great bodies, but they are not the bodies that designer clothes are made for. There is a ton of adjustments going on, because this area [Texas] is not known for small chests. Either women are having dresses completely butchered, or we're selling them separates with a top and skirt in different sizes. (Wilson, 2005)

Thus, what seems to be emerging as the millennium ideal female body is a tantalizing mix of hypersexualized porn chic expressed by large breast size coupled with the fitness ideal emphasizing well-toned legs and a fit, tight belly. The combined visual effect is the core message of the sexy empowerment icon: "Get hot, get powerful!" The perceived linkage of breast enhancement to increased self-esteem and confidence is particularly used to appeal to the teenage market, with Opplinger (2008) citing newspaper articles recounting stories of girls getting implants as graduation presents and sweet-sixteen birthday gifts.

Genital Waxing: From the Bikini Line of the 1970s to the Millennium Brazilian Wax

Contemporary genital-waxing grooming practices for women can be traced back to two different cultural shifts. "Bikini line" genital waxing or shaving as a fashion-related trend emerged in United States and Britain in the 1970s along with bikini-style swimsuits for women. This twentieth-century feminine grooming practice focused on trimming the pubic hair left uncovered by the new, more revealing swimsuit, focusing on hair on either side of the pubic region that was not covered by the high-cut sides of the 1970s bikini styles. The second shift occurred as a result of the mainstreaming of pornography ideals at the turn of the millennium. With this, waxing rather than shaving became the norm, and pubic styles became more defined, popular, and pronounced, with Desmond Morris (2004, pp. 199–200) listing eight different styles:

- *The Bikini Line*: This is the least extreme form. All pubic hair covered by the bikini is left in place. Only straggling hairs on either side are removed, so that none is visible when a bikini with high-cut sides is being worn.
- *The Full Bikini*: Only a small amount of hair is left, on the Mound of Venus (the mound pubis).
- *The European*: All pubic hair is removed "except for a small patch on the mound."

- *The Triangle*: All pubic hair is removed except for a sharply trimmed triangle with the central, lower point aimed at the top of the genitals. It has been described as "an arrowhead pointing the way to pleasure."
- *The Moustache*: Everything is removed except for a wide, rectangular patch just above the hood at the top of the genital slit. This is sometimes called "The Hitler's Moustache," or "Chaplin's Moustache."
- *The Heart*: The main pubic tuft is shaped into a heart symbol and may be dyed pink. This is a popular style for St. Valentine's Day, presented as an erotic surprise to a sexual partner.
- *The Landing Strip*: A cultivated pubic hair pattern in which the hair is trimmed to a narrow vertical strip or rectangle, and all other pubic hair is removed. The landing strip starts from anywhere between the natural pubic hairline to within two inches from the top of the vulva, and ends just above the clitoris.
- *The Playboy Strip*: Everything is removed except for a long, narrow rectangle of hair, 4 cm (1 1/2 inches) wide.

The most recent trend in genital waxing, termed the *Brazilian wax*, is the most extreme. This waxing style is directly linked to millennium trends in the porn industry toward unimpeded and detailed shots of female genitalia on porn websites and videos (Jeffreys, 2005). The Brazilian wax includes complete waxing of the genital region in the front and back, including waxing of the labia and the area surrounding the anus. The safety of this procedure has been a point of debate in the public media due to infection risks when waxing this sensitive area of the body. Popular culture advice columnists have entered the debate, typically supporting the practice and often assigning the unwaxed mound to the wild and primitive era prior to pubic civilization. For example, on the *Cosmopolitan* website a woman writes in for advice: "My guy wants me to try a Brazilian bikini wax that leaves me totally bare. Is that safe?" The sexual health editor for *Cosmo* writes back a reassuring answer linking the need for pubic hair to precivilization: "Generally, yes. Back in caveman days, we needed pubic hair to keep germs out of the body, but now that we bathe and wear underwear, we no longer have much use for it" ("Sexual Health," n.d.).

The connection between good grooming and the Brazilian wax that the *Cosmopolitan* sexual health advice columnist makes is echoed in comments that Dines gathered while she was lecturing on college campuses in the first decade of the twenty-first century: "At a lecture I was giving at a large West Coast university in the spring of 2008, the female students talked extensively about how much they preferred to have a completely waxed pubic area as it made them feel 'clean', 'hot', and 'well groomed'" (2010, p. 99). Female college students talking with Dines attributed their desire for a Brazilian wax to the preferences of their male partners, as did the woman writing to *Cosmopolitan*, who explained her inquiry to the advice columnist by stating, "My guy wants me to try a Brazilian wax." The college students' comments linking their waxing behaviors to boyfriends came out less directly in their conversation with Dines after her lecture:

> As they excitedly insisted that they themselves chose to have a Brazilian wax, one student let slip that her boyfriend had complained when she decided to give up on waxing. The excitement in the room gave way to a subdued discussion of how some boyfriends had even refused to have sex with nonwaxed girlfriends, saying they "looked gross". One student told the group that her boyfriend bought her a waxing kit for Valentine's Day, while yet another sent out an e-mail to his friends joking about his girlfriend's "hairy beaver". No, she did not break up with him; she got waxed instead. (Dines, 2010, p. 99)

In Eleanor Mills's (2010) interviews with young British boys and men, she found the same attitudes toward what she calls the "untended garden." Similar to what Dines reported, British men and boys steeped in pornography expect and increasingly insist on "pornified—i.e., hairless—nether regions" (Mills, 2010, p. 21). Mills captured boys' and young men's reactions to female pubic hair in her article:

> The young men I speak to express disgust at the idea of encountering an unshaven girl. "Gross, I'd get out of there!" said one. "All hairy? No way! That'd be it," said another. One friend in his mid-forties, who dates much younger women, described to me how, as internet porn took off in the mid-1990s, he began encountering what he termed "porn-star privates". He said: "For a man of my generation, it was quite weird, not what I was used to. But now they all do it." (Mills, 2010, p. 21)

The appearance of a woman's genitals after a successful Brazilian wax makes her resemble much more closely a prepubescent girl, making uncomfortable visual connections between the adult woman's waxed pelvic mound and images of naked prepubescent girls found on underage pornography sites. The practice is also linked by Susan Cokal (2007) to pornography's emphasis on serving the male gaze and desire. Cokal argues that the shaving of the pubic region "yields up the vulva's secrets for male gaze, makes the woman more naked, the spectacle—for the female body is always a spectacle—more striking" (2007, p. 139). The solid position of the shaved vulva as the pornography norm is testified to, according to Cokal, by the relegation of unshaved women to so-called dirty alternative porn sites specifically directed toward a male audience preferring a less clean and more natural look.

For men struggling with partners who are resistant to shaving, pornography sites offer online chat room advice. These sites feature discussions by men about shaving their female partners, for example, this posting captured by Sheila Jeffreys in her book:

> One man writes to the "Shaving" section of the Lovers' Feedback Forum: "Found this excellent link on genitals, detailed shaving pictures and methods, etc".
> Another says, "I enjoy giving my wife oral sex, but those hairs just get in the way.... Now I shave her every few months". (2005, p. 81)

The direct tie of shaving to male desire, and some men's lack of tolerance for a natural look, is captured over and over again by Jeffreys. For example, one participant on the AskMan website offered advice to other men with reluctant female partners to "jokingly tell her that you will not give her oral sex until she shaves herself for you.... If she still does not want to do it for you, switch sex partners" (Jeffreys, 2005, p. 81).

While certainly the normalization of the Brazilian wax is linked to heightened exposure to this practice, once restricted to porn sites, through popular culture magazines, Dines and Cokal also attribute this trend to the inclusion of episodes centered on genital waxing in the popular television series *Sex and the City*. Cokal traces the story lines in *Sex and the City* from the early episodes in which Brazilian waxing is treated as a sexual escapade of sorts, ending with the main character eventually growing back her pubic hair, to an episode three years later when the Brazilian wax is normalized and accepted as the route of choice for feminine hygiene for a busy career woman living in a city.

Shaving is also presented within the *Sex and the City* episode as serving to enhance the sexuality of the female character as it provides a fast, easy route to the clitoris since, as one lead character says, "men are too lazy to have to go searching for anything" (Cokal, 2007, p. 148). This moving of a practice primarily directed toward the male gaze into a position of empowerment for women is a classic example of how discourse surrounding sexuality is manipulated to make hypersexualization to a male audience feel empowering to women, while it in fact still supports a patriarchal system focused on male desire.

Designer Laser Vaginoplasty: The Art of Labia Contouring

Related to the genital waxing trend is genital plastic surgery, beginning first with women working as performers in the pornography industry, followed by extension of the practice into the mainstream along with Brazilian waxing. This surgery technique includes the clipping of elongated or asymmetrical lips, injection of fat typically taken from the inner thigh into lips considered too thin, and vaginal tightening. This recent trend in what plastic surgeons have labeled "designer laser vaginoplasty," or sometimes "vaginal contouring," is attributed by plastic surgeons to women's exposure to pornographic ideals of beauty in the mass media:

> Primarily, doctors say, aggressive marketing and fashion influences like flimsier swimsuits, the Brazilian bikini wax and more exposure to nudity in magazines, movies, and on the Internet are driving attention to a physical zone still so private that women do not dare, or care, to look at themselves closely. "Now women shave", said Dr. Gary J. Alter, a plastic surgeon and urologist with offices in Beverly Hills, California and Manhattan who has come up with his own "labia contouring" technique. "Now they see Porn. Now they're more aware of appearance." (Navarro, 2004b)

Plastic surgeons, already cashing in on the gravity effects of aging on women's bodies, also use this argument in their marketing of the procedure, with one surgeon's website stating, "As we age, gravity causes all parts of our body to descend, therefore the pubic hair, mound, and vaginal region also descend, causing an aged appearance" (Jeffreys, 2005, p. 85).

The number of gynecologists moving to this expanding field, now labeled "cosmetic-gyn," has been growing, with *Atlantic* magazine featuring a spotlight article on a 2011 Congress on Aesthetic Vaginal Surgery led by Dr. Red Alinsod, an early pioneer in this surgical specialty. Alinsod is most well known for inventing "a procedure in which the labia minora are completely amputated to create a 'smooth' genital look known in the field as 'the Barbie'" (Myung-Ok, 2011, p. 20). His conference and his procedures are attracting more and more surgeons, with attendance increasing, according to Myung-Ok, at a rate of 20 percent a year. Cosmetic-gyn procedures are not recommended and do not receive oversight by the American Board of Obstetrics and Gynecology. As a result practitioners like Alinsod are providing their services as new-style physician entrepreneurs, focusing on cosmetic aspects of the newly spotlighted female genital area, post–Brazilian wax.

Sexy Behavior: Performing the Porn Chic Ideal

In addition to body modifications made to conform to the porn chic ideal, Eleanor Mills's interviews with girls found they were altering their sexual behaviors to more closely conform to what boys were watching on porn sites. Among the behaviors requested by boys and often delivered by girls at an increased frequency are anal and oral sex. Oral sex has become a party staple, often not classified by teenagers as "real sex," with one of the girls interviewed by Mills dismissing her serious question on the behavior by saying, "You mean blow jobs? Giving head? Oh, that doesn't even count—happens all the time" (Mills, 2010, p. 21).

Anal sex, as an Internet porn staple, is a frequent request from boys. In the minds of young women who have come of age dating men affected by porn, requests for anal sex are directly linked to their partners' exposure to pornography. Again from Mills's interviews, this time with an eighteen-year-old female college student:

> There's a lot of interest from boys in having anal sex. I'm not saying all women hate it and don't want to do it, but certainly it's become normalized. I've been asked several times, but I haven't wanted to. When a group of girls gets together it's become something they talk about quite a lot—about whether they should do it, whether it will hurt. Some couples do it, but it's the kind of thing you'd do in a relationship, not on a one-night stand. I'm sure it is because of porn. (quoted in Mills, 2010, p. 21)

Finally, girl-on-girl sexual action, again an Internet porn staple, has been picked up by girls and young women, who are quick to understand that it is a turn-on for boys and will get their attention. Boys, according to Mills's interviews with girls, often prompt the action and most certainly pay attention to the girls who do it. Again, a quote from a different eighteen-year-old British teenager interviewed by Mills:

> "They're always on us to kiss each other," she giggles. "Girls do it just because it drives the boys wild, because they want the attention and to get the boys going—they're really interested in seeing girls kissing in real life. We play up to it." (Mills, 2010, p. 21)

Porn Chic Makeovers: The Sexy Studio Photograph

The reconstruction and modification of women's bodies to better match those found within the porn industry, and the association of empowerment with sexuality, led in the late 1990s and the first decade of the millennium to a rebirth of the notion of a fashion makeover, updated to fit the new porn chic ideals of the millennium. Focusing more on the body than on dress, the new porn chic makeovers are directed to a wide swath of women under the general term *boudoir photography*, making reference to the highly sexualized content of the images. British and American photographers specializing in this genre typically market their services on a website offering clients a range of different photo shoot styles. In the United States, swimsuit, fitness, and boudoir makeover styles are targeted to the different interests and aspirations of the mainstream female photo subject. In Britain, the photo shoot styles are slightly different, with specialized burlesque, vintage, and erotic options. Online galleries of the different options are posted by the photographers so that potential clients can peruse the website, deciding where they fit within the broad category of boudoir photography.

All varieties of porn chic makeovers, to a greater or lesser extent, are marketed to a broad audience of women, selling the idea that once inside the studio even the most ordinary woman can find her hidden sexy side and be transformed into a fantasy shot. Some photographers working in this genre also offer photography services to professional sex workers, such as call girls. Typically these websites provide separate galleries for these more revealing photographs. Photographers who also serve sex workers often specialize in addressing the mainstream target market that wants an edgier, raunchier, or more explicit porn makeover. For example, "Miss Boudoir" working out of Mossley, United Kingdom, offers photographs for the portfolios and websites of professional escorts and adult entertainers but also offers "Naughty Girls!" portraits, described as "edgy and gritty boudoir-glamour photography with bags of raunchiness. Great for the more adventurous and alternative" (http://www.missboudoir.com/).

Boudoir Photography

As a narrower genre of professional photography directed toward the mainstream market in both the United States and the United Kingdom, boudoir photography focuses on making women of all body types and ages feel welcome. Promotional materials directed toward women emphasize an accepting, fun, and private studio experience. Photographers specializing in boudoir photography use props, poses, and post-shot cleanup to turn all women into sexy divas for a day. *Boudoir photography* is the most "user-friendly" of the terms used by photographers for a porn chic makeover; sessions are offered by professional studios specializing in sexually evocative poses as well as women's exercise studios offering pole-dancing, strip-acrobatic, or burlesque dance classes. Exercise studios typically hire a boudoir photographer for the day and set up a temporary on-site photography studio for the women enrolled in their classes.

Boudoir photography sessions at dance and exercise studios are often timed around special occasions, offering women enrolled in dance classes the opportunity to get a sexy photograph to give to their hubby or partner for Valentine's Day or Christmas. Posted galleries of boudoir photography portraits in both the United States and the United Kingdom are sexually provocative but steer carefully away from being sexually explicit and raunchy. These posted online galleries of real British and American women help make potential customers who do not consider themselves the "porn chic" type of gal feel comfortable signing up and attending the boudoir photography session.

The British boudoir photography categories referred to as "naughty girl" and "provocative and sensual" include more explicit and provocative photographs, including breast nudity, girl-on-girl innuendo, and Lolita, "little-girl" sexuality references. "Fun and giggles" is again a British subset of boudoir photography, with a humorous, "come and get me" attitude directed toward women wanting to get a fun photograph made for their spouse or boyfriend.

Glamour and/or Pinup Photography

Glamour photography is the term used by the industry to describe traditional pinup/centerfold photography, made most famous by Hugh Hefner and *Playboy* and featured in British lad magazines. This form of photography, once the domain of a select few, has been mainstreamed through college coed issues of *Playboy*, the Hooters Girls contests and calendars, and the rags-to-riches stories of glamour girl models that have been picked up by the mass media. Women opting for this type of photo shoot are more apt to have professional or semiprofessional aspirations. As an example of the cross-over, some American Hooters Girls have made the transition from being a Hooters Girl of the Month to making it onto the centerfold of *Playboy*. One of the most famous British porn remakes falling into this category is Katie Price, known as the glam model Jordan, who made her way onto the popular culture stage in the 1990s in Britain with a series of three tabloid-covered breast implants.

Price's elevation to celebrity status in Britain began in the late 1990s when she began glamour modeling topless under the name "Jordan" for the London tabloid

The Sun. A British glamour model is a woman who appears close to naked in tabloids and lad magazines. Jordan started her glam modeling career as a Page 3 girl, posing topless as what *The Sun* labeled "a girl next door." Jordan's story became big tabloid news as the English readership was drawn into voting roles on a series of three breast implants. This extended breast implant story shot Jordan into a celebrity role and earned her a loyal readership. According to Ed Zukerman (2008) it was on the reality television game show *I'm a Celebrity, Get Me Out of Here* that she won over the hearts of British women and girls with her grounded working-class toughness and stage presence. Placed in the jungle competing for the prize with other celebrities, who often buckled under the pressure, Price showed her mettle and won her audience.

The story of Price and her transformation into the glamour model Jordan resonated with young British women, particular those from working-class backgrounds. One of the draws of Price's glam modeling story is the fast route to power she experienced as a result of her ability to court and capture the male gaze. In Madeleine Coy's and Maria Garner's article on the impact of glamour modeling on young British women, she quotes a March 2008 edition of *Love It* magazine featuring an interview with twin sisters from working-class backgrounds who were inspired by Jordan to give up university educations to model in the porn industry:

> In March 2008, an edition of "Love It" magazine featured twin sisters who decided to go into glamour modeling after a childhood of poverty.... In the article they describe the initial awareness of sexualized attention from boys at school as a "surge of power". Later, they say "Jordan had made a fortune by posing in skimpy underwear" and began glamour modeling—"We just wanted to be glamorous and sexy". Subsequently both gave up their university degrees—"My degree could wait, I was addicted to the rush of feeling sexy.... neither of us regret going into the porn industry for a second. It goes to show—sisters are doing it for themselves." (Coy and Garner, 2010, p. 664)

This narrative captures the four key components of the sexy empowerment icon outlined by Rosalind Gill (2008) and introduced in chapter 3. First of all, the script is dominated by the body and the use of the sexual body to gain power. Second, the two sisters are intensely focused on the male gaze and are objectifying their bodies to attract sexualized attention. Third, the sisters stress that it was their choice to give up their university degrees, and they don't look back in regret. Finally, the interview ends with a statement of empowerment, "sisters are doing it for themselves."

This movement of the working-class Katie Price into celebrity role model status in the new millennium is symptomatic of a wider cultural shift in terms of how female role models are being evaluated and elevated. The trend is definitely tilted toward an interpretation of female self-objectification as a choice and as a mark of power. The attitude could be simply summed up as "It is going to happen to you anyway, these women took charge, did it to themselves, and conquered the world!"

Thus, female performers who objectify their own bodies, and then use their sexuality to attain celebrity status and power, rise—in many cases—to role model positions for significant numbers of young women and girls. This model of empowerment thus stretches to include working-class women, like Price, who used self-objectification to turn their lives around and become well-known and recognized success stories.

Swimsuit Photography

Traditional swimsuit portrait photography is offered by commercial photographers in the United States. This style of personal portrait has a broad appeal in the United States, particularly among college students and women in their twenties, likely related to the mass popularity of the *Sports Illustrated* annual swimsuit issue featuring nonprofessional models in sexy poses. The posted photographs I surveyed, either found on commercial photographers' websites or displayed by individuals as profile pictures on Facebook, are modeled after the classic *Sports Illustrated* poses. While many of the photographs require the porn chic customs of a Brazilian wax and natural or surgically enhanced large breasts, the look is "good clean American beach." Similar to boudoir photography, swimsuit photography is easy to classify as mainstream, with little connection to edgy or borderline pornographic raunch. These types of professional photographs have made it onto Facebook profiles as pictures among young college and postcollege women in the United States, many of whom have galleries of these images available to their Facebook friends.

Fitness Photography

American *fitness photography* is a related genre and is the term used for photographs documenting women who are competing in extreme fitness contests or building a portfolio as a professional fitness model. These swimsuit photographs focus intently on the female body as a sex object but also carefully document the physical conditioning of the body. Classic examples of posted fitness photographs feature women with large breasts combined with extremely toned arms, legs, stomach, and back. Similar to swimsuit photographs, these poses remain within the comfortable zone of mainstream but depend heavily on the porn chic conventions of the Brazilian wax and artificial or natural large breasts. The sometimes contradictory desire to have an extremely well-toned body and large, voluptuous breasts results in women in this group turning to breast-enhancement surgery. Online Facebook research I conducted tracing the wall postings of a contestant as she prepared for and went to a national fitness contest revealed the strong relationship between training for and participating in fitness contests and empowerment. After a disappointing finish at a national contest, the reaction of the young woman was to set new empowering goals for fitness and appearance: "I think its okay to be disappointed in great accomplishments if you know that regardless it was a success…but if you aren't reaching further and committing to higher goals then you get stuck at calling it good. Create new and more difficult goals for yourself all the time. The feeling of accomplishment will only get better." As I followed this young woman's Facebook profile and postings through her training regimen and during the actual contest, the posted photographs were revealing swimsuit shots focused on physical strength and fitness. Posted Facebook photographs of this contestant celebrating after the national contest with her boyfriend display a sexy, more provocative version of her identity, still clad in a swimsuit but with lusty sexy props and a "come get me" set of poses much more in conformity with the sexy empowerment icon.

Pole Dancing: Porn Chic Exercise and Fun

> Physical progress stagnating? Bored with aerobics classes? Workouts becoming a chore? Tired of the gym scene? Need to feel confident again? Want to spice things up with your partner?
>
> Get ready to let your hair down and bring out your naughty side! Grab your girlfriends and join us for a great time that you won't soon forget! It is all about the girls!! NO BOYS ALLOWED! (http://www.keescampstore.com/servlet/the-template/pole/Page)

Popular culture exposure to pornography ideals and practices is also affecting how women are constructing leisure and exercise. Pole dancing as a form of exercise and female recreation, particularly focusing on what is commonly marketed as "time out with the girls," has been a fast-growing trend in both the United States and the United Kingdom. In the United States, Las Vegas, as a hub for gambling and all kinds of vice, has served as a certification hub, with dance studios in locations as remote as the rural Midwest opening and advertising that their instructors were trained in Vegas. Pole-dancing studios in the United States and Britain tend to be housed outside of the traditional fitness establishments, with some making direct reference to being a bit "naughty" and others advertising themselves as a "gym" environment but with a bit of spice. The pole-dancing classes attended by Samantha Holland and Feona Attwood (2009) in the United Kingdom for their participant-observation study took place in a room behind the bar area of a modern-style pub in Leeds, with poles temporarily installed for the lessons by the visiting instructors. This is in contrast with the more specialized studio spaces I visited in the United States, which offered multiple sessions of pole dancing at differing levels.

Pole dancing originated as an erotic performance that was widely performed in Euro-American strip clubs in the 1980s, with some linking the practice to Canada (Holland and Attwood, 2009). The movement of this form of dance into the mainstream through the offering of pole-dancing exercise classes emerged in the first decade of the millennium in both Britain and the United States, with the two studios

I researched in the United States offering their first pole-dancing courses in 2007 and 2009, with both studios advertising instructors trained in Las Vegas; Holland and Attwood's British research occurred in 2006. I would concur with Holland and Attwood that pole dancing needs to be understood within a broader cultural movement toward the acceptance of practices once marginalized as "sex work" in the mainstream of women's culture. Along with boudoir photography these "prosex" events are used to mark bonding moments among women, such as bachelorette parties, but also function as protected environments wherein women feel free to express their sexuality without being censored and judged by others.

During the rise of these expressions of girl culture, raunch popular culture was undergoing a makeover in women's sexuality. Through a range of mass media–covered events, women were being encouraged to express, take charge of, and gain power from their own sexuality. Pole-dancing classes emerged as the most popular of a range of different dance offerings including belly dancing, striptease, and lap dancing, all purported to enhance confidence and self-esteem and grant the female class members physical and sexual power. Holland and Attwood point out that burlesque entered the mainstream in Britain through the reality television show *Faking It*, with a purportedly ordinary, and somewhat shy, working-class house cleaner from Wales transforming into a confident and sexy striptease artist in a 2006 episode (Holland and Attwood, 2009, p. 169).

Holland and Attwood's ethnographic study in Britain, which included participant observation in pole-dancing classes and follow-up interviews with pole-dancing teachers and students, revealed the strong correlation between the popular culture presentation of pole dancing as a hot fitness activity by well-known celebrities and the enrolled students' interest in this new recreational sport. Teachers reported that students used pole dancing to latch themselves to the cool new raunch ideals, and as testimony that they are up on the new stuff and not boring. Teachers and students alike who lacked strong fitness backgrounds felt welcome in the classes. They also felt that while the pole-dancing classes linked them to popular culture porn chic, they were a respectable way to get there, and not compromising in terms of including nudity or clear connections to sex work. The social respectability of the classes is underscored by the fact that one of the teachers was using her pole-dancing instructor position as a cover for her less respectable but better-paid position as a real pole-dancing entertainer at a men's club. She felt she was able to tell her family and her friends that she was a pole-dancing instructor and not suffer the same marginalization she would experience as a paid pole-dancing performer.

As the classes progressed, a clear theme that emerged from the participating women was that pole-dancing culture provided a space for girl-to-girl, woman-to-woman support. Students became braver as they became more comfortable with their classmates and with their own bodies, and they began to wear more body-revealing costumes to class. Learning the difficult dance moves enhanced students' self-confidence, with Holland and Attwood themselves reporting, "Our own experiences bore this out: learning to perform very difficult dance moves in very high heels was scary and we felt self-conscious, but doing it with a group of supportive women made it exciting and exhilarating. There is a particular pleasure in knowing that you have performed a sequence of moves in a way that feels good, that you experience as physically enjoyable and that meets with the approval of your 'audience'" (2009, p. 175). The denigration of pole dancing by male audiences as only "a titillating thing" (Holland and Attwood, 2009, p. 176) was in effect successfully rebutted by the women's culture within the class, with others offering encouragement and reward as class members progressed through the challenging dance routines.

The tie of pole dancing to sexual objectification in the mainstream media is less successfully resolved within the classes. What the women attempt to do is to translate their experiences into a model of female sexuality that is empowered by "strength, grace, accomplishment and exhilaration, as well as sexual allure and display" (Holland and Attwood, 2009, p. 177). The women taking the class and the instructors create an empowered space wherein women's (not men's) sexual agency is celebrated and recognized: "Not only does it become an instance of contemporary raunch within the media, used to demonstrate the acceptability of women's sexual agency, it becomes a practice in women's everyday lives which enables them to engage with, articulate and embody a particular set of characteristics which are currently prized in our culture: sexual hedonism, feistiness, confidence, independence, taste, style, heterosexual desire and solidarity with other women. But this set of characteristics is not simply 'given' to them. Rather they are forged through women's engagement and embodiment" (Holland and Attwood, 2009, p. 179). What remains to be asked is a circular question: Can women be empowered by an act that by its very nature is directed toward soliciting male desire? Is the only route to female sexual agency by way of the back door through feelings of sexual empowerment gained by feeling free to be sexy? Is being sexy about courting male desire, or, when it is cheered on by other women, is the experience somehow different, somehow "healthier"? Holland and Attwood end by posing a version of this question: "Being both performer and audience enables women to 'see', 'be', and 'do' sexiness, and doing this while other women cheer on and applaud may be as close as we currently get to a positive experience of sexualization in contemporary culture" (Holland and Attwood, 2009, p. 180).

Sex Toy Parties: Yes, It Is Plastic, but It Isn't Tupperware

In the fall of 2006 I staged a raunch show-and-tell session for my students in a fashion-trend analysis course. I had assigned as required reading Ariel Levy's 2005 book on raunch culture. Raunch show-and-tell was a stand-up-and-tell event including about forty students who shared examples from their lives illustrating the impact of the porn chic cultural trend on a small rural college campus. The buzz of the bright green vibrator was the showstopper at 8:30 A.M. around the middle of the show-and-tell. It was an example drawn from a recent sex toy home sale hosted by one of the students in my class, and it buzzed its way all around the room. In many ways this book is the story of how the bright green vibrator made its way into a classroom on a fairly conservative campus, and why it was at home there in all its buzzy glory!

The movement of vibrators and other sex toys out of the sleazy adult store on the freeway and into the living room, the dorm room, and the kitchen through franchised organizations similar in structure to Tupperware has transferred these once-stigmatized pleasure-enhancing products into the mainstream. The colliding of the old social mores with the new was signaled by the arrest of Joanne Webb, a middle-aged Passion Party representative in Texas in 2004. The arrest was in response to an anonymous report and resulted in a charge against Webb for violating a Texas state law prohibiting the sale of products used to stimulate "human genital organs" (Navarro, 2004a). While there were six other women who were also product representatives for Passion Parties in the local region, Webb attributed her arrest to her propensity to ruffle "some feathers in town," particularly through her role as a leader in the chamber of commerce. Like other women interviewed for the newspaper story, Webb was in the business to make money and was quick to point out the mainstream character of most of her clients: "Most of my customers are housewives just trying to spice up their relationship" (Navarro, 2004a).

At the same time that sex toys began to be sold in living rooms, sex toy stores began to open in mainstream locations. Targeted at women, these stores, such as Babeland with branch stores in Brooklyn, New York City, and Seattle, had names that attracted women and advertising that was directed toward an educated and open-minded clientele. Open even on Sunday from 12 to 7, Babeland offered best-selling products including the "We-Vibe II" as featured in Oprah's *O Magazine* and online alongside a posted "how-to" set of directions and an online video illustrating how to use the product.

Most working in this industry credit a particular episode of *Sex and the City* focused on the Rabbit Pearl vibrator with bringing this sex toy out of the closet and onto the shelf of the local drugstore, along with the tampons and the toothpaste. Large companies that formerly focused only on men's products, such as Trojan, now feature a well-selling line of vibrators, advertised widely on MTV:

> The newest model on the shelves is the Tri-Phoria ($39.99), created by the condom company Trojan after a study the company conducted in 2008 in partnership with the Center for Sexual Health Promotion at Indiana University revealed that over half of American women had used vibrators, and of that group, nearly 80 percent had shared them with their partners. James Daniels, vice president for marketing at Trojan, said: "The idea really came from consumers. They kept telling us vibrators, vibrators, vibrators. And we just laughed. And then we realized they were serious." (Howard, 2011)

Packaging of sex toy products is discreet, mimicking perfume-style packaging, with directions folded up inside the box. Business is dramatically expanding, especially for online retailers, with sex and relationship expert Dr. Berman moving from $100,000 in online sales in 2005 to over $5 million in 2010. Younger women buy other women vibrators for birthday presents, with pop culture–themed products like Hello Kitty moving into this marketing opportunity and audience. Male partners interviewed for the *New York Times* story were supportive of their wives and girlfriends, with one stating, "From my perspective, a woman who has thoroughly explored her own body, both along and with or without whichever toys she finds interesting, makes for a significantly better lover" (Howard, 2011).

Campus Porn: Zines, Mags, and Student Organizations

Playboy began publishing photographs of college women in 1979, starting first with "Girls of the Ivy League," followed by "Girls of the Big 12," and finally "Girls of the Top 10 Party Schools." The frequent visits of the *Girls Gone Wild* film crew to college campuses in the last decade have also established an acceptance of porn chic norms on campus, leading more students to accept being photographed or captured on film in states of undress or nudity, accompanied by sexual content.

Undergraduate sex-themed magazines first appeared on East Coast Ivy League campuses in the first decade of the millennium, beginning at Vassar with the publication of *Squirm* in 2000. The magazines are typically headquartered under a student organization and are mainstreamed as activities for all students to get involved in. For example, the opening of the website at Vassar that lists *Squirm* as a student organization reads, "Vassar boasts more than 120 unique student organizations, ranging from comedy troupes to debate teams. Organizations are entirely student-run, and manage their own annual budgets. Below, read about each of our organizations and begin reaching out to organizations that interest you. Groups are always looking for new members. Are you involved?" (Vassar Student Association, n.d.). The reader then follows the alphabetical list down from Amnesty International, to Asian Student Alliance, to Broadway A Cappella, to Feminist Majority Leadership Alliance to *Squirm,* which is self-described as "a submissions-based magazine about sex and sexuality" that "seeks to create a sex-positive forum on campus for the artistic, literary, and creative exploration of sex."

The sex-themed publications that subsequently appeared on other Ivy League campuses followed Vassar's lead with student organization–based sex-themed magazines at the University of Chicago (*Vita Excolatur*), Harvard (*H-Bomb*), and Yale (*Sway*). These publications walk a careful line between the college administration and the tenets of academic freedom, with the student editors of *Vita Excolatur* at the University of Chicago publication held to administrative review and restricted to full-frontal nudity, void of erection and/or intercourse (Rudoren, 2006). They also work closely with student affairs staff at the University of Chicago to ensure that students who model for the magazine sign releases both before they are photographed and again after they preview the finished photographs prior to publication. *Vita Excolatur*'s distribution is also restricted to currently enrolled students of the university who are over eighteen years of age, thus in some ways protecting students whose photographs appear in the magazine from full-scale mass distribution of these images apart and away from the university campus. Comments from an interview I conducted with a former student editor of *Vita Excolatur* underscored the role of this publication in providing a venue for the expression of women's sexual agency.

In 2005 a senior at Boston University teamed up with a local freelance photographer to independently launch *Boink* magazine. In the beginning stages of production about half of the models and staff were drawn from Boston University; however, that number has decreased, to an estimated one-third a year later in 2006. Unlike the other, student organization–based publications, *Boink* receives no funding from Boston University, which does not recognize the magazine as a student organization and forbids its sale at the bookstore directly on the campus. Prior to the publication of the first issue, Boston University's dean of students issued a statement clearly separating his office from the publication and its content, citing "concern for the treatment of serious sexual health, relationship, and other issues" (Rudoren, 2006).

As a result of this distancing *Boink* goes a step farther than the other student organization–based magazines; in the case of Yale the magazine uses parents as a limiting factor, with the editor stating, "If we can justify it to our moms every step of the way then we know we are in good shape" (Rudoren, 2006). In contrast, *Boink* magazine advertises for models on Craigslist and presents itself as a glossy sex mag targeted to and about college students, with no parents or administrators leaning over the copy and making decisions. The marketing on the website clearly uses the independent status of *Boink* to position it as the college sex magazine that goes the farthest in terms of content, free to do so due to its lack of formal ties to Boston University:

> Last year's debut of *H Bomb* at Harvard made Crimson alumni cringe. After being approved by the Committee for Campus Life in March and hitting newsstands at the end of the semester last May, *H Bomb* received media attention from as far away as France and Germany. But across town, 38-year-old photographer Christopher Anderson, whose work appeared in *H Bomb*, and 21-year-old Boston University student Alecia Oleyourryk saw the Harvard magazine and wanted to take things a bit further. Soon they started working on *Boink*, a magazine that debuted this February and "explores a little more off the boundaries," said Oleyourryk. (Sisson, n.d.)

A male college student who posed nude for the magazine for a cover and eight-page spread that included simulated intercourse uses the experience as party bragging material: "All my friends thought it was pretty cool. Especially if I have a party, the first thing my friends do is bust out my porn" (Jacobs, 2007). Not surprisingly, the cover shots of issue 2 of *Boink* magazine and the promotional images on the website are shots of women who conform to the genital-wax porn standards discussed earlier in this chapter. The freedom to express women's sexual agency that so much dominated my interview with the female former editor of *Vita Excolatur* is absent from the cover and content of *Boink*, with its clear focus on a mainstream male audience steeped in porn.

Exploring the Contours of Raunch Eroticism

Focus on the White Heterosexual Male Gaze

Trends in how women groom and prepare themselves for public presentation have been deeply and significantly influenced by the mainstreaming of expectations of sexual appearance popularized by the porn industry. Increasing rates of breast implants coupled with widespread trends toward pubic waxing and shaving can both be directly linked to imagining oneself to be an object of the male gaze and desire. The growing use of online pornography by boys and men to facilitate sexual arousal has affected men's expectations of their female partners, with many requesting conformity to porn standards of appearance, such as the Brazilian wax. The saturation of popular culture media with sexuality has influenced daily dress habits, with young women and girls dressing to court the male gaze and desire in more daily appearance styles, as well as dress worn out in the evening for a date or to attract a possible hookup. The porn norms have even extended into influencing sexual behavior, including normalization of casual oral sex, heightened pressure from boys and men for anal sex, and performance of girl-on-girl kissing and sex acts for the pleasure of a male audience.

The mainstreaming of pinup photography, facilitated in part by contests on college campuses for being a college *Playboy* centerfold or a *Sports Illustrated* swimsuit model, and by the popularization of glamour modeling celebrities such as Katie Price, has resulted in new genres of posed photography marketed to women. From standard boudoir photography, to classic American swimsuit photography, to the edgier British "naughty girl" genre, these new photography genres are pictures of women posed to attract the sexual attention of men.

The opening up of pornography to a wider audience has resulted in a wider diversity of materials available to a changed audience. Pornography's traditional audience of young men has expanded to include offerings to the gay and lesbian community, bisexuals, and transsexuals, as well as materials produced by and for women; a key question needs to be raised, however, as to the continuing domination of the male heterosexual, in terms of both the materials produced for that market and also the materials produced for other markets.

Sexual Objectification of Women

The dividing up of women's bodies and the development of porn and popular culture standards for each part of the body are part and parcel of the movement of porn standards into normative practice in the millennium. Standards requiring increased breast size, influenced by mainstreamed porn celebrities like Katie Price, have resulted in dramatic increases in breast-enhancement surgery, moving into the teenage market in some communities and regions.

The cover art for *Boink* magazine brings into the daylight the common practices of female college students in terms of grooming their pubic areas to match those on display on porn sites, with Gail Dines (2010) reporting that young women who resist this trend are subject to rejection and/or negative comments from their male partners on campus. Back shots of some students for college sex-themed magazines, or bootie shots taken by *Girls Gone Wild* film crews, require not only frontal waxing but also the full Brazilian wax, including the area visible from the rear. Perhaps the epitome of the sexual objectification of women's bodies is the new vaginal-contouring plastic surgery procedure coming on the heels of the genital-waxing trend, creating yet another a new zone for scrutiny, comparison, and improvement.

Self-Objectification

Porn chic makeovers perhaps best exemplify the influence of sexual objectification on how women and girls view themselves. The ability to turn themselves into *Sports Illustrated* swimsuit models by hiring a photographer to take them to the beach to do sexy swimsuit shots draws women who are eager to attract male sexual attention, and perhaps also the positive reviews of their female peers. The posting of these images online as Facebook profile pictures and within galleries broadens the audience dramatically, again adding fuel in terms of young women choosing this mode of self-presentation.

Similarly, the new genre of boudoir photography in the United Kingdom and the United States is premised on self-objectification and conformity to the pinup standards set by Hugh Hefner in the early and subsequent years of *Playboy*. These images, often shot to give to male partners to display in personal spaces like the bedroom, embed self-objectification in rituals and relationships, thus serving to normalize self-objectification of women within families, homes, and communities.

The often female editors of campus sex zines frequently play the role of sexually objectifying both their male and female peers. The editorial power to work with photographers to determine story lines and images empowers these female editors in terms of how male and female sexuality is explored within the spread or cover. Magazines vary in how much cultural norms leaning toward sexual objectification of women are challenged, but within these college publications some discourse regarding sexual objectification occurs.

Sexual Attention and Sexualized Practice as Power

The presentation of glamour modeling as a lucrative career choice as captured in the interviews with British young women conducted by Madeleine Coy ties empowerment to sexual objectification. The young women's dismissal of a college education in order to experience the rush of power that went along with a glam modeling career directly expresses the feelings that young women experience and why those feelings are so persuasive in terms of leading women toward this form of empowerment: "My degree could wait, I was addicted to the rush of feeling sexy" (Coy and Garner, 2010, p. 665).

Similarly, young women who upload erotic photographs as Facebook profile pictures and wall postings receive comments from a wide audience of viewers, resulting in a surge of sexual attention and feelings of power. While most of these young women do not cross over into professional shots, there are examples where what begins as personal postings of erotic self-portraits results in professional modeling careers in porn or soft-porn venues.

Finally, in the sexual behaviors of teenagers captured by Eleanor Mills in her cover story for the *Sunday Times Magazine*, young girls and women clearly perform sexual acts and behaviors that they are not enjoying in order to gain male sexual attention. Girl-on-girl kissing and sexual display, an extremely popular current cultural trend, is, in the words of a girl interviewed by Mills, all about driving the boys wild. Boys interviewed by Mills were clearly impacted by the sex acts they were exposed to on porn sites. Tom, one of the young men Mills interviewed for the article, goes as far as to say that he came close to raping his first girlfriend based on the brusque, rough sex he was exposed to growing up: "I was very excited and not very sensitive to the situation. If I'm honest, I was a bit brusque, a bit rough…maybe even more than a bit. It didn't happen in the end, because we were walked in on, but I was incredibly close to taking her virginity in a really rough manner…like almost forcing her" (Mills, 2010, p. 19).

Private Is Public

The privacy afforded to women to explore their own sexuality either online, in pole-dancing classes, or in private sex toy parties with their girlfriends has opened up discussion, behaviors, and products focused on women's sexuality. The open discussion of and photographs capturing campus sex life move what was a private world into a more public domain but also create space for discourse and change. Similarly, the posting of erotic photographs online on blogs or Facebook pages moves the private world of individual sexuality into the extremely public domain of the Internet.

Extreme, Up the Ante

As part of my research for this book I followed the Facebook site of a former design student over the course of several years, watching her personal posted portraits move from a more artistic documentation of body adornment, principally tattoos with some piercings, to increasingly professional and erotic portraits clearly directed

toward attracting the male gaze and desire. As she moved in this direction, her fol-
lowers increased, as did their comments, definitely validating the increasing emphasis on sexuality in her most recent postings. This trend is not isolated, as testified by
Boink's marketing strategy, based on being the campus sex mag that contains the
riskiest material. Given the widely accessible menu of sexual material available in
the millennium, the pressure is on for those presenting either themselves or others to
up the ante, show a little bit more, get that audience back that one may be losing to
a competitor.

Young men's exposure to raunch eroticism on porn websites is affecting their real
relationships with their girlfriends and female peers, with rising levels of rough and
brusque sex and requests in casual relationships for intimate acts like anal sex. This
heightened level of expectation has helped to create the millennium hookup norms
where acts such as oral sex are dismissed by the girls interviewed by Mills as happening all the time. Young girls and women, attempting to court and retain the attention of the male gaze, are driven to behaviors they are not comfortable with, such as
anal sex, or sexually stimulated by, such as making out with another girl.

Misogyny

The flood of Internet pornography has had the effect of upping the ante in terms of
attention-getting sexuality. With so much to choose from, the Internet browser is
courted by ever-increasing varieties of sexual experience and increasing levels of
raunch and violence. Gonzo porn, an extreme category featuring violence and degradation of women and children, has increased in popularity. As these porn images
make their way into the mainstream, the spreads of the edgier versions of campus
sex-themed magazines and the images in boudoir photography follow suit, gradually increasing the violence and degradation within the popular culture mainstream.
Perhaps most alarming is the effect of exposure to porn violence on the expectations
and behaviors of young men, most notably the story of Tom, who came close to raping his first girlfriend, perhaps in part influenced by his exposure to Internet porn
violence.

–7–

Playboy Fantasies, Hooters Girls, and Coyote Ugly Tattoos

Corporations that hire women full-time to use their sexual appeal to represent their brand create hiring policies, company conventions, and self- and corporate policing behaviors that successfully package the distinct versions of sexuality they deliver to their mostly male audience. This chapter begins with a review of the Playboy Bunny brand, moving forward in time to more mainstream marketing approaches at Hooters, Coyote Ugly, and select other sex-themed food/beverage bars/restaurants and/or coffee shops. For each case study comparisons are made in terms of branded

Figure 7.1 *Spilled (Coffee).* Courtesy of Nicola Bockelmann.

sexuality in the following four areas: (1) body type, (2) self-presentation, (3) makeup and hair styles, and (4) demographic profile. Entertainment and music industry giants such as Disney and MTV use a popular culture icon to sell product. Similarly, this chapter explores the branding of licensed product based on the corporate image of female sexuality by *Playboy*, Hooters, and other companies whose profits rest on turning the wide range of female sexuality into an identifiable and salable commodity, a brand. The brand images of *Playboy*, Hooters, and Coyote Ugly are heavily influenced by their creation stories and their founders. We begin in America with Hugh Hefner.

Playboy: The Brand That Started It All

When Hugh Hefner put together his first *Playboy* issue including the now-famous Marilyn Monroe cover and centerfold, he built his brand image based on a widely accepted British American genre, "the pinup." These images, now considered classic, were either photographs or paintings in a calendar or loose poster format intended to be pinned up to the wall. Pinups most often found a home in male-dominated spaces such as auto repair shops at gas stations and army barracks during World War II. The term *pinup* became a part of American and British popular culture during the 1940s with the wide distribution of reproductions of the hyperrealistic but clearly idealized paintings of scantily clad women by artists such as Earl Moran and Gil Elygren.

Marilyn Monroe began her career working with some of the best-known pinup photographers and painters of the 1940s. These photographers and painters worked hand in hand with Hollywood, often serving to help launch the careers of young female actresses. The Marilyn Monroe centerfold that launched the *Playboy* magazine and brand was an image originally run as part of a pinup calendar series. Hefner, sensing the power of this image to express his magazine's brand, negotiated the rights to include this well-known Marilyn Monroe pinup in his first issue. Along with the launch of the magazine came the creation of the *Playboy* brand.

Background and History of the Brand

Hugh Hefner started *Playboy* on a mere $8,000, working out of his small apartment in Chicago. The opening issue with its famous Marilyn Monroe centerfold was literally an overnight success. In some ways the magazine was a logical step for Hefner, who while editor of his college humor magazine created "Shaft's Coed of the Month," a spotlight column on a pretty girl on campus. Expanding on this concept, and adding in an array of other content with appeal to young urban males, Hefner used his market sense to create exactly the right magazine at precisely the right time. By 1959 one million men a month were purchasing the magazine. According to Hefner the message was a simple one: "Sex is ok...these are nice girls, this is the girl next door." This very sellable message was couched within a broader array of topics of interest to his male audience including jazz, contemporary fiction, and politics. The male rabbit-head symbol dressed in a tuxedo was created by Art Paul, the magazine's first art director, and was intended by Hefner to reference the sophistication of the *New Yorker*'s male icon symbol while also taking it into the sexually adventurous world of the urban playboy.

According to the film version of his life, *Once Upon a Time*, Hefner spent the 1950s creating a fantasy lifestyle for the young urban male. In 1959 he reinvented himself as the quintessential Chicago playboy, with parties first at the Playboy Penthouse, with notable performers such as Dick Gregory, Dizzy Gillespie, and Lenny Bruce, leading into the opening of the first Playboy Club and the Playboy Mansion on State Street in Chicago. While the Playboy icon dated back to the second issue of the magazine, the crystallization of the image of the Playboy Bunny occurred with the opening of the Playboy Club. In 1959, 90,000 men spent $25 each to purchase a key opening the door to the Chicago club, the portal to the fantasy world of Hefner's urban playboy. The fantasy was brought to life for the men who walked through this door by the creation of the Playboy Bunny.

Profile of the Playboy Bunny

Hefner's fantasy must be seen in light of the repressive and moralistic culture in which he and other men of his generation were raised. Citing the haunting role of the Depression as an influence, coupled with images of the remembered 1920s, Hefner talks in his autobiographical film about his desire to create the party he felt somehow he had missed. The Playmates Hefner recruited for his centerfolds, beginning with Marilyn Monroe's opening centerfold, evoked the sexual fantasies of an urban male young adult, steeped in the Hollywood dream sexuality of the Depression and war years. Like the World War II pinups, Hefner's centerfolds showed mature adult women, presented as interested and courting your sexual attention.

Hefner was challenged early on, in one case in a well-publicized television interview with Dan Rather, as to whether his magazine was anything more than a smut journal. From the magazine's launch Hefner stressed the importance of the context of the images, the magazine's focus on publishing editorials and interviews, well-reviewed and avant-garde fiction, sophisticated cartoons by leading artists, and a diverse range of political commentary. This focus continues to lead the magazine, with the editor in chief in 2010 stating, "*Playboy* has always been about the record to lay, the drink to mix, the car to drive, and the clothes to wear to get the girl" (Robertson, 2010, p. 14). The magazine was designed for the fully actualized urban male, adding in what Hefner claimed was the most important ingredient, sex.

The meticulous care Hefner put into the early centerfold shoots, in terms of designing a particular version of sexuality for his male readership, included choosing not only a particular type of woman for the shoots but also props and poses that created sexual fantasy rather than hard-porn displays of raw sexual acts. This attention to stylized detail was brought into Hefner's development of the Playboy Bunny archetype, whose sexual persona in large part created the fantasy world of the early Playboy Clubs. The idea of using the Playboy rabbit logo as an inspiration for a bunny costume for the waitresses at the newly opening clubs came from the girlfriend of Hefner's playboy sidekick and promotion director, Victor Lownes. The costume prototype was put together by the mother of Lownes's girlfriend and then modeled for Hefner and Lownes. Typical of Hefner's meticulous eye, he made the call to raise the leg on the swimsuit style to enhance the length of the leg, resulting in the now-famous and patented costume. The original costume that opened the Chicago club included the high-legged swimsuit style, bunny ears, and a tail; the signature collar and cuffs were added later (Scott, 1998, pp. 54–55).

The costume was modified as Playboy Clubs opened across the country and abroad. In some cases local modesty norms influenced more revealing leg styles (Miami) or more conservative cuts (Boston). Holidays included specially designed costumes, as did the VIP room, where the Bunnies in all clubs wore blue velvet costumes. As local and international contests for Bunny of the Year were developed, silver (local club) and gold (international) costumes were created to mark the status of these specially designated Bunnies. The opening of the London Playboy Club in 1967 was particularly dramatic, with the introduction of a Mod-inspired patterned costume for the desk Bunny (Robertson, 2010, pp. 42–43).

The final crystallization of the Playboy Bunny image took place in the training program developed by Hefner's brother Keith. In the standardized introductory remarks Keith Hefner made before each Bunny training, the essence of the Bunny is captured:

> A Bunny—like the Playboy Playmate—is the girl next door. She is the American romanticized myth…beautiful, desirable, and a nice, fun-loving person. A Bunny is not a broad or a "hippy". She may be sexy, but it's a fresh healthy sex—not cheap or lewd. The Playboy Club is more like show business than the saloon business, and the Bunnies are the stars. (quoted in Robertson, 2010, p. 62)

The linkage to both the "girl next door" and a star in show business brings together the two essential elements of the sexuality brand created by the early Playboy empire. What Hefner so successfully brought together is the memories of the beautiful woman men grew up with, but may not have gotten to date, and romantic star appeal. This linkage is specifically made by Keith in the final introductory comments he made to the newly hired bunnies, wherein he compares them to the 1950s beauty and star Elizabeth Taylor.

> You—the stars—are what bring the people into the Club. You are what gives the Club its glamour. We stress that Bunnies should not get too familiar with customers for just that reason. Men are very excited being in the company of Elizabeth Taylor, but they know they can't paw or proposition her. The moment that they felt they could become familiar

with her, she would not have the aura of glamour that now surrounds her. The same must be true of our Bunnies. (quoted in Robertson, 2010, p. 62)

In Hugh Hefner's autobiographical video, Keith recounts the creation of the now-legendary Bunny Dip, a choreographed method of serving customers a drink at the Chicago Playboy Club. The Bunny Dip remains central to the image of the Playboy Bunny, with *The Bunny Book: How to Walk, Talk, Tease, and Please like a Playboy Bunny*, released by Playboy Enterprises in 2007, still including a description of the classic move:

> The idea is to look elegant and sexy in a *tasteful* way while serving a drink, rather than exposing your cleavage to everyone at the table. Your feet and legs should stay together, with one foot slightly turned out, its heel at the arch of the other foot. Stand with your tail toward the client and reach, bending at the knee and keeping your legs closed, to serve the drink. *Et voila',* the Bunny Dip! (Playboy Enterprises, 2007, p. 63)

The bend-and-serve motion, with the serving tray held high and off to the side, created a dance of sorts with individual male patrons that played off of the fantasy first created by Hefner in the centerfolds, then brought to life in the first Playboy Clubs. You weren't just served a drink at the Playboy Club; you were the focus of attention—the Bunny was all yours, for just a moment in time.

The elegance of the Playboy Bunny and the exclusivity of her costuming were carefully maintained in the early Playboy Club years. Along with the Bunny Dip, Playboy Bunnies learned a sexy, elegant way of standing, the Bunny Stance, and a way of sitting on the edge of a table or stool, the Bunny Perch. Bunnies were instructed in the training manual and in the daylong training session to never smoke, drink, chew gum, or eat in the presence of keyholders. In the section of the manual labeled "Stylized Service Table Procedures," newly hired recruits were told that "a Bunny NEVER says or does anything that is not representative of the feminine beauty and grace that is the 'Bunny Image'" (Scott, 1998, p. 27). Training topics included not only decorum but background on the cultural atmosphere and good life Hefner used to sell his brand, in terms of both the magazine and the early clubs. Kathryn Scott, in her book on the inside story of the early clubs and the women who worked there, quoted a letter she wrote home to her family describing her training to work as a cigarette bunny in the New York Playboy Club. This young woman's words capture the excitement of moving into a world of sophistication and international glamour: "We *really will* have classes on exotic and gourmet foods and wines. I was told that Bunnies are supposed to be as elegant and knowledgeable as a *garcon* in an expensive French restaurant" (Scott, 1998, p. 21).

The transformation of a pretty girl into a Playboy Bunny at the New York club was turned over to a feisty former singer and tap dancer named Elizabeth Dozier Tate, known to all the bunnies as "Betty." In her first-person account, Scott described the first time she was dressed by Betty, and how the famous wardrobe queen solved Scott's lack of conformity to the bosomy Playboy Bunny ideal by stuffing the bottom of her bra with plastic cleaning bags. Scott recounts that the less endowed

Bunnies—in this pre-implant era—used a number of items to complete the needed lift, including extra bunny tails and wadded-up socks.

The tantalizing pairing of overnight financial success with sexual objectification was an early draw for the young women who worked the first Playboy Clubs. In her personal account Scott captures this sentiment as she explains why many young women decided to become Playboy Bunnies:

> For the first time, daughters were graduating in almost equal numbers from college with sons. But what was waiting in the real world was in reality not terribly different from what their mothers had faced. There was no clear-cut path from a four-year university to Wall Street or to corporate America. Now suddenly there was this opportunity for many of us to earn more money than our fathers, in what was essentially an interim job, while exploring options that would otherwise have been beyond our financial means. Here was an opportunity for a young woman to pay for a college independently or stockpile funds to start a business, invest in real estate, travel the world or realize any number of other dreams. (1998, p. 3)

Debbie Harry, later the lead singer for Blondie, who was a Playboy Bunny in 1968 in New York City, stressed the role of intelligence as well as sexiness in the job of a Bunny:

> Being a Bunny involved a rare combination for a woman in the workplace. It was an unusual perception of women that they could be beautiful, feminine and very sexy, and at the same time ambitious and intelligent. At Playboy those women had a place where they could use those attributes to make money—and also be really valued as employees. Bunnies were the Playboy Club. (Scott, 1998, p. 184)

This feeling of empowerment captured by the quotations from both Harry and Scott needs to in part be read within the context of the time period and the relatively limited options open to women. Also, Scott notes, the route into the Playboy Clubs was unusually open in terms of race, as she comments that the Playboy Club locker room in New York in 1963 had "every ethnic combination under the sun" and that "you would have to wait a couple of decades to see as much multiculturalism and ethnic diversity on a college campus" (1998, p. 34). Further, she argues that there was a diverse range of body types, from what she refers to as "waifs to heiresses to statuesque show girls" (1998, p. 34), a point I think could likely be argued but that still, given her former Bunny status, is worthy of note.

Hooters: From the Glamour Marketing of Playboy to Selling Knockers and Wings

When I drove into my very first Hooters parking lot, the number of pickup trucks there confirmed what I had read about the restaurant's appeal to men, particularly pickup-driving boys and men. The actual composition of the parties eating in the restaurant for lunch on a weekend surprised me. A relatively small percentage of the tables were occupied by exclusively male customers. A vast majority of the tables included women, and two large tables included significant numbers of children. One table including children was made up of a set of grandparents and a family of four. The second table of children was an all-girl birthday party for a five-year-old, with grandma and grandpa and parents supervising the activities, and balloons supplied by Hooters. One of the birthday party "take-homes" appeared to be little-girl-size Hooters T-shirts (with the famous owl logo) for all the girls attending the party. A second birthday party was happening at a table for two, where a college-age woman was treating her boyfriend to a Hooters lunch, and a bouncy serenade from all the Hooters Girls, to celebrate his special day. I was convinced by this first visit to Hooters that the brand was truly mainstreamed—even to the point of offering theme-based birthday parties to little girls with their grandparents in tow.

The first Hooters opened as a beach-theme restaurant in 1983 in Clearwater, Florida. The founders included Ed Droste, a Midwestern transplant to the beach state, along with five of his buddies. Five of the six men were in their thirties, with one older retired service station owner. None of the men had a background in running a restaurant, but they all shared the idea of opening a neighborhood beach bar with good fast food, pretty girls, and a jukebox with oldies but goldies. Like Hefner, they started the franchise on a shoestring and a concept; the initial investment in the bar was $140,000. In 1984 Hugh Connerty, an industry insider scouting locations for expansion possibilities for his franchise, stepped into the Clearwater Hooters and knew instinctively that these six men had created a strong brand that could be marketed across the country. A *Fortune Magazine* company profile outlines the original deal, put together by Connerty and the founding six on a napkin at the Clearwater bar (Helyar, 2003). The six cofounders received $50,000 and ownership of the owl trademark, plus three cents on every dollar earned by the franchise. They also kept the right to build franchises in a surrounding six-county area and Chicago. Connerty got the rights to franchise the brand across the rest of the country, as long as he stayed true to the original concept of the Clearwater beach bar.

Bob Brooks, the current man behind the brand, first entered the picture as a business partner providing loans to finance the expansion of Hooters as a national brand. Brooks took over franchise leadership from Connerty in 1988 when he requested that loans be repaid and Connerty didn't have the funds to do so. The man behind the expansion of the chain that followed is described in the *Fortune Magazine* profile as a "Methodist family man who grew up on a South Carolina tobacco farm" (Helyar, 2003). Brooks's expansion philosophy was pretty straightforward and simple. Hooters franchises spread across the country offering down-home country cold beer, simple food, and pretty, friendly girls who advertise on the backs of their T-shirts that they are "delightfully tacky, yet unrefined." In addition to the original concept Brooks added the growing sports bar trend of the 1980s. Currently, Hooters positions itself in the restaurant market as a comfy sports bar primarily directed toward male customers as a neighborhood hangout, a place to meet the guys and watch a game, and watch and interact with the waitresses.

Droste, one of the six founding members, was a man raised in the Midwest. As a graduate of the agricultural university dubbed "Moo Roo U" in the popular lingo, Droste had his hand on the pulse of mainstream middle-class men in the 1980s. The Hooters Girls and the brand of humor were described in a quote from the *Fortune Magazine* case study as "naughty but not too naughty, [a form of] an elaborate PG-13 joke" (Helyar, 2003). This folksy, down-home sexuality and humor coupled with the fund-raising Hooters did for local charities went a long way toward cementing Hooters as an acceptable brand, despite its overt sexual objectification of women for profit, as captured so perfectly in the brand logo. The result was a restaurant that, while primarily marketed to men, actually serves a much broader clientele, with only 68 percent of the customers served at Hooters being male and 10 percent of the parties served including children, such as the parties I observed during my first Hooters visit.

"Delightfully Tacky, yet Unrefined": The Hooters Girl

While what may be most apparent are the clear differences between the Playboy Bunny and Hooters Girl, the one similarity dating from the two founders' original concepts was the connection both brands make to the "girl next door." Similar to Hefner's marketing plan the Hooters brand was in large part successful as a result of creating a place for men to go with sexy women who connected back to their memories of real cheerleaders, homecoming queens, and the often unattainable pretty girl next door. The big difference between the two brands is not so much the young women they recruited to represent their brand but the market segment of men they were targeting. Playboy created a sophisticated fantasy for the young, urban, well-educated man interested in fiction, politics, jazz, and very nice sports cars. The classic Playboy VIP look was a polished urban male in a very nice suit with a Playboy Bunny perched on each arm. In contrast, Hooters positioned itself to appeal to the young truck-drivin' male who has a set of blue balls hanging on his trailer hitch and loves chicken wings. Policing of white male heterosexuality is accomplished by a wooden sign hanging on the outside of the Hooters men's bathroom door, which features a line-drawing cartoon of a white male standing up and taking a whiz along with the words "Most Men." If you are not white and not quite man enough to stand up to whiz, beware. In contrast, the Hooters women's bathroom has a wooden sign featuring a line drawing of a woman sitting down and using the toilet, along with the words "All Women."

The contrast between these two market segments is acted out in the construction of the original Playboy Bunny, who is elegantly sexy, and the Hooters Girl, who when she turns her back on a customer proclaims that she is "delightfully tacky, yet unrefined" from the rear of her skintight white jersey. With the franchising of the

Hooters brand, and the passion of the original founders to maintain some degree of control over the brand, recruiting standards and uniform dress guidelines were developed for Hooters Girls. Similar to the Playboy Clubs, Hooters Girls are outfitted in standardized uniforms worn at all franchise locations, with the Hooters look carefully staying within what Hooters refers to as an "All American Cheerleader" look. Sizing is standardized, with shirts sized to fit very tightly, with "NO BAGGINESS." Shorts are prescribed to fit tightly but "NOT SO TIGHT THAT THE BUTTOCKS SHOW" (Hooters, n.d., p. 3). Hairstyles falling within a range labeled normal by the Midwestern middle-class founders are also prescribed, with an implied preference for long, sexy locks and not what are termed "bizarre haircuts, styles, or colors" (Hooters, n.d., p. 2). Tattoos and multiple piercings are not permitted. Makeup is also limited to the mainstream, with fingernail length and color kept within a modest range. Hooters standards for applying makeup are available to servers both on the website and in an information packet supplied to newly hired waitresses. Hooters Girls are not pierced, punk, and edgy; they are friendly Midwestern or Southern beach girls, there to make you happy. "Thou shalt always smile" is both number one and number ten in the "Ten Commandments of a Hooters Girl," with the implied connection of this down-home girl next door to homespun Christianity.

The very first Hooters Girl was Lynne Austin, and in many ways she defined the brand and shaped the future employee-recruiting strategy. Droste, one of the co-founders, literally recruited Austin off the Clearwater beach and put her into an outfit he had spotted on an employee at a charity softball tournament. Austin was a vivacious, bubbly blonde, quick to smile and quick to make people feel happy to meet her. As the first Hooters Girl she became a well-known sidekick to Droste as, in a fun way, he sold the first Hooters to the community through a series of radio appearances and charity events. Droste marketed his own background as a kid who grew up in Iowa, and he sold Hooters as a place where rural Middle America hospitality was served along with lots of attention from "down-home" friendly Hooters Girls. The appearances with Austin were funny and community oriented, bringing home the idea of Hooters as a neighborhood/community bar where you could go and have a good time and feel welcome. In 1986 *Playboy Magazine* recruited Austin to be a centerfold, resulting in a broadening of the market for Hooters and to some extent a democratization of the Playboy image to include the kind of working-class appeal of Hooters.

Customer interactions with Hooters Girls contrast with the romantic distance from the Playboy Bunnies established in the early Playboy Clubs. While the Playboy Bunnies at the Playboy Clubs were instructed not to date customers in order to maintain a glamorous and respectful ambiance within the clubs, Hooters Girls, as described in April Pederson's (1998) inside look at the chain, frequently date customers and store management. Part of the familiar down-home feel of Hooters is the courting of regulars by particular waitresses, with customers entering the door and being escorted by their "regular" Hooters Girl to a table. The careful avoidance of a direct display of cleavage to individual customers by such stylized serving as the Bunny Dip is taken in exactly the opposite direction at Hooters, with the entire brand focused on the exposure of bounce and cleavage. Pederson captures this sentiment in number six of her list of "Top 10 Statements You'll Never Hear at Hooters":

> 6. customer to manager: "Could you tell my waitress to keep her boobs out of my food?" (1998, p. 47)

As a result the male customers feel less formally separated from Hooters Girls than the Playboy Bunnies, with many waitresses having to cope with inappropriate comments, gestures, and pursuit from male customers. The feisty banter that can occur between waitresses and male patrons at Hooters is in marked contrast to the orchestrated glamour of the Playboy Clubs as established by the Hefner brothers. The level of disrespect allowable within the culture of Hooters leads to not only disrespectful comments but also behavior that ranges from customers shooting strategically aimed straws and spitballs at waitresses' bodies to teenage boys ordering "um, chicken...b-breast...yes breast, breast I'd like a BREAST!" This actual order was placed by a teenage boy with Pederson, who with the fast punch-back of an experienced Hooters Girl, glibly says to the reader of her Hooters memoir (but not to the actual teenage customer), "Yeah, well so would every other guy in this restaurant" (1998, p. 206).

In part to contradict some of the negative stereotypes about Hooters Girls brought to the attention of CEO Coby Brooks when he took part in the reality television series *Undercover Boss* in February 2010, the company launched the "Orange Pride Campaign." This campaign focuses attention on the community-service contributions of Hooters as well as promoting the accomplishments of former Hooters waitresses on the webpage and as part of some public events programming. With the slogan "We're Orange with Pride to be Hooters Girls," the online campaign includes testimonials by successful women who were once Hooters Girls. One of the three women profiled is a physician, a second is an entrepreneur now running a painting construction company, and the third is a woman who worked her way up through the corporate ranks at Hooters while also balancing a career as a "showcase" Hooters Girl appearing in Hooters commercials, as well as branching into a successful separate career as a swimsuit and fitness model. This campaign coupled with the hypersexualized Hooters Girl persona very successfully embodies the sexy empowerment icon for the mass audience, clearly linking self-objectification to power.

The mainstreaming of Hooters into American culture is perhaps symbolized by "Give a Hoot for Self Help," a nonprofit promotional event held in the summer of 2011 in the rural Middle America hometown of three of the Hooters founders, with benefits from the events donated to international relief. Starting off the real Hooters way, the four-day string of events began on day one in a local bar with Hooters Girls on hand for customers. This was followed the next day with a lunchtime calendar signing by Hooters Girls at a local sports bar and an evening party for sponsors of the Hooters Fore Self-Help golf tournament, happening the third day. The Biggest Ever Hooters Iowa event ended with the "Give a Hoot 5K and Family Picnic," with families from throughout the area taking part in the events.

Coyote Ugly Saloon: Tattoos Encouraged!

Coyote Ugly is a franchised saloon started by a female entrepreneur who started out in the trenches waitressing and bartending. Liliana Lovell, the founding CEO, quickly learned that flaunting her sexuality increased both tips and business. Her life story, published on the Coyote Ugly website, stresses her lower-middle-class Catholic upbringing, thus creating a fast bond with working-class Christian Americans. She even professes to liking the nuns and giving them credit for "making me believe I could accomplish anything." "Although," she adds "I am sure that they had different plans for me instead of dancing on top of a bar and sucking every last dollar out of my customer's wallets" (Lovell, n.d.). The not-accidental use of the word *suck*, the position of this young female entrepreneur up on the bar, and her bold assertion that she is out to get the money out of her male customers' wallets begin to paint the portrait of this brand, which contrasts with both the Playboy Bunny brand and the more easily likable and less threatening Hooters Girl.

Lovell's breakthrough was the opening of her own bar with the backing of a "friends' friend, Tony." Working as the jack-of-all-trades at the first Coyote Ugly in New York City, she made a name for the bar as a hopping place with a hot bartender who, when the lights got low, would "dance on the bar, sing to the crowd and insult anyone who wasn't man enough to take me on in a drinking contest." The business plan she put together while launching this first successful saloon follows some of the same script as the early Playboy Clubs and Hooters. In a nutshell, Lovell created an easy-to-brand public venue, provided food and alcohol, and solidified the chain's identity with a particular type of sexy server: "I developed my business plan and that has propelled me to where I am today: beautiful girls + booze = money. I began training my girls to perform my shtick. Some were good dancers, some were good singers, and others could yell at the crowd and entice them to drink. Very few had all three qualities, so I had to improvise. I would pair up the dancer with the comic yeller. Maybe the singer can be trained to dance a little better and it all began to work" (Lovell, n.d.).

But like Hooters, Coyote Ugly took the Playboy formula and refashioned it to appeal to a distinct market segment of men. Promotional events include motorcycle biker season-opening and -closing events, and merchandise includes custom black Coyote Ugly riding gloves with the middle "fuck you" finger highlighted with a white reflective surface. Coyote Ugly girls, like the founder, are rough and have attitude, tattoos, and, of course, very large and exposed breasts. Portraits of Coyote

Girls contrast vividly with both Playboy Bunnies and Hooters Girls. Unlike the girl-next-door sexuality marketed by Hefner and the Hooters franchise, Coyote girls have pierced tongues, dyed hair, hard-edged rather than artistic tattoos, and the language and attitude to match.

Cowgirls Espresso

The simple concept that one way to draw a crowd in and sell them food and beverages is to hire waitresses willing to flaunt their sexuality, and the growing mainstream acceptance of this strategy, has given rise to a small flood of enterprises all operating with essentially the same business plan. Cowgirls Espresso was founded in 2002 in Seattle, Washington, by another female entrepreneur, self-credited with the invention of the term *bikini barista*. The drive-through espresso franchise took off when the owner began to feature "Bikini Wednesdays," followed by "Military Mondays" featuring hot military looks, at a location close to an army base. Windows at the drive-through kiosks were designed with a large window for maximum view of the barista. Like the Hooters Girls, Cowgirls Espresso employees were hired to smile and interact with the customers. The link of this type of service to prostitution was close enough to have a rival start-up company in the same region end up with bikini baristas charged with illegal solicitation in 2009. This resulted in Cowgirls Espresso making a public statement distancing the company from these charges, a disclaimer that is still posted on the current website.

Exploring the Contours of Raunch Eroticism

Focus on the White Heterosexual Male Gaze

The business strategy for all of these business establishments, as so succinctly stated by Liliana Lovell on the Coyote Ugly website, is predicated on the simple formula that sexy girls will draw a male audience. The eating and drinking establishments range from an elegant urban nightclub, to a sports bar, to a rowdy saloon, to a coffee bar, but all have been successful due to the mainstreaming of the sexual objectification of women in service roles within the food and bar industry. The formula isn't new. Gentlemen's clubs have always tailored their performances and advertising to court the male gaze and desire, and less blatantly many restaurants and clubs have used attractive and sometimes scantily clad women to popularize themselves with the local male clientele. What is different in this case is the intentional creation of a branded hypersexualized female icon that comes to represent and popularize the franchise to a mass audience. The movement in the millennium is away from the notion of an exclusively male club environment, with women welcome on invitation only, to restaurants, bars, and coffee bars that are open to everyone regardless of gender but are clearly directed toward and serving the heterosexual male gaze and desire.

Sexual Objectification of Women

The early success of Playboy Clubs, Hooters, Coyote Ugly, and Cowgirls Espresso emanates from the purposeful and lucrative practice of sexually objectifying women for profit. Hefner's decision to turn his servers into Bunnies for the enjoyment of his playboys began a process of looking at female employees as stamped-out uniform symbols of the brand of sexuality being sold by the employer. Hooters' name and logo transform breasts into a male expletive, a male way of describing a really sexy pair of breasts. The Hooters Girls thus wear T-shirts stamping them as valuable in terms of their ability to attract the male gaze and desire through flaunting of this sexualized part of the female body. Even a practiced and authentic feminist has trouble *not* focusing on breasts when she enters a Hooters, due in large part to the branding of the franchise with a name used to rate this part of the female body. The stumbling language of the teenager trying to order a chicken breast sandwich, and also be funny in front of his peers, gives testimony to the focus on the breasts that the name generates for customers.

Self-Objectification

The hiring and training practices of franchises focused on making money based on attracting a male clientele through sexy service providers place the female employees in a position where they self-objectify and also sexually objectify other women working for the same organization. Standards of breast size were talked about in both the employee memoirs I read for this project. The former Playboy Bunny talked about Betty, the club costume director, stuffing the tops of underendowed Bunnies to fill out their bras and make them look like the rest of the girls. While April Pederson is quick to point out that breast implants are not required by Hooters, and that those waitresses who have elected to get them have done it "solely for their own personal reasons," she then adds, "Some of these girls ended up with such fantastic-looking ones that I'll probably even get them soon myself" (1998, p. 17). The normalizing of things like breast implants captured by Pederson's Hooters memoir is part and parcel of working within an organization where your primary value is measured by a part of your sexual body, in this case the breasts.

Sexual Attention and Sexualized Practice as Power

The impact of the sexy empowerment icon has infused millennium business strategies to the point that male entrepreneurs and business owners like Hooters CEO

Coby Brooks use the philosophy to argue that a viable route to real power is through sexual attractiveness. Hooters' creation of the Orange Pride Campaign directly ties the stories of Hooters waitresses with histories of winning choice spots on the Hooters annual calendar to their moving into positions of power and influence. Even more directly, the life story of Liliana Lovell pays testament to the sexy empowerment icon's promise to deliver the goods to women willing to use their sexuality to get ahead. In the case of Lovell, she literally bases a part of her business plan on the ability of a hot bartender to strip the money out of a male customer's wallet through a combination of sexual attractiveness, wit, and tenacity. The television news story covering Cowgirls Espresso compared and contrasted the average tips earned by servers working as mainstream baristas with those of the bikini-clad baristas working at this success story, with average baristas earning $20 a day in tips while what the newscaster refers to as the "bodacious baristas" top out at $700 for a day's work.

Private Is Public

The trend toward mainstreaming of sexy service providers as a means of attracting business points toward the moving of the viewing of objectified sexuality out of the private realm of individual pleasure and into the public realm experienced by everyone. Certainly it can be argued that individuals can opt out of going to Cowgirls Espresso or a Hooters chain restaurant. What is less avoidable is public news coverage of Cowgirls Espresso or the late-summer Hooters golf tournament and fun run held at the local park. Public events sponsored by organizations like Hooters that take place in local parks and advertise themselves as family-friendly events move porn chic into the public zone for even those attempting to steer clear of the trend.

Extreme, Up the Ante

The story of the transformation of Cowgirls Espresso from just another coffee bar to a hot and happening bikini coffee bar attracting not only customers but also a steady stream of press attention illustrates why the trend toward sexual objectification in mainstream eating establishments is attracting entrepreneurial interest and funding. The founder of the espresso bar started out with the idea of creating a unique drive-through coffee bar painted white with big black spots to mimic cowhide. The idea of having the baristas dress in bikinis came from one of the employees, who wanted to start Wednesday Bikini Day during the hot months of the summer. The owner checked in with the local mayor, who told her to move ahead and that it was a great idea in terms of positioning herself with the strong competition in the area. The extreme success of Bikini Wednesdays resulted in the transformation from a traditional coffee bar to a well-known and very successful bikini coffee bar.

The moving of sexuality into an untapped marketplace worked well for this entrepreneur, with the local television news coverage touting the coffee bar in full-story format, opening with "There is a new java joint that has the fastest, hottest, and definitely the sexiest coffee in the country." The movement of scantily clad baristas into the mainstream through the evening news and men's daily trips through the drive-through ups the ante for competing coffee establishments. This type of business also creates a model for other entrepreneurs in terms of using sexualized service personnel to move product and attract business.

Misogyny

The first step toward misogyny is the turning of women into sexual objects. Once a woman becomes a sexual object, she is no longer automatically conferred basic levels of human respect. When this is coupled with alcohol consumption, the stage is set for obnoxious, degrading behaviors ranging from comments about a server's body to spit wads shot into her cleavage. In the millennium age of raunch, the careful distance between the Playboy Bunnies and the keyholders created in Hefner's early clubs has dissolved, giving rise to a range of degrading behaviors toward sexy servers often bordering on or expressing misogyny.

–8–

Construction of Cyber Raunch Identity:
The Private Becomes Public

> Hers was the rear that launched a thousand blogs. "Pip Pippa Hooray!" wrote the *Daily Star.* "Her Royal Hotness", the *Daily Mail* christened her. Swooning Twitter users from both sides of the Atlantic made her a trending topic. Someone started a Facebook group devoted to appreciating the Pippa posterior (it now has more than 160,000 members). (Lyall, 2011)

In 1968 Andy Warhol made the now often quoted prediction that "in the future, everyone will be world famous for fifteen minutes." The opening of the World Wide Web granting individuals the ability to broadcast their identities to international audiences instantly has both validated Warhol's insight and also dated it. Warhol was absolutely right that the future held the promise of potential fame (or infamy) for everyone. However, in the new millennium fame is no longer measured by minutes in the spotlight. Individuals seeking or cast into Internet fame don't hold the whole world's attention at any one time but instead become an online identity that gets epic numbers of hits, repeated visits back to a YouTube video, a Facebook account, or a website. Fame and infamy is measured by how many people read about you, look at you, or watch your YouTube video, and whether they walk away with a memorable nugget that they then text-message on to their contact list.

The celebrity launch of the sister of the royal bride into the international spotlight based on Internet postings and cell phone tweets proclaiming the excellence of her ass points both to both the raunch we are all creating and the ones who are responsible for the situation, us. At a point not long ago a tabloid might have published a page and a picture about Pippa's stunning debut at her sister's wedding, but now we are doing it ourselves, in epic numbers, and in the raunchiest manner possible. And while the *New York Times* would not have stooped to publish a story about the magnificent ass of the royal sister, this respected newspaper did deem it worthy to write a story about the pop culture construction of a porn chic identity for the royal bridesmaid. A month later respected news sources were drawn into covering Anthony Weiner's sexting scandal, with ABC posting "exclusive" cell phone images of Weiner including the now-famous lower-body bulging-briefs photograph.

It is elemental to the human condition that the person willing to do the raunchiest act ever will get attention. People love to see, read, and talk about sexuality, and quickly the Internet became a means of getting instant fame for those willing to upload videos and images of themselves or others containing sexually explicit images. It also became a way for fame to be bestowed on those not expecting or seeking it, through the broadcast of private acts to an international audience. Perhaps the most famous of these incidents was the broadcasting of a homemade sex video of New York socialite Paris Hilton and her boyfriend, which was leaked and broadcast on the Internet in 2003, then later made into a for-sale video. The resulting instant fame helped to launch her reality television show the next week and also propelled her into the international spotlight as the New York rich It Girl to follow; this fame set her up to enter popular culture as a designer, actress, and singer without the typical requisite skills and background. Not surprisingly Hilton was also captured by Joe Francis on a *Girls Gone Wild* tape, which was later circulated on the web at a site entitled Parisexposed.com.

This same instant route to fame on a smaller scale was experienced by college students I interviewed as a part of my *Girls Gone Wild* research. With the advent of the cell phone camera and the capability of the web, young female students who had flashed for several years in the relatively private confines of a college bar district suddenly found their bare-breasted images being broadcast internationally on websites devoted to college girls flashing. Similar, but more tragic, is the fall 2010 story of the gifted Rutgers University freshman whose sexual encounter with another male student was, without his knowledge, captured on webcam and broadcast over the web, resulting in his suicide and the prosecution of the two fellow students responsible for the act. I examine this case study in more detail later in this chapter.

This chapter focuses primarily on the intentional creation of online identities by individuals seeking attention and/or fame using sexuality and raunch as a means of hooking the web surfer. Social networking sites abound on the Internet and range from dating and hookup sites to professional networking sites. All these networking sites are based on an individual taking the initiative to create an online identity to attract the attention of others served by the site. The opening of this chapter focuses on the most influential and successful of those ventures, Facebook. The second section of this chapter focuses on the creation of online identity through the posting of YouTube videos. This section is followed by a discussion of the potential damage wrought by the posting or forwarding of sexually explicit photographs and/or videos of oneself or others, leading in some cases to suicide and permanently altered and damaged lives. The chapter ends by focusing on the construction of cyber-identities that enter into computer-based sexual relationships with other cyber-identities through cyber chat rooms.

Facebook

Facebook in its current form is an international social networking website headquartered in the heart of computer geek country, Palo Alto, California. The central headquarters of this innovative firm employs 1,400 people and had a likely revenue of close to $1 billion in 2010 (Kirkpatrick, 2010). Facebook is a mega-broadcaster of both information and images, with David Kirkpatrick citing monthly postings of "20 billion pieces of content" by Facebook members, with the uploaded images making the networking site "by far the largest photo-sharing site on the Internet" (2010, p. 11). Launched from its college student founder Mark Zuckerberg's dorm room on February 4, 2004, the website had 650 students registered in just four days, 10,000 active members after one month, and, with its launch on other campuses, 20,000 Facebook accounts by mid-March and 100,000 on thirty-four campuses by the end of May (Kirkpatrick, 2010). As of February 2010, Kirkpatrick reports that there were 400 million active accounts on this site and that "20 percent of the 1.7 billion people on the Internet worldwide now use Facebook regularly," with "mind-bending" growth rates of "about 5 percent a month" (2010, p. 16). It is a truly international site, boasting seventy-five different languages, with 75 percent of current users based outside of the United States (Kirkpatrick, 2010, p. 16).

The site was originally named after the Harvard University system of storing student pictures, and the term *Facebook* is now a commonly used verb, "I am Facebooking my friends," and has engendered the term *Facebook Effect* to describe the impact of the network on social life in the millennium:

> The Facebook Effect happens when the service puts people in touch with each other, often unexpectedly, about a common experience, interest, problem, or cause. This can happen at a small or large scale—from a group of two or three friends or a family, to millions.... Facebook's software makes information viral. Ideas on Facebook have the ability to rush through groups and make many people aware of something almost simultaneously, spreading from one person to another and on to many with unique ease—like a virus, or meme. You can send messages to other people even if you are not explicitly trying to. (Kirkpatrick, 2010, pp. 7–8)

Very early in its development, Amelia Lester, then a student at Harvard, now the managing editor of the *New Yorker* magazine, picked up on the voyeuristic and exhibitionist potential of the website. Created in what Michael Kimmel (2008) has called the most intense dating environment of a lifetime, a college campus, Facebook had from the beginning a "let's check out who's hot" potential that attracted the male gaze but also an appeal as the ideal place to strut your stuff, which attracted female students eager to get noticed by the right guys on campus. During the launch year at Harvard, when it was barely out of the racing gate as a website, Lester wrote in the student newspaper: "While the facebook.com isn't explicitly about bringing people together in romantic unions, there are plenty of other primal instincts evident at work here: an element of wanting to belong, a dash of vanity, and more than a little voyeurism" (quoted in Kirkpatrick, 2010, p. 33).

Facebook was launched on my home campus in the rural central United States in June 2004, just four months after the Harvard grand opening of the site in February.

I set up a Facebook account for myself in the fall of 2004 at the same time as students in my classes were beginning to experiment with the social networking technology. At that point in time, of the 2,000 community colleges and universities in the United States, only 882 were served by Facebook, and those accounts were restricted to users currently enrolled in and working at the host institutions. While fewer than half of all campuses in the United States were served by Facebook, on active campuses, 85 percent of the students had Facebook profiles.

When I created my faculty Facebook account, there were a total of 3.85 million student members in the United States, with 60 percent of those students logging in every day and 80 percent logging in at least once a week. Statistics for faculty and staff were not gathered at that point, but suffice it to say that in those early years it was relatively rare for a faculty member to be active on Facebook. When I presented a research paper on the cultural construction of cyber-identity on Facebook at a national research conference in the fall of 2006, many of the faculty in the audience were unaware of or had only a very vague understanding of the social network. In contrast, students across the country were committed to and actively using Facebook to construct identities and social connections.

At that early stage in the development of Facebook, the network was exclusively found on college campuses. Privacy settings were set up so that only those officially connected to a particular campus through an e-mail address could access profiles on that campus. I became involved early in part due to my gender-violence prevention role on campus. Campus police and victim service providers were detecting relationships between female students' posting of information such as class schedules, cell phone numbers, and photographs and incidents of stalking and interpersonal violence. Also, as a researcher primarily focusing on the cultural construction of gender, I was very interested in both male and female students' use of Facebook to construct cyber-identities.

When I came into class and talked about Facebook and showed students my profile page, they reacted much the same way as the students at Harvard did when they came back to campus in the fall and President Summers told them he had been studying their Facebook sites over the summer. Their first reaction was shock that a professor, or, in the case of Harvard, the president, had spent time on Facebook and possibly looked at their profiles. The second reaction of my class was excitement; they were stimulated by the idea that this was something to analyze and think about, a fun research area in terms of identity formation, and very much at the center of student life at that time and now.

The research I conducted with my students (Lynch, 2006) was based on content analysis of university student Facebook accounts on three different campuses in the rural central United States. One of the premier findings was the increasing impact of raunch culture on college students during that same time period. Not surprisingly, a dominating theme, particularly of first-year female students' profiles, was the concentration on constructing a cyber-identity that would attract the male gaze and attention.

This fit with other research I had conducted in the late 1990s that indicated changing patterns of Thursday and Friday night bar dress as female students moved through their college years (Lynch, 1999b). This earlier research, also conducted with the assistance of undergraduate students, found that first-year students were the most apt to dress to attract sexual attention at the bars, with older female students more often wearing what they called "bumming-around clothes," particularly those young women who either had active boyfriends or had a serious commitment to a career. The less apt a young woman was to have career aspirations, the more apt she was to continue to dress provocatively throughout her four to five years of college. Similarly, women who entered into committed relationships also toned down the dress styles they wore to the bar on Thursday and Friday night.

This pattern was replicated on Facebook profile sites. By far the most sexually explicit profiles were those of the entering first-year class. In addition to posting pictures of themselves in hot Thursday and Friday night bar fashions, first-year female students were more apt to use the ability to post favorite quotations on Facebook to speak about themselves and their willingness to party. The following quote is taken from a first-year student's Facebook site that featured a profile picture taken in a bar with her hand on her hip and her arm around a drunk-looking fellow with a bottle, paired with a classic "come and get me" pose taken right out of *Playboy*:

> It's COLLEGE…Make MISTAKES. Make the same mistake TWICE because it is too good to only make it once. FORGIVE others. Forgive yourself. Forget things. PARTY on a weekday. PARTY HARDER on the weekends. Forget that you partied at all. Get SICK. Get so sick you don't remember how you got sick. Skip CLASS. Watch movies instead of doing homework. Stay up all night before a final.

Another feature of the early Facebook site was the ability to create Facebook groups that you could invite other Facebook members on your own campus to join. First-year women were also prone to creating sexually provocative Facebook groups directed toward a male audience, with Britney Spears sites particularly popular. Facebook group sites, like individual profiles, featured a signature picture expressing the essence of the group. In the case of the "Drunk Girls Gone Lesbian and Are Crazy for Britney Spears" site, the group profile picture was the famous kiss between Britney Spears and Madonna at the MTV Awards. Facebook group sites also featured a profile quote explaining the purpose and membership of the group. This Britney Spears group defined itself as follows: "If you've EVER made out with a girl when you are drunk, then this is the group for you! But only if you think that Britney Spears is undeniably hot and aren't afraid to admit it!! Woooo Go Britney! We love you!" While certainly the site was intended to attract female members, the girl-on-girl sex emphasized by the site was staged for a male audience. There were also girl-on-girl sites created by male students, such as "Oh I love to watch Drunk Girls Make Out," described by the membership as "for everyone who loves to watch girls making out.

There is just something about two beautiful women going at it. To put it simply: its just fuckin' hot."

One of the most popular early types of Facebook groups started by male students on these relatively large state-supported public campuses was a "hottest freshman" rating site. These "rate the coed" websites, created under a range of different group names, were in many ways similar to an early website that Facebook's founder Zuckerberg created but quickly took down at Harvard. These websites were invitational sites for women, run by men. Male members of the Facebook group invited women to apply for membership using their Facebook pictures. The male members of the group would then vote to accept a certain number of top applicants. One site was entitled "50 Hottest Broads @ [name of campus]." The description of the group explained the rating system: "This group will showcase only the 50 most beautiful females on campus. Candidates will be selected for membership based on strength of Facebook photo.... bribery is not only accepted but it is encouraged. Those of you who are invited please do not think you are safe. If there are 50 hotter girls than you, you will be herded off this list. Once the group has reached its limit you can challenge one of the members for their spot."

Stereotypical unapologetic bad boy behavior centered on the link between alcohol and sex was formally endorsed with Facebook groups such as "I Like My Women Like I Like My Coffee...Filled with Booze." This Facebook group was self-defined as being the online home "for all those animals out there who just don't give a rat's ass whether you're sober for work, or whether your late night hook-up is either." Cult leaders among these self-defined campus bad boys, like Tucker Max, entered Facebook early in its development with fan pages. Max's was named "Dude, Here's My Book," with the description of the writer coming directly off his website: "His name is Tucker Max, and he is an asshole. He gets excessively drunk at inappropriate times, disregards social norms, indulges every whim, ignores the consequences of his actions, mocks idiots and posers, sleeps with more women than is safe or reasonable, and just generally acts like a raging dickhead." The Facebook profiles of members of the Tucker Max fan club were in some cases blatantly misogynistic, with one featuring a profile picture of a woman lying down with a black eye and man standing above her, with the slogan "Punch her in the face—to prove you are right."

Facebook rhetoric has continued to popularize porn chic, with the term *raunched out* used in the spring of 2011 by an alumna of my university to describe a photo album she posted on her Facebook profile. The gallery featured photographs of risqué Halloween regalia worn by the Facebook profile owner as well as her friends but also other sexually provocative bar and party photographs. As Facebook spread into high schools, parents and schools were brought into the mix in terms of policing the images posted by their children and teenagers. A friend of mine with a seventeen-year-old daughter told me about trying to convince her daughter three years ago that posting a Facebook profile picture of herself lying on a bed, even though she was dressed, was provocative and not a good idea. At age fourteen her daughter listened and removed the photograph. It was more difficult this year, when her daughter was older and the same type of problem emerged again. This time her daughter was more resistant. At this point the daughter is still living at home, and the mother was able to persuade her daughter to take down the photograph. These parental interventions typically no longer work once children are launched and living away from home.

YouTube

YouTube was developed and launched in June 2005 by a set of three Silicon Valley entrepreneurs who were former employees of the online commerce website PayPal. It was an extremely timely innovation and was picked up quickly by Google, which purchased YouTube for $1.65 billion in October 2006, just over one year after its launch. YouTube became the most popular entertainment website in the United Kingdom, and in early 2008 it became a top-ten-rated entertainment site worldwide (Burgess and Green, 2009). The website's growth has been unprecedented and exponential, with its links to Facebook enhancing its appeal for social networking and its ability to facilitate cultural construction of cyber-identity. YouTube dominates the video-upload market. A March 4, 2009, press release from comScore.com, a leader in measuring the impact of digital technologies, reported that Google Sites, owner of YouTube, controls 43 percent of the online video market, with Fox Interactive Media ranked second with only a 3.7 percent share of the video-viewing marketplace (comScore. com, 2009).

Jawed Karim, one of the three developers of the original YouTube site, credits the success of the site to four key features outlined by Liz Gannes (2006) and Jean Burgess and Joshua Green (2009), three of which facilitate easy dissemination of videos to social networks:

1. The ability to recommend videos to others
2. An e-mail link to facilitate easy sharing with others
3. The ability to make comments and link to social networking sites, particularly Facebook
4. An embeddable video player

The combination of being able to easily upload a video for your own viewing and forward it on to friends with comments has made videos part of daily life for many computer users. *TechCrunch*, a web blog focused on leading computer technology start-ups, reported in 2009 that these latest figures in real practice translate into "pretty much everyone on the internet, on average, watching one YouTube video per day" (Arrington, 2009).

Accompanying the development of user-friendly websites like YouTube that make video uploading and sharing easy for the average Internet user are camera technologies that have made the video production process cheaper and easier. Dedicated-use video cameras have been successfully challenged in the marketplace by cell phones and image cameras that also capture short videos for amateur filmmakers. One of the very latest camcorders introduced in a *New York Times* technical review in November 2010 is a headlined as a "Life Partner," an extremely small and lightweight camera that fits over the earlobe or on a headband, allowing for ease of recording and literally capturing video as you live it (Eisenberg, 2010). I couldn't help but immediately think about my fieldwork observing *Girls Gone Wild* flashing on my home campus and the explosion of privacy issues that occurred after the development of cell phone cameras. This type of easily hidden device when coupled with the ease of uploading provided by sites like YouTube and Facebook has the potential to cause dramatic increases in abuses related to the exposure of private lives by third parties, as is discussed in the final section of this chapter.

YouTube is both a bottom-up platform, a place where literally anyone with a camera and a computer can upload their own videos, and a top-down platform used by commercial interests for distribution, particularly to young, hard-to-reach consumers. As a top-down platform the power of entertainment distributors to mass-promote music, films, and other popular culture has been changing, with the young, sometimes termed the *YouTube Generation*, turning to their PCs and iPhones to watch streaming videos of television shows, movies, and music videos. While certainly YouTube affects a broad band of Internet users, perhaps the most vulnerable group are young preteens and teenagers in the process of formulating their identities.

The old-fashioned process of dressing up like your favorite pop singer and wiggling to their music in front of a mirror has been transformed into dressing up and lip-synching to your favorite entertainers on YouTube. A vernacular video genre referred to as bedroom dance videos has emerged in response to this new technology. This new genre was both mass-introduced and in part defined by an early YouTube hit entitled simply the "Hey Clip." This amateur video produced by two girlfriends lip-synching, dancing, and playing air guitar to The Pixies' song "Hey" was viewed by several million visitors by mid-2006 and over twenty-one million by March 2008. One of the two instant YouTube stars had this to say to the newspaper *USA Today* about the production of this extremely popular video: "We just turned on the camera and danced funny....I keep asking people why do you like it, and they say, 'Because it's reality'. You see it's homemade, that we're so spontaneous and natural—dancing, having fun. It makes people remember when they were young and danced in front of the mirror" (Kornblum, 2006).

YouTube success stories like the discovery of popular teen singer Justin Bieber in 2008, coupled with the enormous popularity of bedroom dance videos like "Hey Clip," fueled young people's investment in self-produced and -uploaded music videos. The teenage YouTube upload story does not always end in interviews for *USA Today* or contracts with music producers. During the course of my research for this book, I talked with a mother of a high school student who was frantically trying to figure out how to remove her daughter's YouTube video from a website devoted to linking men to Asian call girls. Her daughter had naively uploaded a bedroom dance video of herself dancing to a Lady Gaga song, and it had been picked up by the call girl website through its username, which included an Asian girl reference.

The influence of media on identity formation is in part facilitated by the relatively large amount of unsupervised time youth are spending in their bedroom spaces, which are often equipped with PCs, music systems, and televisions. European studies of what is termed *bedroom culture* indicate that access to media in bedrooms increases the amount of time nine- to ten-year-olds spend in their own rooms in the house while at the same time decreasing parental involvement in monitoring media use by their children (Bovill and Livingstone, 2001). The development of handheld Internet-capable devices like the iPod Touch and smart phones further decreases parents' ability to police the YouTube videos and websites viewed by their children, particularly within the relative privacy of their own bedrooms. The resulting increase in easy access by children and tweens to the Internet points toward the escalating impact of media images and messages on how young people are taught to construct gender identity.

Capturing the media habits and play of tweens within the privacy of their bedrooms and within the relatively closed confines of their homes is challenging. In two separate studies Sara Louise Baker was able to effectively get inside the private spaces and play of Australian preteen girls. In Baker's first study (2004), she used a combination of a tape recording and photography diary kept by individual girls capturing their lives within their bedrooms. Her second, follow-up study (2011) was based on fieldwork at an afterschool facility serving teenage girls. Within this afterschool program, Baker used a combination of direct observation and participant observation to get inside the process of self-representation through play that is so central to identity formation among preteens.

Using Richard Schechner's (1995) concept of play as formative and transforming, Baker's results and analysis explored the role that music and pop stars played in these young girls' explorations of emerging female identity. One of Baker's key subjects, assigned the pseudonym "Kate," used her tape recorder to create a simulation of her favorite local radio station. With Kate playing the role of DJ and a range of popular female pop singers, Baker's analysis captures the private play of her subject: "In her bedroom, tape recorder in hand, Kate's play enabled a slipping into Otherness as she *became* pop singer Mandy Moore or radio DJ Amanda Blair. In her play, she was both DJ and pop star, announcer and singer, and always the performer.... By opening up a sensual space to understand the cultural processes of radio, DJing and pop stardom, Kate's play resonated with the possibilities of self-representation" (Baker, 2004, pp. 83–84). Baker's tape recorder and camera empowered Kate to capture versions of herself that emerged as she played with the self-presentation of female pop musicians and, in this case, a lively female DJ working at the radio station in her hometown known for providing the "hotter mix of the 80s, 90s and today" (Baker, 2004, p. 81). YouTube technology moves the possibilities of self-representation into video format, with girls literally able to project themselves as their favorite singers on videos that they can easily upload to the Internet. Thus the line between private and public is blurred, leading some tweens and teenagers, such as my friend's daughter, to post videos connecting them to potentially dangerous strangers and websites on the Internet.

Baker's research also captures the agency demonstrated by young girls as they play with the music of their favorite pop musicians. For example, Rosa, another of Baker's subjects, actually inserts herself into the music production process, at times turning down the volume of a male lead singer so that she can take over the lead role in the song (2004, pp. 86–87). Rosa used the research camera to capture herself with the microphone performing one of her favorite songs. This image, according to Baker, is capturing more than Rosa simply trying to duplicate her favorite pop star Christina Aguilera but rather "Rosa struggling with the process and multiplicities of becoming: becoming-girl; -woman; -popstar; and ultimately becoming Rosa" (2004, p. 88). Unfortunately, YouTube uploads add the unintended risk for young girls of becoming a Lolita to an unknown and potentially dangerous stranger.

Rosa as a research subject also demonstrated another path between mainstream popular culture and porn, which is the dangerous play zone often trekked by tweens and teenagers. A part of "play" is transgressing permissible boundaries, experimenting with the forbidden. In the case of Rosa she records a version of herself singing an Australian lout's version of "Merry Christmas," including the lyrics "Ho ho fucking ho, what a crock of shit," and almost being caught by her mother (Baker, 2004, p. 89). This is an example of Schechner's (1995) concept of dark play wherein participants purposefully cross normative boundaries and take on and play with the identities of people from forbidden zones. For Rosa this is one method of exploring and testing the rules for what it means to be a girl, a woman, within the peer-policed boundaries of Euro-American femininity (Bordo, 1992).

Transgressing the boundaries through dark play was also a theme in Baker's fieldwork conducted with some of the same preteen girls at a casually supervised after-school care facility for older grade school children. In this setting Baker was able to observe over the course of several weeks as the preteen girls explored porn websites using a Britney Spears website as a cover. The technique used by the girls to hide their porn viewing from supervising adults was to minimize the porn site when their private cyberspace was threatened, leaving only the Britney Spears site up on the screen for adult scrutiny. This porn-screening device succeeded in much the same manner as the method used by Tom in chapter 6, who hid his favorite pornographic images inside of Word documents during his teenage years in a British boarding school (Mills, 2010, p. 22). Baker, by this time a trusted confidante of the girls, was afforded an equal seat in front of the screen and was thus able to personally observe the girls' reaction to both the Britney Spears website and also multiple porn sites.

Similar to Rosa's behavior as she played in her bedroom pretending to be the DJ and a pop star, as the girls viewed the porn site they played with the identities on the screen, mimicking the videos of the porn stars dancing and stripping for their screen audience. In particular, one young girl named Emlyn had acquired what Baker (2011) termed *kinetic knowledge* from repeated study of both the porn sites and the Britney Spears site and was able to reproduce the provocative dance moves and behaviors of the websites for her friends. To stress again, the ability to move from simply playing with porn identity through replication of dancing and stripping behaviors to the uploading of YouTube videos of oneself or one's friends dancing like a porn video blurs the private and public and also opens young people to scrutiny and abuse by an unbounded Internet audience. While this was not the focus of Baker's research, YouTube placed within the bedrooms and/or the daycare facility ratchets up these behaviors and moves them from private explorations of self into public displays of identity that have the potential to be used and manipulated by others.

The girls also learned to both self-objectify and name the parts of the body through studying the Britney Spears website and the porn sites. One point of special interest to the girls was the study of Spears's breasts, with their debates focused on whether she had breast implants or not. The porn websites taught the girls to name parts of their body using the terminology of the male gaze and also to focus on things like breast implants. These websites taught the girls how the male gaze views the female body. The girls then used this viewing system on others as well as to evaluate their own bodies.

Baker's description of this fieldwork incident also provides a window into how underage users navigate through the world of Internet porn, finding images and videos despite supposed barriers to access to the sites by minors and unregistered users:

> Without a credit card their registration was not accepted, but this was only a minor setback as the next thing Emlyn did was enter a different URL nine.com, in the hope it would contain similar content. This URL redirected the girls to a different website, pussy. com. At the sight of the word "pussy", the girls literally fell about laughing again. Emlyn, legs slightly parted and pointing to her crotch said, "It's weird how they call pussy cat the same as there." "Because they're both furry," giggled Kylie. At the moment Emlyn noticed how close the OSHC [adult supervisor] was and frantically told Kylie to, "Get it down, get it down. Put Britney page back on." (Baker, 2011, pp. 179–180)

This field note nicely captures how the girls used the Britney Spears site to mask their viewing of the porn sites, similar to Tom, the boarding-school boy interviewed by Mills, who hid his pornography in Word files that were easily minimized if he was close to being caught (Mills, 2010, p. 21).

The potential of vernacular YouTube videos to both contribute to and create dialogue about hypersexual objectification of girls and women can be explored through a single case study example of the YouTube videos created as a response to the hugely successful MTV music video release promoting "Barbie Girl" by the Danish dance-pop band Aqua. The song itself was controversial enough in its references to Barbie as a sexual object and a bimbo to prompt a Mattel lawsuit:

I'm a Barbie girl, in the Barbie world
Life in plastic, it's fantastic!
you can brush my hair, undress me everywhere
Imagination, life is your creation
I'm a blond bimbo girl, in the fantasy world
Dress me up, make it tight, I'm your dolly
You're my doll, rock'n'roll, feel the glamour in pink,
kiss me here, touch me there, hanky panky...
You can touch, you can play, if you say: "I'm always yours,"

The music video, whose success launched the career of its Danish director, Peder Pedersen, cleverly deconstructed, quite literally, the plastic body of Barbie and also the cultural meaning of the doll in terms of the male gaze and sexual objectification.

The vernacular YouTube videos that were created in part as a response to both the song and the MTV video vary widely in terms of intent and visual content. The most famous of the group was created by two young men whose goal was to promote their rock band through YouTube. Their performance, though done by two men, falls within the genre of a bedroom lip-synch and dance YouTube video. One of the young men, wearing a fake mustache, plays the role of Ken, while the second young

Figure 8.1 *Porn Chic VI.* Courtesy of Nicola Bockelmann.

man, who eventually strips down to his Speedos, plays the role of Barbie. "Barbie," stripped to his Speedos, rubs his tits and ass as he coyly lip-synchs, "you can touch me here, undress me everywhere." The casting of both characters by men and the deliberate sexual objectification of the male playing Barbie creates dissonance and humor, effectively challenging the cultural norm of hypersexualization of women to perform for the male gaze as found in this era of raunch eroticism.

In contrast, a stream of less popular but abundant bedroom dance and lip-synching YouTube videos of "Barbie Girl" produced by preteen and teen girls twist the meaning of the lyrics back to supporting sexual objectification of girls and women. The humor and clever deconstruction of the Barbie doll as cultural icon is absent and is replaced by the conventional interpretation of Barbie as played with by young girls everywhere—sexy and directing her attention to the male gaze. For example, in one video I watched, which was created by girls who appeared to be between ten and twelve, the girls are both dressed in short pink skirts and tight white Hooters-style shirts, and they present themselves as sexual candy for the audience, drawing this response from a viewer: "nice sluts."

Sexting: The Risks of Internet Uploads of Explicit Material

A *New York Times* front-page headline on March 27, 2011, read eerily like a pulp tabloid: "POISONED WEB: A Girl's Nude Photo, and Altered Lives." The story took place in a small town in the northeastern United States. An eighth-grade girl followed the emerging national dating trend and sent her new boyfriend a frontal nude self-portrait, a photograph she took of herself in front of her bathroom mirror. Isaiah, the young man Margarite sent the picture to, explained in an interview how the sexting began:

> How had the sexting from Margarite begun? "We were about to date, and you'll be like, 'Oh, blah, blah, blah, I really like you, can you send me a picture?'" Isaiah recalled.
>
> "I don't remember if I asked her first or if she asked me. Well, I think I did send her a picture. Yeah, I'm pretty sure. Mine was, like, no shirt on."
>
> "It is very common," he said. "I'd seen pictures on other boys' cellphones." (Hoffman, 2011)

The story goes wrong from this point on. The first indication of a potential problem was the relatively fast breakup of the early dating relationship, leaving the sexually explicit photograph on the cell phone of a boy no longer committed to the relationship. Isaiah, reportedly unaware of a falling out between Margarite and her best friend, honors her former close friend's request to forward the picture. The friend, who is a friend no longer, forwards the picture to a long list of contacts on her personal phone along with the following text message: "Ho Alert! If you think this

girl is a whore, then text this to all your friends" (Hoffman, 2011). The county pros-
ecutor had a tough case on his hands, made much harder by the fact that the sexting
had gone beyond the dating couple and had been mass-distributed on the Internet. The
story of the arrest of the eighth graders is chilling as recounted in the *New York Times*
front-page story:

> He decided against charging Margarite. But he did charge three students with dissemina-
> tion of child pornography, a Class C felony, because they had set off the viral outbreak.
>
> After school had been let out that day in late January, the police read Isaiah his rights,
> cuffed his hands behind his back and led him and Margarite's former friend out of the
> building. The eighth graders would have to spend the night in the county juvenile deten-
> tion center. (Hoffman, 2011)

Charges against the eighth graders were eventually amended from the child pornography felony to a gross misdemeanor of telephone harassment, making the three
teenagers eligible for a community-service sentence, keeping them out of court and
out of detention. The debated photograph became viral and remains available online,
haunting the recovering victim.

The answer as to where the behavior comes from is fairly direct and easy. A first
point of influence is popular music that makes reference to the behavior. Hoffman
directly quotes the song lyrics of two popular music celebrities: "Take a dirty picture
for me," urge the pop stars Taio Cruz and Kesha in their recent duet, "Dirty Picture.
Send It to Me. Snap" (2011). In this song Kesha not only requests a dirty picture but
also provides the sound effects, the snap of the camera shutter. Also surrounding
these young people are news stories covering the sexting escapades of popular culture heroes like Brett Favre and a 2010 Super Bowl advertisement for a Motorola
phone in which "the actress Megan Fox takes a cellphone picture of herself in a
bubble bath. 'I wonder what would happen if I were to send this out?' she muses.
The commercial continues with goggle-eyed men gaping at the forwarded photo—
normalizing and encouraging such messages" (Hoffman, 2011). Adding all of these
popular culture influences together, it becomes easier to understand how eighth graders in Lacey, Washington, end up set loose with technology capable of damaging
multiple lives as fast as a snap, text, and forward.

The problems are intensified on college campuses, where students are concentrated into dorms and other living communities at precisely the time period when
they are most sexually active. The suicide death of eighteen-year-old Tyler Clementi,
a first-year student at Rutgers University, in September 2011 served in some way as
a tragic marker of the seriousness of Internet distribution of sexually explicit material on college campuses. Clementi's suicide followed his discovery of a streaming
video of an intimate encounter between him and another man that had been captured
on camera and transmitted live via the Internet. This incident happened despite pro-
active programming on the part of Rutgers University, which, like my own home

campus, had been the recipient of federal funds to work to prevent and respond to these types of incidents. In fact, the *New York Times* front-page article on the incident reported that "the news came on the same day that Rutgers kicked off a two-year, campus wide project to teach the importance of civility, with special attention to the use and abuse of new technology" (Foderaro, 2010).

Walter Kirn (2010), writing a commentary in the *New York Times Magazine* following Clementi's suicide, points out that what is difficult about preventing or policing this behavior is that it "dwells inside us." It is "us," not a sinister Big Brother surveying us from behind a hidden curtain. We ourselves have created a system of surveillance that we impose on each other without asking permission or clearance. In Kirn's words we are being watched by a "new, chaotic regime of networked lenses and microphones that point every which way and rest in any hand" (2010, pp. 17–18). This network of surveillance and documentation, argues Kirn, allows us to focus lenses "on ourselves as easily as we aim them at one another," merging our public and private lives and selves, as well as those of the people who surround us. Driven by what, you might ask, and Kirn ends his commentary by stating the obvious motivating factor: We "turn our lenses on ourselves [and others] in the quest for attention by any means" (Kirn, 2010, pp. 17–18).

Cybersex Chat Rooms

One of the opening sections of Howard Stern's autobiography *Miss America* recounts the story of bringing the women he had met and had cyber relationships with onto his radio show. Stern's Internet seduction by multiple fantasy divas named Puppetgirl, Rubberbaby, and Cyberqueen ends with his screen partners' disappointing exposé as ordinary-looking housewives. Dennis Waskul points out the ability of cybersex chat rooms to offer a zone of transformation to participants:

> On the Internet, everyone can be anyone: personhood is transformed into an ostensibly unlimited discursive performance. Even seemingly stable elements of self—race, ethnicity, age, gender, sexual orientation, and physical appearance—are made into infinitely mutable self-selected variables to be toyed with as part of an elaborate kind of "self-game." (2004, p. 9)

Waskul used an ethnographic interview approach to study Internet sexual experiences, most commonly referred to as *cybersex*. He defines the term in this way:

> Cybersex strictly refers to erotic forms of real-time computer-mediated communication. Through typed text, live video, and sometimes spoken voice, cybersex participants meet one another for erotic encounters in the ether of computer-mediated environments. Regardless of the form, however, cybersex always entails meeting someone else in these

decidedly liminal "places" where real people communicate with other real people for the purposes of explicit sexual communication, arousal, and/or gratification. (2003, p. 71)

Waskul's research included 152 open-ended interviews gathered in real time while he himself was online in a chat room. His findings tell stories of distinct experiences online, providing information on the creation of online identities, motivations for joining chat rooms, and effects on and comparisons with offline personal relationships.

The creation of cybersex identity, according to Waskul, begins with the creation of one or more screen names that, like dress and appearance choices in the "outside world," are used to symbolically communicate identity to others. Waskul charts the process of identification that occurs within chat rooms related to screen names:

> As chat participants select, change, and manipulate various screen names, they begin a process of toying with their self in what will become a uniquely situated identity game. That is, by selecting a screen name, participants associate themselves with a self-selected label that is intended to convey crafted meanings. As chat participants quickly learn, their screen name is the prominent indicator of who they claim to be, their interests, and motives for interaction. (2003, p. 39)

Cybersex chat rooms allow vast experimentation with a wide range of sexual identities without risk, thus opening up possibilities not only in how you look but also in how you project yourself as a sexual being and the types of experiences you allow yourself to sample. To illustrate the flexibility of Internet identity, Cleo Odzer's testimonial regarding Internet sexual experiences:

> With the freedom to be and do anything, I had sex with three men at once. I had sex with a woman. I had sex with three men and a woman at once. Posing as a man, I had sex with a woman. Posing as a gay man, I had sex with a man. Posing as a man I had sex with a man who was posing as a woman. I learned all about S&M, as the sadist and the masochist. I had all sorts of sex in every new way I could think of. (1997, p. 43)

Stern also captures this behavior in what he dubs his final dive into the cybersex world, after which he is planning to rise "above my primal sexual urges":

> I started getting it on with some hot little cutie with a D cup named AllOverTan. I'd let you read the transcript but I burned it. You see, I found out the next day that AllOverTan was a guy. A big fan of the show who knew it was me the whole time. I was stroking my cock with a fucking guy at the other end! What a loser!! I was finished with computer sex. (1995, p. 49)

Thus Stern was able to end his cybersex testimonial with a scenario policing the lines around masculinity, to make sure his readership understood loud and clear that he knew you could pose on the Internet as whoever you wanted to be but that he, Howard Stern, was always a "man's man."

In more general terms, even though in text-based cybersex participants are theoretically free from the cultural conventions surrounding normative definitions of male and female sexuality, cybersex identities by and large conform to and reinforce mainstream cultural expectations. Women typically define themselves by their sexual attractiveness and glamour, and men focus on broadcasting their virility by advertising their penis length and width and declaring that "it is hard as a rock." Elizabeth Reid's (1994) research found that in a virtual space where everyone has the power to be beautiful, appearances must be stigma free in order to compete on a level playing field with others. Examples of posted physical descriptions cited by Waskul for, first, a man and, second, a woman include:

> My hobbies include workin' out; I have a 46 inch chest, 32 inch waist, and 22 inch biceps/great and nice and firm and thick 9 inch cock.

> I'm 5 foot 7 inches, Long Black Hair, Brown Eyes, 46DD-30-36, 125 lbs.

Thus in most cases cybersex participants chose to create identities that conform to idealized cultural expectations of beauty for women and strength/virility for men. According to Waskul,

> when the body is transformed into a discursive performance without necessary commitment to the physically real, performances become ideal—a reflection of that which is culturally and socially defined as appropriate and desirable. These performances draw meaning from well-established socio cultural scripts for behavior. (2003, p. 88)

Therefore, he goes on to argue, online cybersex identities generally serve to promote cultural norms rather than offer alternatives or challenges.

While Stern felt compelled to somehow make the cyber real, through identifying his partners and making sure all of them were women, interviewed cybersex enthusiasts stress the erotic turn-on of the open-ended fantasy, seemingly not focused on actually meeting partners:

> It's erotic, it turns—me on—the mystery of it. Not knowing who is really on the other end is really erotic—you can be anything. I may stretch truth, and live out fantasies.... It allows you to be with who ever you want—no inhibitions. (Waskul, Douglass, and Edgley, 2004, p. 20)

The ability to start over with a new screen allows participants to stretch beyond their comfort zones and then retreat if necessary, coming back onto the screen with a new identity and a fresh set of normative expectations from other members of the chat room.

Along with this widening of sexual experience through Internet cybersex spaces come visual images and expectations that move visual expressions of once-marginalized sex practices such as S&M into the mainstream. Televideo cybersex changes the experience for participants significantly as they exchange not only text messages but also images of parts of their bodies. Names that participants assign to their cyber-identities on these websites often are self-objectifying, highlighting parts of the body that will be displayed during the computer interchange. Waskul's (2004) participant-observation research found that men outnumber women on televideo sites and often use self-objectifying screen names like "HardWood," "HungDude," and "BIG COCK" to attract female attention. In the case of men as well as women partici-pants, the body is objectified into sexual zones that are captured on camera and used to arouse one's partner or partners. One of the appeals of the site is anonymity, allowing participants to experience sexual arousal and orgasm without strings attached, and often without disrupting a real monogamous relationship with a partner or spouse.

For female participants one of the draws into the world of televideo cybersex is the opportunity to be naked in front of an audience of men who appreciate and become aroused by parts of their bodies. In the words of one of Waskul's female participants:

> When someone is turned on by watching me, it makes me feel that I'm sexier than I truly believe I am....It's nice to get compliments on...the body....I just think it's sexy that people can masturbate and think of me.
>
> Having a few dozen guys tell you how hot you are, etc., really gives you a great out-look on how you see yourself sexually. Positive reinforcement! (2004, p. 47)

Thus, some women enter into cybersex chat rooms conscious of the male gaze and focus their attention on the gaining of indirect power through sexual attractiveness. This fits with interview data gathered from male subjects as well, who describe par-ticipating in the site from a point of privilege where the men are there to watch the women and get turned on. For example, a male subject interviewed by Waskul states, "I'm just like most males, I get hard just watching a pretty girl putting on a show" (2004, p. 44).

As pointed out earlier, unlike in the real world, the number of available men on the site greatly exceeds the number of women, so women can literally shop the merchandise. Some interviews from women emphasize that while turning on others attracts some women to the site, others are seeking their own sexual satisfaction, often outside of a monogamous relationship that is no longer as lusty as it once was: "Hubby is older than I am. He knows nothing of this. I'm not a complainer, but he does not have the passion or the desire, or at least he doesn't know how to show me....It's hard for him to tap into the part of my brain that triggers the stimulation. I'm a very erotic person. The feeling of being naughty is a turn-on too. See I'm bad, but I love it" (2004, p. 49). For both men *and* women a form of what Waskul refers to as "looking glass eroticism" appears to operate within this cyber environment, with participants experiencing a turn-on as a result of someone else watching them take off their clothing, touch their body, or masturbate.

In the case of both text-based chat rooms and televideo cybersex the computer opens up the range of partners and sexual experiences to participants, offering someone entering the sites a relatively risk-free world of sexual experimentation that seems to participants to be "risky" and a bit "naughty." The entry of these experiences into the popular culture lexicon through raunch celebrities such as Howard Stern brings discussions of sexual practices that fall outside of conventional monogamy into the mainstream. As these types of experiences become both normalized (lots of people do this) yet highlighted as "a bit naughty" by celebrities like Stern, they become an element of mass culture raunch eroticism, rather than classified as a legitimate expression of acceptable sexual practices, which some might argue is more warranted. The high level of control by a small number of entertainment industry giants over the mass media largely confines the presentation of cybersex experiences within mainstream media to those recounted from the perspective of the male gaze.

Exploring the Contours of Raunch Eroticism

Perhaps more so than any of the other topics in this book, the world of Internet networking and cyber-identity offers the most potential for a democratic and inclusive dialogue focused on raunch eroticism and its cultural impact. At the same time as I argue this, I must also point out that Internet broadcasting has an almost unfathomable power to facilitate and support the power of the male gaze to continue to influence female identities and behaviors. The fact that all of us can choose at our own discretion to project images and commentary about ourselves and others onto a worldwide communication system is both phenomenally empowering and at the same time tragically crippling in terms of the cultural construction of identity and personal agency. Determining which is happening the most, some type of quantitative measurement of "how much" discourse, compared to "how much" conformity, is virtually impossible given the enormous number of YouTube videos, Facebook profiles, and cybersex chat rooms on the web. Given that reality, the analysis of the seven points is by necessity specific to the small sampling of case study examples discussed within this chapter.

Focus on the White Heterosexual Male Gaze

A study of the history of the development of Facebook reveals the underlying focus on the male gaze that directed Zuckerberg and his friends as they explored the potential of the Internet for social networking on a college campus. "Facemash," the early program developed and briefly launched by Zuckerberg, was a rating system used by male students to rate and compare the appearance of female students. Male students' tendency to continue to see all social networking sites as potential methods of checking out and finding attractive women followed Facebook to its launch on other campuses, leading to the development of "100 Hottest Freshmen" websites as discussed earlier in this chapter. A random study of Facebook sites on college campuses still indicates that young women, particularly those entering into new social environments during the peak dating years, tend to choose Facebook profile pictures that are directed to attracting the male gaze, as I found in my earlier research.

A comparison of male profiles to female ones reveals gender patterns in the posting of Facebook profile pictures. Males more often post Facebook profile pictures celebrating or recognizing accomplishment, in terms of either profession or physical ability—for example, a photo taken at the end of a marathon race. Women, in contrast, tend to post photographs clearly chosen because they will attract male attention or photographs documenting a relationship with a partner or, when older, with children or other family members.

Similar patterns emerge in a random review of vernacular YouTube videos posted by amateurs. Young male YouTube video producers often focus on innovative use of the YouTube technology in the creation of the video, whereas the focus for the typical bedroom dance videos uploaded by girls and young women is delivering a hot, sexy performance directed toward a male audience. Commercial interest in YouTube by the leaders in the entertainment industry brings the normative cultural patterns of that industry to what is mass-distributed on the website. Thus, the overall pattern that women are most often presented by these industry giants as objects of the male gaze and desire continues to dominate this side of the YouTube business.

Probably more so than Facebook and YouTube, cybersex chat rooms flip the customary pattern of women being put into positions that serve the male gaze and desire. More men than women frequent the sites, and men are put in the position of competing for the few women trolling the net. In this context the male participants tend to create screen names that will attract women, often related to the size or hardness of their penis, whereas select women often have screen names related to their own desires such as "like them big." The translation of this behavior into the pop culture mainstream through celebrities like Howard Stern moves it back into the normative cultural lens of focusing on the male gaze and desire.

Sexual Objectification of Women

Early Facebook history on college campuses, particularly as designed and utilized by young male students, set up a system of sexual objectification of women through Facebook groups focused on measuring the "hotness" of a parade of coeds, with no attempt to look deeper than sexual attractiveness. YouTube and other forms of video uploading have dramatically increased the access of boys and men, and girls and women, to nude bodies of women void of content. The ability to replay again and again images of the same girl dancing creates a different audience dynamic than a live performance, wherein you are reminded at points of entrance and closure that this is a real person, not just a sexy body in motion.

Cybersex venues objectify everyone's body, creating a world of sexual parts disconnected from real people, where the focus becomes only arousal and orgasm. Despite the objectification of both men and women on cybersex sites, male participants outnumber the women and tend to provide more vocal feedback on their experiences. The result is that the written comments focus more attention on sexual objectification of women. While the new dating trend is to exchange nude or partially nude cell phone pictures as a part of the courtship ritual, the tendency is for girls to reveal more, with boys more typically taking their shirts off for the shot or sending a fully clothed picture, in some ways conforming to the patterns found on male and female college student Facebook pages.

Self-Objectification

The Internet has opened up an interactive lesson plan for young girls to mimic and rehearse the lessons of self-objectification either by themselves or with their friends in their real and cyber private bedroom spaces. As shown by Baker's (2011) research, porn sites are easily accessible to not only young boys but also girls who are learning how to become sexual adults. The popularity of bedroom dance videos gives testimony to the power of the Internet to create even stronger patterns of self-objectification among younger and younger audiences of girls. This self-objectification pattern moves into the creation of both Facebook profile pages and the world of cybersex, where self-objectification for both women *and* men is the norm.

Sexual Attention and Sexualized Practice as Power

The fastest and surest route to getting Internet attention for women and girls is through exposed sexuality. Attention is power on the web. The creation of bedroom YouTube videos by young girls in which they mimic the moves and actions of their favorite female pop icon literally teaches the girls the moves, style, and dress of the sexy empowerment icon. The comments and following generated by the YouTube videos created by these girls provide reinforcement and also give them power within their schools and peer cultures. The walk-away message becomes the staple of the sexy empowerment icon: The route to being the "It Girl" is through flaunting your sexuality.

Contrasts between the Facebook profile pictures and self-portrait galleries of young men and women entering into college dating culture as first-year students clearly demonstrate the normative reliance of young women on sexual attractiveness as a means of gaining social power. Cybersex sites reduce both men and women to sexual objects, with the much larger number of male participants courting the sexual attention of the relatively small number of female participants by emphasizing the size of their biceps and their penis.

Private Is Public

The Internet is the millennium version of Warhol's fifteen minutes of fame, with our private worlds made public instantly. A big difference between the 1960s and now is that it is no longer fifteen minutes of fame; it is viral. The implications of the viral upload are extremely underestimated by individuals broadcasting themselves, and those capturing others, as is made evident by the case studies summarized within this chapter. What is also made evident is the lack of preparation of parents, schools, campuses, and judicial systems to prevent and respond to violations of privacy using the Internet, digital imaging, and cell phone technology. Walter Kirn's thoughtful commentary following Tyler Clementi's suicide, with its emphasis on the complex network of phones, microphones, and computers that we have created to document the minutia of our lives and those that surround us, forces us to acknowledge the very primitive need for attention within the core of the human psyche. The attention-grabbing nature of the erotic makes it ripe for coverage by the web of broadcasting apparatus that now structures our lives.

Extreme, Up the Ante

The Internet is an intensely competitive arena where there is a seemingly endless supply of Facebook profiles, YouTube videos, and cybersex partners for the web surfer. To compete with other college coeds, young women are driven to create "the raunchiest" photo album ever. Men in cybersex chat rooms with other men create screen names like "Largest Dick Ever" to set themselves apart from the pack. Young girls creating bedroom dance videos wiggle and shimmy their way onto call girl sites, simply trying to get the largest number of hits on their YouTube site. Popularity is linked to attention, and Internet posts and cell phone uploads are a means of getting your peers to notice you. This drive for attention ups the ante in terms of trying to beat the competition using explicit sexuality, virility, sexual attractiveness, raunchiness, and audacity.

Misogyny

Peer-supported misogyny within Facebook groups is viral, creating networks of support for bad boy behaviors made popular by media entertainers like Tucker Max and musicians like Eminem. The entrance of this discourse into a publicly accessible space makes it feel normative and also opens the door for women and girls to buy into the misogyny as a means of gaining attention and acceptance. Facebook groups created by men featuring the "Top 100 Sexiest Freshmen" rely on female students participating by sending in their pictures for evaluation and judgment.

Private worlds created by tweens and teenagers, in which they move into spaces haunted with misogyny with the aid of handheld iPods, Internet-capable cell phones, and computers, take away the power of parents and other caregivers to play an editorial role in what children are exposed to as normal and acceptable. The proliferation of popular culture media validating violence and degradation of women in video games, music, YouTube videos, and films makes the risk of a young person absorbing misogyny as a cultural lesson very real and very probable.

–9–

"Va-Va-Voom Goes the Soprano"[1]:
Engaging Discourse on Porn Chic

LONDON—An opera about Anna Nicole Smith: The American sex symbol, Playboy Playmate, hapless model, laughable actress and fortune-hunting wife of a billionaire nearly 63 years her senior? Commissioned by, no less, the Royal Opera House, Covent Garden? (Tommasini, 2011)

Raunch eroticism is trending at an epidemic rate in the new millennium, popping up in high and popular venues. This chapter focuses on popular and high-culture efforts to create conversation and discussion focused on raunch eroticism. Public discourse on porn chic took a very high-culture turn with the intensely anticipated and media-hyped opening of the opera *Anna Nicole* at the Royal Opera House, Covent Garden, in February 2011. For those readers not familiar with the sordid details of her life, the *New York Times* critic Michael White provided a fast two-paragraph summary in his preview article about the opera:

For those who may not remember, Ms. Smith was a poor girl from Texas who found fame exposing her surgically enhanced breasts serially and showing there were no depths to which a determined social climber couldn't profitably sink. At 26 she married an 89-year-old billionaire who obligingly died a year later; she became embroiled in tangled legal actions over the inheritance, then died herself at 39.

In between, she was a stripper, pinup, small-time actress and reality-TV star. And the highs or lows of her colorful existence included having a Caesarian delivery live on television; appearing in Pieta-style photos with her dead son (who died from a drug over-dose in her maternity hospital room); having a whole posse of men claim paternity of her daughter (one of them a masseur married to Zsa Zsa Gabor, Frederic Prinz von Anhalt); and playing the part of an extraterrestrial kick-boxer in a film in which her mission was to save Earth. (White, 2011)

For the British, hungry for a more tantalizing and dramatically dead version of Katie Price, *Anna Nicole* fit the bill. It was also reviewed as an artistic triumph for the British composer Mark-Anthony Turnage and the British librettist Richard Thomas. It was perfect for the millennium: a high-culture take on the underbelly of porn chic.

Commentary and engaged discourse on the themes underlying this book are explored creatively throughout the opera. The decision to present the story of Anna Nicole's life as a series of interviews with frenzied, invasive, and rude reporters, who function in operatic terms as the chorus, aptly represents the key role of the media in promulgating the prominence of porn chic as a cultural influence. The casual acceptance of the language of porn chic into mainstream culture is captured in the opera's score, with an absurdly big-bosomed and ripe Eva-Maria Westbroek belting out, "I want to blow you all, I want to blow you all, I want to blow you all," and then, after the audience laughs, "a kiss." The mythology underlying the emergence of the sexy empowerment icon is brought to life within the opera, with early scenes in the production focused on Anna Nicole's early feelings of entrapment, first in a small Texas town and later in Houston, where she works at a fried-chicken fast-food restaurant. Similar to the life story of her British counterpart Katie Price, Anna Nicole's route out to celebrity status starts with multiple breast implants. Who would have predicted that this pretty girl from Texas would end up the subject of an opera, with her initials "A n R" replacing Queen Elizabeth's on the Covent Garden, Royal Opera House stage.

Parsing out what emerged by way of cultural discourse on porn chic as a result of this production is difficult. Clearly, the high-culture status of the Royal Opera House elevated the conversation about the impact of porn chic, prompting the best critics in the country and thoughtful audiences to respond to this cultural trend. Conductor Antonio Pappano's published comments underscored the role of the opera in getting the audience to consider the impact of this cultural trend on daily lives: "Here's a white-trash American symbol but also a symbol of what's wrong with a lot of today's society: fame at all costs, the fetishistic relationships of the cameras and the public, and ambition. It's sordid, it's lurid, it's funny and pathetic, but ultimately the story is very sad. For me, that's what makes it interesting" (quoted in Gillie, 2011). Not all cultural commentary on porn chic intersects with such a high and visible stage as the Royal Opera House. The remainder of this final chapter explores cultural responses to porn chic in a number of different venues and voices, analyzing each example in terms of four distinct levels of discourse.

The first stage of creating meaningful discourse on porn chic is to create a space for open expression of female sexuality. This requirement is seemingly quite easily met given the cultural normative shift toward raunch eroticism. We are literally inundated with competing sexually objectified images of women being used to brand, sell product, and more generally catch our fleeting attention in a cultural landscape littered with pop culture distractions. The next three stages are much more challenging and in some ways function as tests for whether a visual or performing artist is able to compete with the litter of mass culture successfully enough to create true discourse on porn chic. The second stage requires a conscious consideration of the impact of the male gaze and desire on the cultural construction of female sexuality. The question needs to be asked, are we really looking at, experiencing, hearing the voice of female sexual agency or rather a pose constructed to serve a patriarchal audience of male desire? The third stage of meaningful engagement on this topic is to address commodification. On the most basic level the question needs to be asked, is what we are experiencing yet one more expression of female sexuality being used to generate funds, sell product, or create a branded image? Does the audience understand the challenge to commodification, or are they simply attracted, once again, to hypersexualization? The fourth and final stage is discourse and dialogue. Do we walk out, as the opera conductor hopes, talking about the impact of raunch eroticism on our lives and the lives of others?

The Female Tucker Max: Karen Owen's Viral PowerPoint

Perhaps the most effective starting point for this discussion is to go into the trenches and examine the attempt of a young woman living within a college environment literally submerged in raunch eroticism to make a statement about her predicament. The now-infamous and widely distributed PowerPoint created by Duke undergraduate student Karen Owen was on the surface an attempt to do a Tucker Max on Tucker Max. Owen's presentation was a self-conscious attempt to use the same formula of reporting back on college sexual exploits that was made famous by Tucker Max but to do it from the woman's point of view. Unlike Tucker Max, who also began his morning-after tell-all blog while enrolled as a student at Duke, Owen originally shared her PowerPoint only with three friends. The movement of the PowerPoint to the web occurred as the PowerPoint went viral, eventually reaching a national audience and provoking commentary in a number of publications, including an articulate analysis by Caitlin Flanagan in the January/February 2011 issue of *Atlantic* magazine. Flanagan does my job for me as she deconstructs and ultimately rejects Owen's efforts as an act of sexual agency in her thoughtful analysis: "If what we are seeing in Karen Owen is the realization of female sexual power, then we must at least admit that the first pancake off the griddle is a bit of a flop. What rotten luck that the first true daughter of sex-positive feminism would have an erotic proclivity for serving every kind of male need, no matter how mundane or humiliating, that she would so eagerly turn herself from sex mate to soccer mom, depending on what was wanted from her" (2011, p. 89).

Flanagan's comments are supported by studies of college hookup culture, perhaps most notably that of Kathleen Bogle (2008), that have concluded that sexual behavior on college campuses has evolved toward a culture favoring the male preference for casual and uncommitted sexual encounters. Bogle's research observations, based on interviews with seventy-six former and current students from a large state-supported university and a smaller faith-based private university, speak directly to the fact that while on the surface both male and female students appear to be expressing sexual agency and choice, the reality is more complex, often shifting power and control to the male involved in the hookup:

> For those on the outside looking in, it may appear that men and women are on an equal playing field in the hookup culture on campus. Upon closer inspection, however, it becomes clear that college men are in a position of power. First, men are able to sustain the hookup system on campus despite the fact that it is not working for the majority of women. Most of the students indicated that college men favor casual sexual encounters or casual relationships, whereas women prefer more committed relationships. Therefore, while the hookup system works for men, it does not provide a good way for women to get what *they* want. Men's power in the hook up culture is also demonstrated by the fact that men control the intensity of relationships. They are able to keep most women as "just a hookup partner" and they decide if and when the relationship will turn into something more serious. (2008, p. 125)

Elaine Eshbaugh and Gary Gute's (2008) statistical research on college hookup culture also underscores the price female students are paying, with empirical results indicating a relationship between casual sexual intercourse and sexual regret for the 152 surveyed students who took part in their study.

Tom Wolfe's exploration of similar terrain at private and public Ivy League universities led to the 2004 publication of a novel documenting and exploring the impact of college hookup culture on a young female character who was a first-year scholarship student from a modest background at a campus modeled after Duke University. Wolfe's focus on the private Ivy League campus that spawned both Tucker Max and Karen Owen makes his novel, largely based on his own firsthand fieldwork at Duke, a mirror of the culture that surrounded both students as they created their highly publicized sex chronicles.

Duke University has had an infamous reputation for at least the last two decades for an often lethal and damaging mix of entitled privilege, passionate commitment to nationally ranked sports programs, a social scene dominated by a solidly entrenched fraternity and sorority system, and an extremely ambitious and competitive student body focused on making it—"it" being money and also the related bonus to money, power. The sense of entitlement conferred by the heady combination of class, the institution's status, and fraternity membership is captured early in Wolfe's novel as Hoyt, one of the male protagonists in the novel, stands looking over the Grove, an ornamental masterpiece of gardening and a strong symbol of the aura of privilege emanating from this Ivy League institution:

> The Dupont campus...The moon had turned the university's buildings into a vast chiaroscuro of dark shapes brought out in all their sumptuousness by a wash of pale white gold. The towers, the turrets, the spires, the heavy slate roofs—all of it ineffably beautiful and ineffably grand. Walls thick as a castle's! It was a stronghold. He, Hoyt, was one of a charmed circle, that happy few who could enter the stronghold at will...and feel its

invincibility in their bones. Not only that, he was in the innermost ring of that charmed circle, namely, Saint Ray, the fraternity of those who have been chosen to hold dominion over...well, over everybody. (Wolfe, 2004, p. 11)

Tucker Max, an undergraduate alumnus of the University of Chicago, another pillar of privilege, was a full-scholarship law student and fraternity member at Duke when he began his sex-exploit blog, depicting in real life the sex lives and attitudes of fraternity men brought to life by Wolfe in his novel.

In marked contrast to the insider and privileged position of Tucker and Hoyt, both Charlotte Simmons, for whom the novel is named, and Karen Owen share a marginalized status at Duke (Dupont). Charlotte Simmons is a full-scholarship student from the Appalachian Hills, where she grew up in a small house where the picnic table had to be literally carried out of the kitchen and into the yard for her graduation party. She is an academic prodigy mentored by her teacher, and the first student in her small rural community to be given a full scholarship to Dupont, a university considered by those living in her community as an unattainable symbol of class and privilege. In order to break through and gain the attention of men of status and position, both the fictional Charlotte Simmons and the real Karen Owen resort to using their appearance and sexuality to gain attention and favor. Charlotte's anxiety to please Hoyt, considered the top fraternity catch on campus, is first expressed in a manic need to dress herself right to fit into the fraternity world she has to enter to thank him for intervening for her in an altercation with a very drunk male lacrosse player. A financially strapped scholarship student reduced to living on her stipend, Charlotte goes out and spends $80 (of her total of $320 for the semester) on a pair of high-end "must-have" jeans that she feels she must wear in this first real meeting with the fantasy fraternity man.

In the end both the fictional Charlotte and the real Karen Owen allow themselves to be sexually used and abused by men of status on campus. Charlotte loses her virginity to Hoyt at his senior fraternity formal. A very drunk Charlotte, who wants to say no, is brutally assaulted by Hoyt, and she, even in the midst of the pain of the assault, is focused on whether she is pleasing her male partner:

> "Mmnnnnh", she said, her eyes watering, wanting to say, "NO IT'S NOT OKAY! THIS HURTS! THIS HURTS, THIS HURTS, THIS HURTS, THIS HURTS"—but he kept moving in, out, in, out to THIS HURTS, THIS HURTS. Animal grunts, animal grunts. She looked at his face blearily, her eyes were watering so. *His* eyes were closed. He was sweating, groaning, biting his lower lip. She *couldn't* tell him to stop, couldn't even tell him to slow down because...because that look of rapture on his face was what she had wanted from the beginning, and what she did not want to go away. She was at this moment all that life could hold or mean for him. He was...Charlotte Simmons's, down to the last molecule. (Wolfe, 2004, p. 480)

After the assault Hoyt dresses quickly and heads out the door to party some more, with Charlotte in her drunken stupor overhearing a laughing conversation between

Hoyt and his male and female friends where he refers to her as a "freak" with a "hillbilly beaver" that he had to "knock the dust off," returning again at the end of his dismissive comments to the fact that Charlotte was not properly waxed and that it was "like fucking Astroturf" (Wolfe, 2004, p. 486).

Owen's sexual experiences were similarly focused on male pleasure and often included violence, drawing this response from Flanagan: "For all the attention Owen has received as a boundary-breaking, sexually empowered new woman, there has been almost no discussion of the fact that the kind of sex she most enjoyed was rough to the point of brutalizing. One encounter that occurred during an alcoholic blackout was still, as Karen Owen would say, 'baller', because in the shower the next day she found bruises on her body" (2011, p. 88). The memorable moments she recalls with a lacrosse player are focused on the attention he bestowed on her in front of other team members; for example, he said to his friends, "She's so hot, isn't she so hot? Her breasts…they're just exquisite, so exquisite." The negatives Owen notes for this encounter include "It was over too quickly. And it was a tad bit painful," pointing to the focus of the sexual act on male pleasure and her willingness to suffer pain to satisfy her high-status partner. Owen seems almost to be playing to a male audience attracted to the intersection of violence and sexual acts as she positively reviews very rough, aggressive sex that leaves her unable to walk the next day.

Similar to Charlotte's experience with Hoyt, Owen recounts being used and discarded by many of her thirteen partners. In one encounter she describes having the earrings she mistakenly forgot in the bedroom of a high-status tennis player thrown outside for her to pick up the next day. This story is strikingly similar to a Tucker Max exploit in which he reports throwing a fat girl's clothes out the window rather than have her reenter his apartment in front of his roommates. Owen documents a pattern of noncommitted hookups with comments such as "neither of us ever spent the night, nor was there any cuddling. It was always simply sexting, sex, and goodbyes, a routine I anticipated and enjoyed, due especially to the complete lack of clinginess or drama associate with it." Again, what Owen appears to be doing is courting male attention by conforming, to the point of absurdity, to her male partners' preference for uncommitted sex—no emotional strings attached. Links to common pornography staples such as the "cum shot" on the face pop up in Owen's PowerPoint as well as behavior patterns that characterize college hookup culture, such as making requests for sexting nude pictures.

The sexual double standard was definitely applied in the case of Owen, who was dismissed as an outsider by sorority members from Duke in an editorial in the student newspaper. Rightfully offended by an article previously published in the student newspaper, which referred to Owen as a "sororstitute," the Duke sorority presidents go on to clearly articulate Owen's marginal status on campus by emphasizing she "was not a member of a Greek organization during her time here" (Feinglos, 2010). In contrast, Tucker Max became an insider folk hero among his Duke fraternity brothers as well as those at other universities across the country for his accounts of his sexual exploits while a student at Duke. Similarly, in Wolfe's fictional account, after the assault Charlotte is ridiculed by not only Hoyt and his male friends but also the sorority women who had attended the formal.

The first stage of creating meaningful discourse on porn chic is to create a space for open expression of female sexuality. Certainly it can be argued that Owen brought one woman's sexual experiences on a university campus into the spotlight, not only on her home campus, but across the United States. What becomes problematic is the second level of analysis, which focuses on whether we are looking at, experiencing, and hearing the voice of female desire and sexual agency. What I often experienced in reading her exploits, having come fresh from both meeting Tucker Max and reading his two books, was that she was taking Tucker Max stories and trying to make them appear to come from the female partner's point of view. While certainly the sexual encounters may be her own, her experience of those encounters as captured in her PowerPoint feels forced and performed for a male audience. The sensibility as well as the content and focus are most often, as also articulated by Flanagan, "shaped not by her own desires but by a particular male sensibility, in fact a particular male: Tucker Max" (2011, p. 89).

The third level of analysis addresses commodification. Are we encountering just another way to make money off of women's sexuality, or is this an authentic challenge to the selling of products, web hits, and brands through porn chic? In this case the question that needs to be asked, one that really has no answer, is why Owen made this PowerPoint. Did she truly want her PowerPoint to be seen only by the three friends she self-reports that she sent it to? Or was her intent closer to that of her mentor, Tucker Max: to get famous, get a book deal, and attract the attention of peers and possible future sex partners? Certainly in the end she created a large following; her PowerPoint became a commodity of sorts, with some still predicting she will get a book offer.

One thing that Owen did accomplish was to prompt a cultural conversation on raunch eroticism as experienced on university campuses in particular. This highest stage, level four, asks us to assess what happened afterward, who talked about it, who responded to it, how much it mattered in the end in terms of discussions surrounding how we construct male and female sexual desire and behavior. Did this PowerPoint in fact challenge us to consider the impact of porn chic on real people? While this was not Owen's intention, I think the answer to this question is yes. The creation of a copycat female version of Tucker Max moved the work of this unapologetic bad boy from being easily dismissed as just another example of sophomoric humor to a more serious questioning of the misogyny underlying many of the current norms functioning on campuses across the United States. It also both propagated and provoked discussion focused on the link between being sexy and being powerful, with a female student from Duke telling a reporter on the *Today Show* that Owen's PowerPoint brought out "the inner feminist in me" (Flanagan, 2011, p. 92) and with others, myself included, using this teachable moment to ponder how very far we are away from authentic mainstreamed feminism in the millennium.

Vivienne Westwood's Subversive Fashion: "I Always Wanted to Cut a Dash"[2]

Vivienne Westwood was born the daughter of a cotton weaver, and her father's family made their living making shoes. She herself started out as a schoolteacher, drawn into the fashion industry first through collaborating with Malcolm McLaren in the creation of streetwear as cultural commentary. McLaren, in talking about the function of these early fashions as cultural commentary, stated, "I was very excited by this idea of taking culture to the streets and changing the whole way of life, using culture as a way of making trouble" (quoted in Wilcox, 2004, p. 10). The concept that dressing the body was about transforming how people think is central to understanding Westwood's body of work as cultural commentary and, perhaps most important, a cultural catalyst.

Westwood first entered the London fashion scene in the late 1960s and early 1970s as what might be termed a street artist. Working in partnership with McLaren, Westwood began to transform notions of femininity, experimenting with her own street looks first, in much the same pattern as Coco Chanel in the earlier years of the twentieth century. Surrounded by London shops selling hippie and ethnic apparel, Westwood and McLaren set out to create a new, rebellious look speaking to the class and gender divisions of the period. The punk look emerged from their creative partnership, transforming then obscure fashion fetish elements into fashion.

As pointed out by Claire Wilcox, "one of the most important factors of punk was that it gave license for women to dress assertively" (2004, p. 14). The assertiveness of punk in part came from the fact that it challenged viewers, particularly the male audience, to rethink the meaning of sexual fetish dress styles from the woman's point of view. Punk girls found in the London streets wearing plaid schoolgirl skirts and dog collars made conventional men uncomfortable, causing them, almost despite themselves, to reconsider women's sexuality. While Westwood moved on from this early work with McLaren and became a more traditional, lauded, and successful designer, what remains within all of her collections is the persistent demand she places on her audience to consider the wearer's own sexuality.

From her early Pirate Collection, with its swashbuckling buccaneer styles, to her experiments with underwear as outerwear, to her reinvented ballet crinolines of the mid- to late 1980s, Westwood has consistently used fashion design to focus on the sexuality of the woman in the clothes, rather than turning her attention to the imagined audience of men. Caroline Evans and Minna Thorton reflect on this aspect of Westwood's creative power:

> All her work pivots around the idea of a sexuality which is autonomous and subjectively defined. When she talks of what is "sexy" the stress is on what will *feel* sexy to the wearer, so that the issue becomes one of the wearer's libido, rather than one of "being attractive". Westwood fosters the idea of a self-defined feminine libido, however demented, which communicates itself idiosyncratically through dress. (1989, p. 154)

Central to Westwood's tenacious grip on subjectively defined female sexuality is her insistence on playing with historical as well as contemporary feminine shapes and forms. Rejecting the masculine styles being applied to women's bodies in the mid-1980s she introduced a reinterpretation of the ballet tutu, the 1985 Mini-Crini collection, with an emphasis on how the collection felt on the wearer's body. Regarding the meaning of this collection, Westwood stated:

> The thing that really interests me is when it is used as an undergarment, as it's intended to change the shape of women's clothes. For the past ten years clothes have had shoulder pads and tight hips—that's supposed to be the sexy look, the inverted triangle—but I think people want more feminine fitting. Women want to be strong but in a feminine way. These dresses give you balletic posture and are very, very elegant. You feel like a ballerina…it gives you presence and swings in the most sexy way. (quoted in Wilcox, 2004, p. 20)

Note that in Westwood's commentary her focus is entirely on how the Mini-Crini is experienced as a garment on the wearer, with the sensuality of the swing felt, rather than on the garment as a means of gaining male attention.

In terms of analyzing Westwood's impact, her work clearly brought women's sexuality into the public eye and at the same time challenged the notion that sexy fashion should focus on attracting the attention of the male gaze. Instead, she stresses staying true to exploring women's own sexuality, many times through the refashioning of historical looks for modern women. In terms of commodification, Westwood's work has never been about using women's sexuality to attract money and brand interest. For her the motivation to work has to do not with making money but, in her words, with "that incredible need to just question everything" (quoted in Wilcox, 2004, p. 32). In terms of creating discourse, Alix Sharkey articulates the immense power of Westwood's work to challenge and create reflection and transformation: "For her, clothes should intensify and refine the wearer's sense of physical presence; provide a reaction, charge the atmosphere with sexual and political tension; they should directly alter the physical reality of the world around them. Clearly, this kind of clothing poses questions, and challenges us to explore, to consider the unknown. It can make us uncomfortable, this fashion that works like a drug that alters our state of consciousness" (quoted in Wilcox, 2004, p. 33).

Red Hat Societies: "GlamMa" Comes Out of the Closet

UrbanDictionary.com now has a name for an older woman with a grandchild: "If 60 is the new 40 then GlamMa is the new Grandma, a woman with a sense of self and style." A GlamMa is also "hot," according to Gwyneth Paltrow, who revealed in a televised interview that her mother, Blythe Danner, wanted to be called "Wolf," to skirt the aging stereotypes of the traditional term *Grandma* (Zissu, 2011). The celebrity comedian Goldie Hawn's son Oliver thought up the term *Glam-Ma*, which caught on with a wider audience, making it into the popular culture lexicon with its listing in the online dictionary. The feelings of these two celebrity grandmothers are echoed by many older women who in a range of ways have rebelled against the stereotypes of the past and the domination of the fashion system and mass media with their ideals of youthful beauty. In response to the emergence of this newly fashioned older woman, I began to work with a team of colleagues researching Red Hat Societies in the 1990s. This collaboration resulted in a series of articles that, together with the time I spent at the New Year's Day Parade in London with Red Hat Society members, supported the writing of this section (Lynch, Stalp, and Radina, 2007; Stalp, Radina, and Lynch, 2008; Stalp, Williams, et al., 2008; Radina et al., 2008).

The Red Hat Society got its official start in 1997 when Sue Ellen Cooper, a midlife white California native, bought a red fedora on a whim in an Arizona thrift shop while on vacation. She discovered that wearing the hat made her feel free to have fun again as she did when she was younger. Cooper wanted to share this experience with her friends, so she started a tradition of buying her female friends red hats for their fiftieth birthdays and sharing with them the Jenny Joseph poem "Warning" (1961), excerpted here:

> When I am an old woman I shall wear purple
> With a red hat that doesn't go, and doesn't suit me,
> And I shall spend my pension
> on brandy and summer gloves

Cooper's group of friends named themselves the Red Hat Society and began meeting in public spaces wearing their red hats. Their activities quickly earned them public and media attention, as well as e-mail interest from women throughout the country. The Red Hat Society has grown in the United States to include both chapters officially registered on Cooper's Red Hat Society website and regionally based unofficial chapters, and around the world, with its founder working full-time on the organization (Walker, 2005).

Chapters are typically small (under fifteen members), to allow restaurant dinner reservations to be easily made for meetings and to ensure bonding between the group members. When assembling, a chapter elects a Queen Mother and selects a name for their group, typically incorporating the color red as well as adjectives describing the attitude of the group. Examples of the names of groups not participating in this study include Red Hat Rubies, Diamonds in the Red, and Red Foxes (Cooper, 2004). Activities, meeting times, and frequencies of gathering vary by chapter. Chapters meet for lunch or high tea, travel regionally to cultural exhibits and events, do wine tastings, and even meet to quilt or knit. The "fun" each group has depends on each chapter's members. Red Hat Society activities also include national and international conferences, including the annual London New Year's Parade convention featured as part of this case study.

Official Red Hat Society membership is restricted to women who are fifty or older. Those younger than fifty interested in being involved in the chapters can wear pink and lavender and are referred to as "pink hats." Pink hats are red hats in training and in more formal groups undergo at fifty what is called a "red-uation." A red-uation is when women graduate from pink and lavender to red and purple. Important to note, red hat women are rewarded for their rising age, instead of punished for it as typically occurs in mainstream society (Calasanti and Slevin, 2001; Cooper, 2004). As Red Hat Society membership has grown, as Rob Walker (2005) points out, the group's subversive ability to make the surrounding culture look at female aging differently has grown proportionately. Fun apparel styles and accessories are now custom-made for the Red Hat market, and Red Hat events are heavily covered by the local and national news. Most recently, in 2011 Katie Couric covered the donation of the first hat purchased by Cooper to the Smithsonian Institution. This granting of attention to older women, combined with the "bling" and sexual vitality expressed by the group, make the Red Hat organization a strong challenge to the stereotypes of largely invisible older women playing supportive but not dramatic roles in British and American culture.

Appearance Management of Aging

The sociologist Gregory Stone (1965) established that the dressed body establishes a two-way communication system, with the wearer creating a program of dressed appearance that is reviewed by an audience, creating a discourse on the meaning of the dress. As a result of this communication exchange, dress can be altered by the wearer to achieve a more positive review or maintained to challenge existing norms or standards. Studies on the management of identity through dress conducted prior to the emergence of the Red Hats indicated that older women respond to society's negative review of aging female attractiveness by using cosmetics, undergarments, and custom-tailored garments to try to appear younger and hide the aging process (Bartley and Warden, 1962; Ebeling and Rosencrantz, 1961; Jackson and O'Neal, 1994). John Schouten (1991) found that plastic surgery is more often used by individuals during periods of personal transition, or movement from one phase of life into another, such as movement into perceived old age.

Women's efforts to hide the aging process have been shown to be linked to the stigma attached to female aging, in contrast with more open attitudes toward male aging. Research shows that women's attractiveness to men decreases significantly with age, while men's attractiveness to women is not impacted significantly by the aging process (Mathes et al., 1985). Related research supports the finding that age plays a fundamental role in ratings of female attractiveness, with older models receiving lower ratings than younger models in image-based quantitative studies (Korthase and Trenholme, 1982; Nowak, 1975; Sorell and Nowak, 1981). Aging has also been shown to be a fundamental component of physical attractiveness for aging women, with middle-aged women describing a thin and young ideal of beauty (Lennon, 1997). These differing attitudes toward male and female aging have made aging more difficult for women due in part to a culturally maintained reliance on attractiveness as a measure of female accomplishment (Kaiser, 1997) throughout the female life cycle.

The results of the preceding research can in part be explained using the gender-role dichotomy outlined in chapter 4, which establishes key differences in how males and females in the United States are socialized to measure accomplishment. On the one hand, boys and men learn to measure themselves based on an agonic standard in which active definitions of self are used to mark success; therefore, men often gain power and attractiveness as they age. Girls and women, on the other hand, learn that physical attractiveness is a key to positive reviews, leading to heavy reliance on youthfulness and beauty and a related loss of attractive power with aging. Women therefore experience higher degrees of negative stereotyping and stigma related to aging than their male contemporaries.

Susan Kaiser and Joan Chandler's (1984) work concluded that aging correlated with feelings of fashion alienation for women. Women over fifty reported frustration regarding finding suitable and/or unique dress styles available in stores for their age group. Older women also expressed a lack of understanding of or identification with fashion symbols used in the mass media. This research indicates that due to the natural process and the inability to follow fashion trends due to sizing and availability issues, older women are stigmatized, with little route into the mainstream arena of fashion culture.

Using the early work of Erving Goffman (1963), *stigma* has been defined within the dress literature as "possession of an attribute that is undesirable or difficult to understand," leading to classification of an individual as "different from others" (Feather, Rucker, and Kaiser, 1989, pp. 289–290). Goffman's definition of stigma as an attribute that has the power to marginalize individuals, making them feel separated from mainstream culture, aptly fits older women in current American culture. According to Goffman, one of the methods that individuals use to manage stigmatized identity is to join together with other members of the stigmatized group and present a positive image to others, often through shared dress and appearance styles. One of the goals of our research thus became understanding how dress, appearance, and behavior within chapters of the Red Hat Society offered members a positive means of managing their stigmatized identity and, in the case of this book, how these dress styles allowed older women to reclaim "bling" and their sexual identity.

We came to an understanding of the meaning of Red Hat dress, appearance, and behavior through a combination of in-depth interviews,[3] focus groups, and participation in national and international conferences. A typical response from the women, when asked about stereotypes of aging, was to create distance from how they experienced their own grandmothers: "I remember when we looked at our grandmas and they were OLD people! My kids and grandkids don't think of me as old! And it isn't like we are not at the age they were, but all they did was make cookies and stay home." Red Hat women clearly identified with the idea of being GlamMas, not Grandmas, with one interview subject retorting, "Old, gray-haired and old, that just doesn't fit anymore.... We are changing that attitude!"[4] Most frankly admit to their age early in the interview and stress that the Red Hat Society is not about hiding or masking aging but is rather a celebration of the freedom and joys that come with the aging process. For example, one woman stated, "We are admitting to our age, but we are saying we don't care about our age, we are old people who are having fun!"[5] There is also a stubborn streak expressed among the women regarding being written off by younger generations. One woman quipped at the end of an interview, "Hey, don't write us off yet, we're not gone. We can still have fun!"[6]

Dress is clearly the most powerful symbol of cohesiveness for group members. Women repeatedly brought up how critical the dress was to making the group fun and cohesive: "The same group can go out and there is not an air of giddiness at the breakfast without the outfit. When we have the red hat and purple on there is an air of fun. I don't know how to explain it, but it is there, it is the common thread, and everybody's there for the same reason. Wearing it makes the difference."[7] Many women emphatically declared that the hats are worn only when the group gets together, with very few women claiming they wore their red hats in other situations. One interview subject went as far as to say, "I don't think any one of us would choose to dress in purple and red hats. The only reason we do it because it is part of being in the group."[8]

The security Red Hat members get from all being dressed up in like colors and similar styles is clearly stated in the interviews: "Well some people, when they put on that red hat their ego gets a little big, more ego, more outgoing. Some people really change when they are dressed up. But it is fun when everybody has on the red hat, then you don't feel singled out."[9] The confidence of being a part of the larger group results in a lowering of inhibitions, with dancers at the London New Year's evening party drawing reluctant dancers up to the dance floor. This confidence led several Red Hat participants to shimmy in a sexy dance with a young man helping out with the Red Hat London tour, to the great delight of the Red Hat audience.

While members of the Red Hat Society can be interpreted as coming together to battle aging stereotypes as a group rather than individually, a strong secondary adhesive holding the group together is a common stage of life and shared histories. The majority of women stressed that most of their lives they had been taking care of others and that the Red Hat Society was the opportunity to finally focus on the self: "Oh, I just like the idea that we can be free. And I guess I am of that generation where I did a lot for my kids all the time, and now it is kind of time to sit back and just relax and have fun."[10] So while the Red Hat Society is a response to stigma through group behavior, the strength of the bonds holding the women together is deepened by a set of shared experiences drawn from the time they all played the invisible but critical roles of raising children and doing community service.

Antiaging Behavior and Dress

Interviewed Red Hat Society members continually make reference to the Jenny Joseph poem as they explain the meaning of the dress and their own behavior. The poem links the wearing of what one Red Hat member referred to as "bodacious" dress to behavior that challenges aging stereotypes that assume that older people are serious, slow moving, largely invisible, not very fun, and always well behaved: "It is the poem with the outfit, the poem dictates to make up for the sobriety of your youth and then you decide how you are going to do that. At the picnic, we brought watermelons so we could learn to spit. That is part of the poem. The poem to me is huge. The poem dictates that you wear the colors and have a good time. It always goes back to that."[11] Ignoring ladylike manners and having the freedom to be visibly loud and a little bit naughty in public are central to the feeling of youthfulness women experience as Red Hat Society members. The customary invisible role that older women often play in this culture is set aside by the members as they go out together wearing their hats with pride and zip: "We can be very loud and kind of obnoxious because we do just have fun and act goofy and laugh."[12]

Part of the fun of the public events is the violation of proper dress rules they learned as young adults. Women describe being overdressed, overdone, and over the top in terms of accessories, colors, and behavior, as if to visibly announce, "We will not be ignored!" For example, one woman stated, "People my age love being ourselves, being able to wear clothes that don't necessarily match."[13] Another recounted, "I never wore red. I had red hair growing up, I never wore red. This is the first red article that I have ever purchased, but I am over fifty and I am proud of it. I do wear red now, and I don't care!"[14] Red Hat Society members feel that membership allows them to feel young and have fun again, with some making references to their childhoods. Women give central importance to the group, stating that without the group they would not feel the same freedom from rules and responsibilities: "I think it just empowers us to be more free. And maybe do some things that we normally wouldn't do. I think when you are in a group, a large group like ours, where everybody else is doing these silly things, you can do things and not feel like everybody's just sitting there staring at YOU because you are being silly. But there are so many of us doing it, that you know, it is accepted."[15]

Another aspect of youthfulness that emerged as an important theme in the interviews was a renewed power to attract hedonic attention, particularly from men, but also from other observers. Many women brought up how delightful it was to get compliments on their appearance when they appeared as a group, with some expressing amazement that men would be complimenting them on their appearance at their age: "A lot of times it will be the men that will come up and make a comment about it. Which, I don't know, in a way it is kind of amazing. I mean, you know, it is kind of like, they like to see that feminine side again…a lot of times they will come up and just have that comment. That, 'you look so nice in your red hat.'"[16] The act of revealing the feminine and sensual side of themselves through the wearing of hats and accessories, and the public recognition they receive for the behavior, gives Red Hat Society members feelings of hedonic power that many have not experienced for a long time: "We went out to eat at a restaurant you know and that is a lot of fun to do because like I said, you go in and you definitely get noticed because you've got there eight or ten women sitting around with their hats on."[17] Regaining the power to attract positive attention through their appearance, particularly from men, is cited repeatedly as part of Red Hat Society fun. One woman stated, "There is something about women in red hats I guess. Men will come up to us and say how do I join this group? Oh they just love it."[18]

Why Red Hats, Why Boas?

The choosing of hats to symbolize group identity for women in this age group must be analyzed in light of their history with hats as they were growing up and at earlier stages of their adult lives. These women grew up and came of age during an era when hats were commonly worn by women in public. For them, the wearing of hats during these earlier stages of their lives had to do with following rules, being proper, and in many cases dressing up and going to church: "We wore hats. We were Catholic and had to wear hats to church. And so we wore hats a lot, we wore hats when we dressed up, even the people who weren't Catholic. And I mean we had to wear them to church and our three daughters all had to wear them to church. We thought it would be terrible if they did not keep their hats on in church."[19] For these women the symbolic meaning of hats is related to following the rules and wearing the "proper" matching dress and gloves. So for this generation of women, the violation of the rules, so central to the fun of being a Red Hat Society member, is ideally expressed in the wearing of improper and ostentatious hats.

Red feather boas were also a crowd favorite among the Red Hatters as they dressed up for the 2011 London New Year's Day Parade and the party the evening before. For the oldest members of the Red Hat Society I talked with, boas were directly associated with burlesque performances of their youth and symbolized flamboyant sexuality. This symbolic connection of the boa to burlesque was formally marked in 2007 at the fiftieth anniversary of the Burlesque Hall of Fame's Striptease Reunion, which opened with a multigenerational lineup of burlesque divas bumping and grinding down the length of a half-mile pink boa. For younger Red Hat members the boa also spoke directly to the expression of sexuality, with a younger member saying that as a Red Hatter, "It's perfectly permissible to be bodacious and when I am feeling bodacious I wear this boa to the meetings."[20]

Finally, the red hats and boas are chosen because of the poem, and the fact that the poem speaks so clearly to women in this age group. For almost all women interviewed, they circled back to the poem as being central to what the organization means to them, and the meaning they derive from the wearing of red hat regalia in community with other women:

> I think the poem explains what the women are really trying to do. When we get on our purple and our red, we are allowed to be silly.... we all still have this little girl inside of us.... society says you are supposed to be prim and proper, you are supposed to use your quiet voice inside.... society says you are old enough that we have taught you your manners, [but when] we put on our red hats and we can be the little kid again, just like the poem dictates.... I shall sit on the street.... I will learn to spit.[21]

And, I will add, when the women get ready to dance the night away at a New Year's Eve party in London, it is the boa that gives them that added sexual confidence to shimmy with the busboy, smiling all the while the smile of a woman who knows she still has it.

Red Hat Society events create an open, free space where older women do not feel judged for letting loose and expressing their more fun, free, and, for some women, sexual side. While certainly our research found that Red Hat women enjoy once again attracting male attention with their eye-catching apparel, perhaps more important they enjoy being able to have fun with other women. At the New Year's Eve party in London, it cannot be denied that the women got a kick out of seeing the young male bus attendant dancing and grinding away with a boa-flipping Red Hatter, but they also most thoroughly enjoyed flipping their boas at each other on the dance floor, without the need to court the male gaze, just having fun with each other. The space to wear apparel that is fun and sexy again, without worrying about being proper, is a real attraction of Red Hat events for older women seeking a space to express their mojo. While certainly the fashion system has responded to this market with Red Hat merchandise, the Red Hatters are still in charge of the identity and driving the product lines.

Burlesque: The Millennium Revival

The burlesque revival in the United Kingdom and the United States is most commonly traced back to the mid-1990s when burlesque clubs began to open in Las Vegas and New York, with follow-up fever spreading to London during the first decade of the twenty-first century. Most recently, Paris is in the wings, with the director of the London-based Burlesque Factory relocating to France to jump-start a studio in Paris. In New York City, the Museum of Sex opened a show titled "The Nudie Artist: Burlesque Revived" in the spring of 2011, with lessons from local burlesque artists offered as a part of the exhibit programming. Drawing on a heady mix of 1930s American folk burlesque, British vaudeville, circus performance arts, and the magnificence of late twentieth-century drag queens, the new burlesque has many guises and multiple agendas. Ranging from very traditional reenactments of 1930s productions, to burlesque classes "for everyone," to performance art, to classes promising sexy and empowered routes to fame, burlesque has taken a place again in Euro-American culture and insists on being noticed.

The history of American burlesque is most commonly traced back to the appearance of Lydia Thompson and the British Blondes on the New York stage in the late 1860s. These early British burlesque performances were spoofs on popular operas, songs, and stories, heated up by scantily clad women and racy language. The British Blondes' first big hit in New York was a mythological story in which Thompson's female cast cross-dressed in tights to portray male roles within the story line, often spiced up as sexual aggressors. The cross-dressing of women in body-revealing male costuming, coupled with roles in which they played the sexual aggressor, created discourse focused on "proper" roles and behaviors for women in Victorian New York City. Thompson's position as not only a performer but the director of the troupe also raised eyebrows.

Thompson's huge success on Broadway spawned some American copycat burlesque theater troupes, with a limited number run by women. As men took over exclusive direction of American burlesque in the 1880s, the emphasis within the performances began to shift toward peep show acts that used any means possible to increase the level of skin exposure by skirting the obscenity laws of the period. Techniques ranged from having the burlesque divas wear see-through tight-fitting costumes to instructing them to move to the wings behind the curtain to remove clothing items to avoid laws forbidding open stripping in front of the audience—thus creating the burlesque curtain-tease tradition of reappearing on stage after a brief departure wearing a scant bit less than what you left with! By 1905 American burlesque theater owners had created traveling circuits for their performers, rotating them in forty-week blocks through whole regions of the United States, where they appeared on large big-city stages, in smaller midsize-city venues, and in small theaters in midsize towns.

Striptease emerged as a burlesque staple as theaters began to struggle for attendance with the first opening of movie theaters in the 1930s, and this literally kept the theaters alive throughout the Depression. Many of the women recruited to the burlesque stage had acting aspirations that were at least in part satisfied by the dancing and routines that were a part of the job description of a good burlesque performer. Burlesque performers prided themselves on their elaborate costuming and experienced their own thrills of delight wearing sensual evening gowns, gloves, and jewelry, which they slowly removed—an act they referred to as "the tease." April March was a burlesque dancer who worked stages in both the United States and the United Kingdom. She dismisses contemporary mainstream versions of strip dancing, indicating that the art of the show is gone now and that all that remains is the raw nakedness, in essence a strip show stripped of the magic, in her estimation:

> Asked if she would become a striptease dancer and do it all over again, April responded, "No way, not today. Today it's not show business. If I could go back and do it in the days

when it was fun, I would. I was always elegantly dressed, did a lot teasing, and performed a good routine. Today they have everything off before they even come out on stage." (Briggeman, 2009, p. 191)

Tony Midnight, at first a female impersonator also working the clubs, transitioned over to designing elaborate costuming for the female dancers. His comments capture the wonder the women experienced through the wearing of fantasy dress, again a pleasure experienced by the wearer in part due to the fact that the dress attracted audience attention, but also due to the delight of wearing a glamorous dress:

> "I got to know them", Tony said, "and when they found out that I could sew, they began to ask me to make things for them. The valet shop at the hotel was empty, so I rented and re-decorated it, then opened my first studio. In a very short time, I had to hire help to take care of all my orders. I got a sequin embroidery machine from Paris and specialized in very elaborate embroidered gowns and costumes. I gave the girls costumes that they never dreamed of owning." (Briggeman, 2009, p. 166)

This attachment to finery makes better sense if one takes into account the life stories of the performers captured in the Leslie Zemeckis's 2010 documentary *Behind the Burly Q*. For many women interviewed for this film, burlesque was a way out of dire poverty, and thus the costuming truly was a sensual fantasy with vivid and real dimensions.

Many of the American burlesque performers during the peak period considered themselves artists. "Blaze Fury" was raised by a mother who ran a chorus line for a midsize American city theater and considered herself a performer with a rich tradition to draw from:

> Blaze was a strong and determined woman. In a 1953 *Cavalcade of Burlesque* magazine interview, she stated, "It's everybody's favorite indoor pastime to psychoanalyze the burlesque dancer. When are people going to realize that we're in burlesque because we like show business and like to dance? Half the girls have mothers or grandmothers who have been in show business. It runs in families, like musical talent. It's also traditional to scoff when you read that a burlesque girl supports a family, attends opera, and reads good books, but that's exactly the truth. We have nothing to be ashamed of. We're proud of our art and our morals are as high as career girls anywhere. In fact, I've heard more vulgar talk among a group of stenographers than I've heard around a dressing room." (Briggeman, 2009, p. 223)

As the erotic entertainment industry moved toward porn standards and away from the elegant play and humor of the peak era, performers like Blaze Fury retired, put off by the explicit body exposure expected in strip clubs from the 1970s onward.

The range of current burlesque performances include historical reenactments of traditional programs from the 1930s, often focusing on performances of burlesque standards such as the fan dance, straight man, circus acts, and the strip. Many also draw from the long history of drag performance, sometimes combining with single impersonators, or troupes of impersonators, other forms of erotic dance such as belly dancing and strip-bar standards such as pole dancing. The promotion and organization of burlesque also vary considerably. Nonprofit and profit-making versions of burlesque have popped up in metropolitan areas, offering classes, opportunities to perform, conferences, and contests. Some burlesque venues and lessons are seamlessly linked to promoters of the more explicit for-profit erotic entertainment of our era, with the burlesque lessons at the popular London-based Burlesque Factory taught by Gerard Simi, the former owner of a well-known London erotic club from 1997 to 2004, who is now moving his burlesque enterprise to France.

On a smaller and more local scale, the Boston Babydolls are a theater company in residence at the Cambridge YMCA Theatre. Cofounded and directed by the Babydolls' self-named impresario and emcee, "Scratch," and the head dancer, "Miss Mina," the theater company offers burlesque classes at the YMCA and also sponsors a three-day conference drawing burlesque performers from the United States and Canada. Les Dames du Burlesque, an American troupe operating out of Iowa City, Iowa, is an example of a grassroots organization put together literally on a shoestring by founder Nelle Dunlap. Dunlap was first exposed to burlesque by a troupe in a neighboring city, followed up by a wider exploration using posted YouTube videos. Excited about the art form, she gave herself the stage name Tough Köokie and used her Facebook connections to put her first troupe together, with an eye to finding a woman with a dance background to help put the show skits together. Similar kinds of groups have emerged in both small and large communities as women with performance art, theater, and dance backgrounds have organized themselves, often in collaboration with other creative community groups, to do live shows coupled with some teaching of burlesque through local venues such as fitness and/or yoga centers and dance studios.

Male-emceed shows tend to fall into the patriarchal patterns of performance that emerged as burlesque norms in the early twentieth century. The role of the master of ceremonies, who appears at the beginning of the show and appears throughout to announce acts, often either implies or directly positions the male gaze as the priority. For example, in introducing acts at the 2009 Burlesque Festival in Boston, Scratch urges the crowd on at the beginning by telling them to "please DO hoot, holler, wolf whistle, cheer, and generally carry on," all stereotypical male responses to female bodies. In contrast, well-known female emcees such as "Miss Kitten on the Keys" speak directly to the women in the audience ("You look like a girl who would love a garter"), blatantly strut their own sexuality, and lavish praise on the artistry of the burlesque performer they are introducing. To balance this statement, however, passionate burlesque promoters like Scratch, who are themselves playing traditional burlesque roles in the productions, often take care to point to the empowerment aspect of the performance for the female dancer. In an interview Scratch articulates much of the appeal of contemporary burlesque to performers and audience members:

> Burlesque is sexy, without being sexual. Good burlesque teases you and makes you feel good about yourself and everyone around you whether you are a man or a woman. It is not overt, it is not crude, it is not raunchy, it is teasing and titillating. It puts you in the right frame of mind to be sexy. If you are a burlesque performer you are powerful. You are charismatic. You are enchanting. You can be sexy, you can be funny. But when you are on that stage if you are doing it right you command the audience's attention. Men like to see women doing that. Women like to see women doing that. It is inspirational.[22]

Worthy of note is Scratch's emphasis on gaining power through attracting and holding the attention of the audience, the classic hedonic indirect power often used by women. In contrast, there is a more direct power that comes from expressing your own sexuality on your own terms. For example, Miss Kitten on the Keys directly confronts the audience with her own sexuality, often opening the show cross-dressed in a male tux, with just a flash of pasties, then changing over to pasties and a tutu to announce the remainder of the show. She, unlike Scratch, is playing with her own sexuality, not just serving up the sexuality of the performers. In her cross-dressing tux at the opening of the show, she challenges the audience to think about the patriarchal roots of the girly peep show and consider how this show is different. This subtle difference in the role of the emcee moves the narrative from a showgirl event put on by a man for a male audience to a show put on by women celebrating women's sexuality. The line between a performer's empowerment based on her ability to attract and hold an audience and empowerment resulting from a performance in which she freely expresses her own sexuality is sometimes gray, but this subtle difference is noticed and is significant in particular in terms of how women in the audience experience burlesque.

The use of cross-gender performance within burlesque to create reflection on dichotomous and restrictive constructions of male and female sexuality was successfully and creatively employed by the creators of a 2011 combined performance of Les Dames du Burlesque and the I. C. Kings, a local drag king performance group. The female-to-male cross-dressed kings performed in erotic skits with the female burlesque cast members, opening up a range of different erotic roles for all the cast members while at the same time, as pointed out by Rhonda Blair's work, serving to "illuminate gender-as-construction" (2006, p. 361). Particular highlights of this performance that spotlighted the concept of gender as constructed included a king's lip synch to Aerosmith's "Dude Looks like a Lady," in which a female-to-male cross-dressed performer was challenged and stripped down by a second, more macho king to reveal the woman beneath the man. This deconstruction striptease included the ripping away of the tape wound round her breasts, in a twirling dance movement like the unwinding of a top, and a grab down the front of the underpants that removed a molded penis-shaped stuffing.

Figure 9.1 Sissy's Sircus, a burlesque troupe located in Cedar Falls, Iowa, challenges audiences to reflect on cultural construction of gender and restrictive constructions of female and male sexuality. Photo provided by Sissy's Sircus.

In Blair's theatrical productions she has used gender switching to effectively move audiences through a reflection process: "The way we played with gender and aggression recast the erotic and sadomasochistic elements of the script. As the configuration of actors changed from male/male to male/female to female/female, the audience was confronted with their own response to aggression, anomie and desire; they were 'reading' the surface male/male text against the gender permutations going on beneath it" (2006, p. 362). Similarly, Les Dames du Burlesque and the I. C. Kings continually played with standardized expectations linked to constructed female and male sexual identity, creating a humorous, sexy, and open gendered performance. The gender cross-dressing of the burlesque diva Tough Köokie (Nelle Dunlap) to lip-synch the classic John Lennon lines, "I want you so bad, it's driving me mad, it's driving me mad," while slowly stripping herself down to her undies literally had the entire mixed-gender audience in the palm of her hand.

In terms of analysis, there are spaces within the revived burlesque movement for open expression of female sexuality that is subjectively defined, particularly in shows like those staged by Les Dames du Burlesque, wherein gender construction itself becomes an element of narrative drama. The patterns of the male-directed girly peep shows of the early twentieth century still produce mainstream profit-driven burlesque modeled on and serving the male gaze and desire, particularly when emceed in a vaudeville style by a male master of ceremonies. The challenge to this pattern happens first with the transformation of the emcee from a traditional male master of the showgirls into another gender guise, which then moves the audience into a more reflective and questioning zone. Content analysis of comments about YouTube videos of burlesque performances captures the differing attitudes of segments of the burlesque audience, with some male viewers rating the videos on the woman's ability to arouse and others writing back, "FYI Burlesque isn't about YOU getting an erection." The strong patterns in mass media dictating that women's bodies are there to arouse a male audience still affect responses to burlesque and also the ways in which events are staged, depending on the intention of the burlesque troupe. Linkages between owners previously running erotic nightclubs and now switching over burlesque heighten the tendency to create events directed toward the male gaze, and also the use of women's burlesque performances to make money.

The appeal of burlesque can be analyzed as itself a commentary on, or public response to, raunch eroticism. For performers as well as audience members, burlesque done well brings the play back, hides just enough to make sex sexy again, treats us to titillating foreplay in a culture that focuses on the cum shot. Burlesque, in contrast with mass media porn chic, includes and celebrates a wide range of body types and gender identities, again embracing a subjectively defined sexuality, not dictated by the surgically enhanced images found in mass media. The simple joy that many performers and audience members experience at low-overhead and low-entrance-fee venues is an outlet for sexual expression that is self-defined, gender-open, and not dictated by a profit-driven media machine.

–10–

The Path toward Gender Justice

This book is dedicated to gender justice. The exploration of raunch eroticism I have led you through has been an attempt to understand the popular culture messages surrounding us that influence how we construct and experience our sexuality. Two central characters emerged within its pages: (1) an extremely unapologetic bad boy and (2) his lusty sidekick, the sexy empowerment icon. What is interesting to behold is the degree of power, influence, and command of the bad boys in our midst. The "player" who gets laid every weekend using alcohol as a rape drug is able to operate undetected because not only do his male peers look up to him, but in many cases so do the women he is pursuing. His father and/or his coach may even laud him for being "a real guy that gets around." And for heaven's sake, everyone does it—listen to Eminem and look at Tucker Max's blog. On the other hand, the girls and women have it harder. The sexy empowerment icon is a charade in terms of authentic power. Yes, sexy women attract men, but the men they are attracting are socialized to view them as whores, as objects, and as dispensable.

This is not to say that healthy relationships don't exist. Thank goodness, they do. It is, however, a partial explanation of why approximately 20 percent of college women will be victims of attempted or actual sexual assaults. It also can be used to explain the dramatic decrease in self-esteem experienced as young girls enter the age of dating, the time period when the sexy empowerment icon is doing battle with their souls. These cultural gender patterns also help to explain why many boys are falling into the muddy ruts of Michael Kimmel's *Guyland* (2008), where underachievement and endless hours spent playing sexually explicit and violent video games seem normal.

A classic social justice technique is reappropriation of disparaging terms, artifacts, and images by the stigmatized or victimized cultural group. The premise of this organizing approach is that by taking back control of words and images used by others to inflict harm the oppressed themselves seize the control over how they are being labeled, imaged, and talked about. In so doing the victimized create the ability to comment on the mainstream disparaging discourse and in some cases transform the meaning of the words and images to empower rather than victimize their cultural group.

The success of social justice reappropriation methods depends largely on their ability to affect those both inside and outside of the stigmatized cultural group. It is easy to have a party and invite only the people who already agree with you. Unfortunately, to cause shifts in power distribution and social justice, you have to invite the tough crowd, the hard-to-convince mainstream audience that not only accepts as normal the damaging labels you are wrestling to change but often has a vested interest in maintaining the labels and language you are battling to transform. To return to the key question opening this book, how do we successfully challenge a sexuality script being written by largely unchallenged unapologetic bad boys whose acts are not only typically excused from reprimand but often held up as cultural emblems of masculinity? If we are really to succeed in changing current rates of sexual violence, those boys have to come to the party and accept that the woman they labeled a slut yesterday is now standing before them owning that word and demanding respect. That is a hard job. This final chapter opens by exploring contemporary attempts by self-declared feminists to use reappropriation of images and words to effect social change and justice.

Eve Ensler: *The Vagina Monologues*

The year 2008 marked the tenth anniversary of Eve Ensler's *The Vagina Monologues*. Opening first in New York, the monologues were self-described by Ensler as the most radical of her career. Ironically, she states in the foreword to the tenth-anniversary edition of her book, it was this radical production that brought her work into the mainstream. In Ensler's own words: "Saying the word I was not supposed to say is the thing that gave me a voice in the world. Revealing the very personal stories of women and their private parts gave birth to a public, global movement to end violence against women and girls called V-day" (Ensler, 2008, p. xiii). Spread it did, from the first productions in New York all the way to a rural Middle America campus where in 2004 I was named a "Vagina Warrior" for working to end gender violence as a part of campus V-week activities in my own community.

An analysis of the strong popular appeal of Ensler's work must take into account the growing porn chic trend during that same decade. At the same time that the mass media were accelerating and intensifying the streaming of women's sexuality directed principally toward a male heterosexual audience, Ensler offered an erotic outlet for those not served by mainstream pop culture. The monologues were authentic stories of real women who were mature, funny, uninhibited, and erotic. Yes, she certainly took on the hard questions, such as the gang rape of Bosnian women, but she also played hard ball with transformations of female bodies and sexuality driven by the increasing access by the mainstream to pornography during this time period.

For example, one of the opening monologues, "Hair," directly confronts the accelerating grooming trend of waxing and/or shaving the pubic hair, driven in part by male partners who are influenced by pornography norms. The monologue also makes clear the uncomfortable tie of the practice to the growing sexualization of prepubescent girls now running rampant in both porn and mainstream culture: "You cannot love a vagina unless you love hair. Many people do not love hair. My first husband hated hair. He said it was cluttered and dirty. He made me shave my vagina. It looked puffy and exposed like a little girl. This excited him" (Ensler, 2008, p. 9). The end of the monologue comes full circle back to affirming the woman's own sexuality through once again loving the hair and, in a humorous finale, declaring that shaving her vagina didn't keep her husband at home anyway! "I realized then that hair is there for a reason—it's the leaf around the flower, the lawn around the house. You have to love hair in order to love the vagina. You can't pick the parts you want. And besides, my husband never stopped screwing around" (p. 11).

The monologue reclaiming the word *cunt*, and making it sexy, is a good example of reappropriation. *The Vagina Monologues* overall were important as they not only reclaimed the word *cunt* but in a very public and visible way reclaimed women's sexuality—helping women say first to themselves, and then to others, that their *own* desire warranted as much attention as that of their male partners.

> I call it cunt. I've reclaimed it, "cunt". I really like it. "Cunt." Listen to it. "Cunt." C C, Ca Ca. Cavern, cackle, clit, cute, come—closed c—closed inside, inside ca—then u— then cu—then curvey, inviting sharkskin u-uniform, under, up, urge, ugh, ugh, u—then n then cun—snug letters fitting perfectly together—n—nest, now, nexus, nice, nice, al- ways depth, always round in uppercase, cun, cun—n a jagged wicked electrical pulse—n [high-pitched noise] then soft n—warm n—cun, cun, then sharp certain tangy t—texture, take, tent, tight, tantalizing, tensing, taste, tendrils, time, tactile, tell me, tell me "Cunt cunt," say it, tell me "Cunt." "Cunt." (pp. 102–103)

In terms of whether the reappropriation promised by the monologues has worked, one needs only to examine the popular culture that sprang up around them like weeds. At the very time Ensler's monologues were spreading like wildfire across cities and campuses, the unapologetic bad boy was doing his work scripting the ever-expanding stage of the sexy empowerment icon. The cultural discussions created by the monologues, though important, have been and still are in many ways confined to an audience of the already converted. The monologues are popular on campuses, where the auditoriums are most often filled with the women's studies students and faculty. They did signal in a very widespread and public manner the felt need on the part of older and younger women to voice their own sexuality, to reclaim not just the word *cunt* but their own subjective sexual experiences and identities.

SlutWalks: "No Means No! However We Dress, Wherever We Go!"

The first SlutWalk, organized and enacted in Toronto on April 3, 2011, was a direct response to comments delivered on January 24, 2011, by a Toronto police officer who, speaking to women enrolled in a university self-protection course, said that "women should avoid dressing like sluts in order not to be victimized" (SlutWalk Toronto, n.d.). The organizers seized the moment and created an easily branded and significant protest directly tied to the officer's own language and focused on taking back the term *slut* to point to the propensity of law enforcement and the public to assign blame to assault victims based on what they were wearing at the time of the assault. Featured speakers included not only women with long histories in the rape crisis movement but also Michael Kaufman, a male Canadian activist whose work, like that of Jackson Katz and Michael Kimmel, has focused on confronting the damage being done by dominant cultural definitions of masculinity and on attempting to create interventions calling men to leadership roles within the gender-violence prevention movement. Reappropriation of the term *slut* was the stated goal of the protest (see later on), with many of the participants dressing in stereotypical hypersexualized apparel to enact the reappropriation of the highly sexualized term. "Historically, the term 'slut' has carried a predominantly negative connotation. Aimed at those who are sexually promiscuous, be it for work or pleasure, it has primarily been women who have suffered under the burden of this label. And whether dished out as a serious indictment of one's character or merely as a flippant insult, the intent behind the word is always to wound, so we're taking it back. 'Slut' is being re-appropriated" (SlutWalk Toronto, n.d.). The spread of the movement was viral, with highly publicized follow-up SlutWalks with large participant turnouts happening in Boston (May 2011), London (June 2011), Lisbon (June 2011), Berlin (August 13, 2011), and New York (October 1, 2011).

Ranges of dress and behavior varied by city and time period, though all marches included a range of provocative dress, with upper-body nudity and stripper poles entering the latest march in New York, perhaps indicating that this widely produced and branded event includes a built-in ratcheting up of behaviors to continue to draw crowds and press to the event. Slogans in all cities tended to focus around the issue of consent: "No Means No, However I Dress, Wherever I Go." In some locations such as Boston, signage clearly linked to the sexy empowerment messaging discussed in chapter 3, such as "It's My Hot Body, I Do What I Want," was also found among the marchers. Organizers I spoke with talked about the appeal of the event to young women not previously drawn to the movement who identified with the branding of the message, perhaps, again, related to the popularization of messaging linking sexuality to empowerment. This was an opportunity to take sexy dressing out into the streets and link it to a powerful message. For young women accustomed to hypersexualized Halloween street celebrations, this event felt right, felt powerful, and gave them a voice.

Debates surrounding the efficacy of SlutWalks in terms of producing social change and awareness have been intense and at times heated, with lines drawn on racial lines and by positions and age within the movement. In particular, the movement has often struck raw chords within the American black community. In the fall of 2011, just days in advance of the New York City SlutWalk, Black Women's Blueprint, Inc., posted an open letter to the organizers of the original Ontario SlutWalk outlining their key concerns with the movement. Speaking from their position as a civil and human rights organization with a mission of supporting and organizing "on social justice issues steeped in the struggles of Black women within their communities and within dominant culture" (Black Women's Blueprint, 2011), Blueprint members expressed concern regarding the use of the racist/sexist term *slut* as a self-identifying organizing tool. Citing the long history of use of sexist and racist terms to denigrate and victimize black women, the open letter underscored that "black women in the U.S. have worked tirelessly since the 19th century colored women's clubs, to rid society of the sexist/racist vernacular of slut, jezebel, hottentot, mammy, mule, sapphire." Further, Blueprint members articulated within the letter that as black women they were still in the process of ridding their community of offensive labels such as *ho* and further that they were unwilling to counsel their daughters to self-identify as sluts, fearing that the label would put their daughters in possible jeopardy. In a strong statement they also indicated that they were unwilling to encourage their sons, husbands, fathers, and brothers "to reinforce Black women's identities as 'sluts' by normalizing the term on t-shirts, buttons, flyers and pamphlets."

On a broader theoretical level scholars and activists have also questioned the organizers' claim for reappropriation of the term *slut* to a more celebratory and positive end. Gail Dines and Wendy J. Murphy (2011) argued early in the movement, after the spring Boston walk, that "the term slut is so deeply rooted in the patriarchal 'Madonna/whore' view of women's sexuality that it is beyond redemption" and that trying to reclaim a word so steeped in misogyny is a "waste of precious feminist resources." Zerlina, responding to Rebecca Traister's *New York Times Magazine* article, similarly comments that she knows why organizers "want to take the misogynistic power out of the word slut, I just am not sure they can," and further goes on to foreshadow the black women's open letter by pointing out that "many of the most disadvantaged women of color who are the very first to be labeled a slut, ho, or trick, may be the least likely to support this type of movement" (online "Readers' Comments" section in Traister, 2011).

As SlutWalks have erupted across the world, they have generated at times heated exchange in a range of media including letters to the editor, interviews captured in news stories posing women for and against the walks, and commentary in publications ranging from the *New York Times* to the *Huffington Post* to personal websites and blogs. Many identified strongly with Traister when she opened her *New York Times Magazine* story in the summer of 2011 by stating that she really "wanted to love SlutWalks" but in the end "mostly felt irritation that stripping down to skivvies and calling ourselves sluts is passing for keen retort." In a similar vein, when the SlutWalk hit the streets of New York the following fall, commentator Keli Goff decried the organizers' predictable use of flesh to gain attention, serving to reinforce rather than challenge stereotypical notions of female power, most often linked to attracting attention through sexuality rather than effecting change through intellect and strategy: "Fair or not, the images from SlutWalk send the message that when push comes to shove, young women will always fall back on taking off their clothes to get attention, even when it comes to making a serious political statement. The same women who probably ridicule the Kardashian sisters essentially employed the same tactics—a little T & A—to get a lot of camera time this weekend" (Goff, 2011). The criticism that the events were often reduced to a YouTube viewing frenzy being watched by the very males the event is trying to hold accountable is supported by a young male blogger who declared after seeing the New York City walk, "This cop from Toronto is a GENIUS! I've been trying my whole life to get girls to show me a little something sexy and this guy makes one stoopid comment and hundreds of girls are stripping!" (comments section in *Daily Mail* Reporter, 2011).

Sady Doyle (2011), writing about the New York SlutWalk, captures this dynamic as she accurately articulates, "No matter how often we debate SlutWalk's politics, what people really want to hear about are the outfits." About the outfits, Doyle reports that the ones that got covered by the press photographers, as well as the young men out for a look, were the corsets, not the more typical T-shirts. In terms of numbers, and the response of the press and crowd, Doyle recounts that women wearing corsets were easy to find—all you had to do was look for the camera crews—but she goes on to report that "more women went topless. This, I soon realized, was brilliant; the press cameras had to stay away from them. The men on the sidewalk were less inhibited; they gathered on stoops, at intersections, or in the fire escapes, holding out phone cameras, rapt with predatory fascination. When the mobile [stripper] pole rolled down Astor Place, men walked out into traffic to get a clear shot" (Doyle, 2011).

Like those of many other self-declared long-standing members of the violence prevention movement writing on SlutWalks, Doyle's review of the event is mixed, ending with saying that participating in the march, particularly having three older women enact their support from a window on the parade route by going topless and waving to the marchers, gave her hope. As a woman who heavily covered *Girls Gone Wild* flashing on my home campus (see chapter 5) I find the power dynamics of SlutWalks disturbing. Both events, in terms of street theater, focused on women playing the role of attracting attention through sexual display and drew men to the event to capture cell phone images of topless marchers, women spinning on strip poles, and corsets. Certainly the rhetoric contrasts, with signage at the SlutWalks insisting on consent and respect, but in terms of street theater the unapologetic bad boys, the ones we are attempting to influence and change, are playing exactly the same roles at both events. I am not at all sure they are getting the message.

What *is* important, and what must be interpreted as an authentic step forward, is that SlutWalks engaged young women who might never have walked in a Take Back the Night event or volunteered in a rape crisis center to mobilize on an issue deeply affecting their age group and culture. While their tactics may rely on what they have been socialized to do to attract attention—reveal skin and sexuality—their message and intentions matter, and it is important that they are being vocal on this issue and attempting to make a difference. Some of the young organizers' unfamiliarity with the history of the movement, and their sometimes naive tendency to assume their own experiences reflect those of other ages and ethnicities, is problematic and sometimes deeply troubling. But as *Feminista* writer Samhita wrote in response to Traister's article, "Sometimes the purpose of activism is in the theatre, in the noise and in the exaggeration.... It may not make quantifiable policy change, but it makes headlines that are funny, ironic and dramatic and sometimes that is enough to get people to change their minds or rethink taken for granted assumptions about sexuality." Perhaps, she goes on to argue, "Women marching around in 'slutty outfits' yelling about injustice is in a way a type of mockery of conventional ideas about sexuality" (quoted in JOS, 2011) that may provide young women with a needed entry point into activism.

Porn Chic: The Paintings of Nicola Bockelmann

The successful parts of the stories told in chapter 9 testify to the performers, writers, artists, and designers who have attempted to reclaim subjective sexuality from the porn chic heap of popular culture raunch. The victims, like Karen Owen, are still caught under the heap, not quite seeing the path away from the Tucker Max builders of the porn chic universe. Perhaps the most difficult thing for women to reclaim or refashion successfully is the images of female sexuality and women's and girls' bodies that permeate popular culture. In the wise words of Susan Bordo, we live in a culture "bedazzled by created images," and "if we do not wish to become prisoners of those images, we must recognize that they are reality" (1997, p. 2). These opening words to Bordo's book on the power of cultural images to affect our everyday lives speak to the importance of Nicola Bockelmann's body of artwork: *Porn Chic.*

Nicola Steffen is a German/British media scholar currently living and working in the United Kingdom with her husband and their two sons. She works as an artist under the pseudonym of "Nicola Bockelmann," working in the traditional medium of canvas and oil. Bockelmann's most recent project, funded by a 2005 grant from the Arts Council England, focused on reproduction of mass-produced popular culture depictions of porn chic. In October, she was a visiting research fellow at GEXcel, Linköping, Sweden, where she researched porn chic as an underlying cause of gendered violence in intimate relationships. She is now collaborating on an international quantitative study about pornography, sexuality, and culture with New York University media researcher Chyng Sun. Bockelmann's body of work functions to spotlight, and in so doing prompt the deconstruction of, representations of gender in the media, with a particular focus on the sexuality of girls and women. She has recently completed a doctoral degree focused on representations of gender, popular culture, and pornography, so she brings both an academic analytical mind to the subject as well the sensibility of an artist.

The subject matter for Bockelmann's *Porn Chic* painting series as captured on this book cover and throughout each chapter is purposefully provocative, including a number of sexually explicit paintings. The advertising and popular culture roots of the imagery lend an edge to the message, as these are not the conjured imaginings of a cultural critic but rather the reproduced images of our real world. Visitors' comments written in the gallery guest ledger speak to the power of the artist's work in terms of creating a space dominated for many by a disturbingly high level of explicit imagery linked to female sexuality. Sensitive to the nature of the work, the Bradford Museum, located in the north of England, divided the exhibit into two parts, with what they deemed the most explicit paintings behind closed doors with a warning of provocative content posted on the door.

Women depicted in the *Porn Chic* series position themselves in relationship to the male gaze using multiple frameworks of desire. Bockelmann's work makes clear and direct reference to the classic pinup shot as made popular in World War II by Betty Grable and later mass-produced by the early *Playboy* magazine in the United States and the first UK lad magazine, aptly named *Nuts*. Bockelmann's reproductions of the classic pinup feature the expected come-and-get-me pose featuring direct eye contact with the viewer coupled with the also-customary provocative and suppli-cant pose. As examples of this pop culture genre as explored in this body of work see Figure 10.1, the over-the-shoulder Betty Grable shot; Figure 10.2, the direct hot stare and parted lips; and Figure 10.3, the bubblebath invitation shot. The gallery audience in Bradford clearly made the connection between Bockelmann's work and this style of photography shot, with one disgruntled gallery visitor writing, "Makes *Nuts* magazine look challenging. I could go on...." Also related to this genre within Bockelmann's body of work are women posed in fantasy service roles to men mod-eled after the quintessential Playboy Bunny and, in the case of Bockelmann's image, the sexy stewardess (see chapter 7, Figure 7.1), and the international playboy, James Bond (see chapter 2, Figure 2.1).

The more sexually suggestive appeals to male desire depicted by Bockelmann, though drawn from popular culture inspirations, cross over into indirect refer-ences to soft-porn fantasy. These include the classic soft-porn genres of the orgasm shot (see Figure 10.4), the archetypal cum shot (for a creative bovine example see Figure 10.5), the oral sex shot (see chapter 1, Figure 1.1), and classic sadomasochism (see chapter 6, Figure 6.1). These images pushed the more conservative gallery visi-tors to write comments that ranged from "Liked them but a bit sick" to judgmental responses such as "We have no need to wonder why young people disrespect society when we display rubbish like this." The history of the gallery as an institution serv-ing young families, and the frequent visits to the galleries by children, also drew out some responses from viewers such as "I appreciated much of the art but the Porn Chic exhibit is not appropriate in a family oriented gallery and I question whether I can recommend people to come" and "I think with art work described as 'Porn' there

Figure 10.1 *Untitled.* Courtesy of Nicola Bockelmann.

Figure 10.2 *Untitled.* Courtesy of Nicola Bockelmann.

Figure 10.3 *Porn Chic V.* Courtesy of Nicola Bockelmann.

should be at least a warning about content and not as readily accessible to children." I reiterate that the exhibit was separated into two parts, with a content warning on the closed gallery with what the museum staff deemed the more sexually explicit artworks.

Commodification, the use of hypersexualized images of women to sell product and brand, is most directly brought to the forefront in Bockelmann's work through its direct link to published advertising copy and pop culture coverage of sexy empowerment icons such as Britney Spears. *Baby* (see chapter 4, Figure 4.1) was inspired by a promotional photograph of Spears and captures the indelible combination of youthful innocence and ripe sexuality that made up the launch of the Britney Spears brand as it hit the cover of *Rolling Stone* in the 1990s. The large scale of the painting created by Bockelmann and its placement within a large gallery of porn chic imagery has the power to force the thoughtful viewer to reconsider the impact of porn chic imagery on contemporary culture, particularly as marketed to an audience of young women. Less thoughtful viewers, particularly young girls who simply responded to Bockelmann's paintings as a cool, very realistic, and very large representation of their favorite pop star, responded at times with a simple "I would love to put this up in my room." These comments point toward the importance of teaching media literacy to tweens and teenagers as a component of standard educational offerings in this era dominated by images and popular culture.

More reflective viewers in the Bradford Museum viewed the set of images as a whole and provided written comments indicating that the exhibit effectively moved the internal and shared dialogue occurring among those attending the exhibit to the

Figure 10.4 *Porn Chic XVIII.* Courtesy of Nicola Bockelmann.

Figure 10.5 *Porn Chic II.* Courtesy of Nicola Bockelmann.

next level, effectively creating a zone of discourse on porn chic within this relatively small city in England and in the surrounding larger city of Leeds: "At first I thought it was crude and gaudy, once I understood what Nicola had done, I loved it! I appreciate art that comments about society. People who complain about it can't understand it unless they close their eyes when they see a billboard out of protest, or don't open a magazine because they know the adverts inside will disgust them."

Some viewers did not feel the work pushed hard enough in terms of making a commentary about porn chic: "I couldn't really understand where the ideas are going—[the artist] identified this thing that is going on in the media but not really showed us repulsion of it. The pictures still seem to have pornographic values." This comment perhaps speaks to the job of the rest of us. Bockelmann has presented the visual evidence but not the solution. As you walk through the show it finally dawns on you what you have passively accepted, what you are raising your children to see as normal. As well stated by Bordo, it is now our job to dismantle the dazzle and take back the real, for ourselves as well as our children. Our first job is to bring the unapologetic bad boy to the table.

Bringing the Bad Boy to the Table

Jackson Katz starts out his stump speech by telling the audience that we need to add an active subject when we are talking about addressing violence against women. What we are really talking about is "men's" violence against women. Therefore, if we want to create a cultural shift away from women and girls being objectified and violated, we need to bring boys and men into the conversation. Katz tells us we need to bring the bad boy to the table and get his friends to hold him accountable. It is not going to work to simply take back the terms men use to degrade women because another word will substitute. *Whore* becomes *slut*, *slut* becomes *ho*, *ho* turns into *cum dumpster.* Until attitudes and normative behaviors are changed, culture will not be changed.

Good men are already at work.[1] I have been partnering with Katz for over a decade, and during that time I have watched the ranks around him grow. While his program is only one of several successful methods of working with men and boys, I close this book with his ideas as a starting point and also direct you toward others. First of all, it is important to understand that while bad boy behaviors have been allowed to dominate the public discourse, a very small number of men commit a majority of sexually violent crimes. So while we live in a culture where fraternity men from one of America's most elite universities feel comfortable chanting, "No means yes, yes means anal" in the front yard of a first-year women's residence hall, we don't live in a culture where a vast majority of those same young men are all committing sexual assault using drugs, coercion, or other nonconsensual methods. In fact, when challenged, many young men who participate in these communal acts of misogyny do not on their own condone or support rape.

David Lisak's research on undetected campus rapists provides some of the most critical background information on how male sexual predators operate within college social systems (Lisak and Miller, 2002). Out of a data set of 1,882 men, 120 of them self-reported acts to Lisak's research team that met the legal definition for rape. A majority of these predators were repeat offenders who on average were responsible for approximately six rapes each, as well as a range of other acts of interpersonal violence. In total, this small number of men (6.4 percent of the total research pool) was responsible for 1,225 distinct acts of violence. Lisak's interviews found that campus predators target and entrap their victims in much the same way as rapists who have been incarcerated for their crimes. This undetected rapist easily blends into a college peer group, but his strategies for scouting targets and increasing a victim's vulnerability, as well as his ability to cognitively distort his crime to be acceptable both in his own mind and to his peers, mirror those of what we consider a criminal sex offender. The key difference, of course, is that while this young man is most typically a serial repeat offender, he is socially accepted into a peer group of men. He also many times has the social skills and often the charisma to be accepted as not only "normal" but also a leader. So while a small number of men are truly very, very bad boys, they are surrounded by a culture condoning and in many cases blatantly celebrating communal expressions of misogyny. In this cultural soup the serial rapist is able to easily operate because his exploits, while not practiced by the majority, are considered both cool and normal by his friends.

Programs and models designed to influence the 94 to 95 percent of men surrounding this predator focus attention on what Katz and others have labeled the bystander. What Katz's Mentors in Violence Prevention (MVP) program educates men to do is to interrupt the patterned misogynistic behavior that supports and surrounds gender violence (Katz, 2006; Katz, Heisterkamp, and Fleming, 2011). Consciously working within the traditional bastions of male privilege—the locker rooms of well-regarded teams, the social halls of prestigious fraternities, and the military—Katz along with his MVP team works with groups of men to get them to use their leadership roles to step in and stop patterned misogyny. From these early beginnings in college sports culture in the Boston area, MVP is now the most widely utilized gender-violence prevention program in college and professional athletics. In 1997 MVP became the first worldwide gender-violence prevention program in the history of the U.S. Marine Corps, with Katz joining the U.S. Secretary of Defense's Task Force on Domestic Violence in the Military in 2000. MVP trainers have been centrally involved in the development and implementation of the Air Force–wide Bystander Intervention Training, a leadership program that all Air Force personnel are required to complete by the summer of 2012. Within my home state we have worked with Katz and his team to move MVP into high school settings and also into the college curriculum we are using to educate future teachers, coaches, and high school administrators. The wide and large-scale implementation of the MVP program within the bastions of men's culture signals hope in terms of reconstruction of manhood away from the popular cultural allure of the unapologetic bad boy.

The successful moving of female pleasure from a direct experience of sexuality to an indirect pleasure derived from imagining the response of a male partner has created a cultural need for reconstructing not only masculinity but also female sexuality as well. It is not enough for women to reappropriate the roles they are cast in within bad boy sexual scripts. Instead, women need to work toward reconstructing popular culture expressions of female sexuality, away from reliance on the male gaze. Bockelmann's gallery of popular culture imagery points us in the right direction in terms of creating discourse about popular culture depictions of women and girls that need to be first deconstructed and then reconstructed as an opening act on the road to gender justice. The female version of Katz's MVP model also challenges young women and girls to step up as bystanders to interrupt the patterned degradation and victimization of girls and women who surround them. We also need to continue to explore the creation of programs that lead girls in the United States and United Kingdom away from evaluating themselves and their peers by the measuring stick of the unapologetic bad boy and toward engaging in authentic self-defined expressions of sexual agency.

Notes

Chapter 5—*Girls Gone Wild*: College Coeds Flash Their Goods

1. Male flashing of any body part as a part of the homecoming celebration was not observed or documented within interviews.
2. Informal interviews with students attending the celebration, chat room website discussions, and observation of license plates surrounding The Hill area documented that men had traveled from as far as Kansas, Illinois, Minnesota, Wisconsin, and Nebraska to attend the event, due to the flashing behavior.

Chapter 9—"Va-Va-Voom Goes the Soprano": Engaging Discourse on Porn Chic

1. The *New York Times* headline for Tommasini's opera review, 2011.
2. From Clair Wilcox (2004, p. 10).
3. Trained undergraduate and graduate students conducted the majority of interviews and focus groups. Interviews are coded throughout using RH (Red Hat), participant number, and the year in the notes throughout this section.
4. RH03-04.
5. RH06-04.
6. RH07-04.
7. RH12-04.
8. RH10-04.
9. RH21-04.
10. RH01-04.
11. RH12-04.
12. RH17-04.
13. RH04-04.
14. RH04-04.
15. RH02-05.
16. RH02-05.
17. RH06-04.
18. RH07-04.
19. RH03-05.
20. RH10-04.
21. RH12-04.

22. Boston Burlesque 2009, "The Main Event," YouTube, http://www.youtube.com/watch?gl=US&feature=related&hl=iw&v=ZzU0pWljmUU.

Chapter 10—The Path toward Gender Justice

1. I would like to recognize the valuable work of many men, including the founders and directors of Mentors in Violence Prevention (MVP); the founders and directors of Coaching Boys into Men, a program housed at Futures Without Violence; the "Iowa Team" of community and campus advocates, administrators, faculty, staff, and students who helped to support and deliver MVP across the three-campus Iowa Regents' university system; the Iowa Men's Action Network; and my husband, Mitchell D. Strauss, for working to make Boy Scouting a better experience for my son, Parker.

References

Abbey, A., C. Cozzarelli, K. McLaughlin, and J. Harnish. (1987). "The Effect of Clothing and Dyad Sex Composition on Perceptions of Sexual Intent: Do Women Evaluate These Cues Differently." *Journal of Applied Social Psychology* 17: 108–126.

Adams-Curtis, L. E., and G. B. Forbes. (2004). "College Women's Experiences of Sexual Coercion: A Review of Cultural, Perpetrator, Victim and Situational Variables." *Trauma, Violence, and Abuse* 5 (2): 91–122.

Alexander, C. S. (1980). "The Responsible Victim: Nurses' Perceptions of Victims of Rape." *Journal of Health and Social Behavior* 21: 22–33.

American Psychological Association, Task Force on the Sexualization of Girls. (2007). *Report of the APA Task Force on the Sexualization of Girls.* Washington, DC: American Psychological Association.

Arrington, M. (2009). "YouTube Video Streams Top 1.2 Billion/Day." *TechCrunch,* June 9. http://www.techcrunch.com.

Bachen, C. M., and E. Illouz. (1996). "Imagining Romance: Young People's Cultural Models of Romance and Love." *Critical Studies in Mass Communication* 13: 279–308.

Baker, S. L. (2004). "Pop in(to) the Bedroom: Popular Music in Pre-teen Girls' Bedroom Culture." *European Journal of Cultural Studies* 7 (1): 75–95.

Baker, S. L. (2011). "Playing Online: Pre-teen Girls' Negotiations of Pop and Porn in Cyberspace." In M. C. Kearney (ed.), *Mediated Girlhoods: New Explorations of Girls' Media Culture,* 171–188. New York: Peter Lang.

Bartky, S. L. (1990). "Narcissism, Femininity, and Alienation." In S. L. Bartky (ed.), *Femininity and Domination: Studies in the Phenomenology of Oppression,* 33–44. New York and London: Routledge.

Bartley, L., and J. Warden. (1962). "Clothing Preferences of Women Sixty-Five and Older." *Journal of Home Economics* 54: 716–717.

Bauer, N. (2010). "Lady Power." *New York Times Opinionator,* June 20.

Beer, L. J. (2004). Interview for *The Way the Music Died,* written, produced, and directed by M. Kirk. *Frontline.* Boston: WGBH Educational Foundation. http://www.pbs.org/wgbh/pages/frontline/shows/music/interviews/beer.html.

Berger, J. (1972). *Ways of Seeing.* London: Penguin Books.

Berman, B. (2010). *Hugh Hefner: Playboy, Activist, and Rebel.* Toronto: Telefilm Canada and the Rogers Group of Funds. Videorecording.

Bishop, M. J. (2007). "The Making of a Pre-pubescent Porn Star: Contemporary Fashion for Elementary School Girls." In A. C. Hall and M. J. Bishop (eds.), *Pop-Porn: Pornography in American Culture*, 45–56. Westport, CT, and London: Praeger.

Black Women's Blueprint. (2011). http://blackwomensblueprint.com/.

Blair, R. (2006). "Performing Gender Disruptions." In H. K. Chinoy and L. W. Jenkins (eds.), *Women in American Theatre*, 361–363. New York: Theatre Communications Group.

Bogle, K. (2008). *Hooking Up: Sex, Dating, Relationships on Campus.* New York: New York University Press.

Bordo, S. (1991). "'Material Girl': The Effacements of Postmodern Culture." In L. Goldstein (ed.), *The Female Body: Figures, Styles, Speculation*, 106–130. Ann Arbor: University of Michigan Press.

Bordo, S. (1992). "The Body and the Reproduction of Femininity: A Feminist Appropriation of Foucault." In A. M. Jaggar and S. Bordo (eds.), *Gender/Body/Knowledge: Feminist Reconstructions of Being and Knowing*, 13–33. New Brunswick, NJ: Rutgers University Press.

Bordo, S. (1997). *Twilight Zones: The Hidden Life of Cultural Images from Plato to O. J.* Berkeley: University of California Press.

Bovill, M., and S. Livingstone. (2001). "Bedroom Culture and the Privatization of Media Use." In S. Livingstone and M. Bovill (eds.), *Children and Their Changing Media Environment*, 179–200. Mahwah, NJ: Lawrence Erlbaum.

Briggeman, J. (2009). *Burlesque: A Living History.* Albany, GA: Bear Manor Media.

Brooks, G. R. (1997). "The Centerfold Syndrome." In R. F. Lavant and G. R. Brooks (eds.), *Men and Sex*, 28–60. New York: John Wiley and Sons.

Burgess, J. E., and J. B. Green. (2009). *YouTube: Online Video and Participatory Culture.* Cambridge, UK: Polity.

Busby, L. J., and G. Leichty. (1993). "Feminism and Advertising in Traditional and Nontraditional Women's Magazines, 1950s–1980s." *Journalism Quarterly* 70: 247–264.

Butler, J. (1999). *Gender Trouble: Feminism and the Subversion of Identity.* New York and London: Routledge.

Butler, J. (2004). "Performative Acts and Gender Constitution." In H. Bial (ed.), *The Performance Studies Reader*, 154–166. London and New York: Routledge.

Cahoon, D. D., and E. M. Edmonds. (1987). "Estimates of Opposite-Sex First Impressions Related to Females' Clothing Style." *Perceptual and Motor Skills* 65 (2): 406.

Calasanti, T., and K. F. Slevin. (2001). *Gender, Social Inequality, and Aging.* Walnut Creek, CA: AltaMira.

Calogero, R. M. (2004). "A Test of Objectification Theory: The Effect of the Male Gaze on Appearance Concerns in College Women." *Psychology of Women Quarterly* 28: 16–21.

Celizic, M. (2009). "Her Teen Committed Suicide over Sexting." *MSNBC.com*, March 6. http://today.msnbc.msn.com/id/29546030/ns/today-parenting_and_family/t/her-teen-committed-suicide-over-sexting/.

Cokal, S. (2007). "Clean Porn: The Visual Aesthetics of Hygiene, Hot Sex, and Hair Removal." In A. C. Hall and M. J. Bishop (eds.), *Pop-Porn: Pornography in American Culture*, 137–154. Westport, CT, and London: Praeger.

comScore.com. (2009). "YouTube Surpasses 100 Million Viewers for the First Time" [press release]. March 4. http://www.comscore.com.

Cooper, S. E. (2004). *The Red Hat Society: Fun and Friendship after Fifty.* New York: Warner Books.

Corsianos, M. (2007). "Mainstream Pornography and 'Women': Questioning Sexual Agency." *Critical Sociology* 33: 863–885.

Coy, M., and M. Garner. (2010). "Glamour Modelling and the Marketing of Self-Sexualization: Critical Reflections." *International Journal of Cultural Studies* 13: 657–675.

Daily Mail Reporter. (2011). "Scantily-Clad 'Slutwalk' Women March on New York after Police Tell Them to 'Cover Up' to Avoid Rape." *Daily Mail*, October 2. http://www.dailymail.co.uk/news/article-2044213/Slutwalk-women-march-New-York-NYPD-tell-cover-avoid-rape.html#ixzz1aaX816XR.

Daly, S. (1999). "Cover Story: Britney Spears." *Rolling Stone*, April 15.

Dines, G. (2010). *Pornland: How Porn Has Hijacked Our Sexuality.* Boston: Beacon.

Dines, G. (2011). "Supersexed: Pop Culture Images of Women in a Porn Culture." Lecture given at University of Northern Iowa, Cedar Falls, Iowa, October 19.

Dines, G., and W. J. Murphy. (2011). "SlutWalk Is Not Sexual Liberation." *The Guardian*, May 8.

Doyle, S. (2011). "SlutWalk NYC: Real Empowerment, Corsets and All." *In These Times*, October 3. http://inthesetimes.com/article/12040/slutwalk_nyc_an_important_success_corsets_and_all.

Durham, M. G. (2008). *The Lolita Effect: The Media Sexualization of Young Girls and What We Can Do.* Woodstock and New York: Overlook.

Duveen, G., and B. Lloyd (eds.). (1990). *Social Representations and the Development of Knowledge.* Cambridge: Cambridge University Press.

Ebeling, M., and M. L. Rosencrantz. (1961). "Social and Personal Aspects of Clothing for Older Women." *Journal of Home Economics* 53: 464–465.

Edmonds, E. M., and D. D. Cahoon. (1984). "Female Clothes Preference Related to Male Sexual Interest." *Bulletin of the Psychonomic Society* 22: 171–173.

Egan, D. R. (2000). "The Phallus Palace: Stripping Spaces, Desiring Subjects, and the Fantasy of Objects." PhD diss., Boston College, Boston.

Eisenberg, A. (2010). "When a Camcorder Becomes a Life Partner." *New York Times*, November 7.

Elliott, C. (2007). "The High Street Porn Brokers." *The Guardian*, October 10.

Ellis, B. J., and D. Symons. (1990). "Sex Differences in Sexual Fantasy: An Evolutionary Psychological Approach." *Journal of Sex Research* 27: 527–555.

Ensler, V. (2008). *The Vagina Monologues.* New York: Villard Books.

Eshbaugh, E., and G. Gute. (2008). "Hookups and Sexual Regret among College Women." *Journal of Social Psychology* 148 (1): 77–89.

Evans, C., and M. Thorton. (1989). *Women and Fashion: A New Look.* London and New York: Quartet Books.

Feather, B. L., M. Rucker, and S. B. Kaiser. (1989). "Social Concerns of Post-mastectomy Women: Stigmata and Clothing." *Home Economics Research Journal* 17: 289–299.

Feinglos, B. (2010). "Monday, Monday Article Offensive, Sexist Excuse for Humor." *Duke Chronicle*, October 6.

Fiore, A., and M. DeLong. (1984). "Use of Apparel as Cues to Perception of Personality." *Perceptual and Motor Skills* 59: 267–274.

Flanagan, C. (2011). "The Hazards of Duke." *Atlantic Magazine*, January/February, 87–96.

Foderaro, L. (2010). "Private Moment Made Public, Then a Fatal Jump." *New York Times*, September 30.

Foucault, M. (1980). *Power and Knowledge: Selected Interviews and Other Writings, 1972–1977.* New York: Pantheon Books.

Fredrickson, B. L., and T. Roberts. (1997). "Objectification Theory: Toward Understanding Women's Lived Experiences and Mental Health Risks." *Psychology of Women Quarterly* 21: 173–206.

Freedman, R. (1986). *Beauty Bound.* Lexington, MA: Lexington Books.

Gannes, L. (2006). "Jawed Karim: How YouTube Took Off." *Gigaom*, October 26. http://gigaom.com/2006/10/26/jawed-karim-how-youtube-took-off/.

Gerber, R. (2009). *Barbie and Ruth: The Story of the World's Most Famous Doll and the Woman Who Created Her.* New York: Harper.

Gill, R. (2008). "Empowerment/Sexism: Figuring Female Sexual Agency in Contemporary Advertising." *Feminism and Psychology* 18 (35): 36–60.

Gillie, B. (2011). "London Opera Portrays Life of Anna Nicole Smith (Trailer)." *Examiner.com.* http://www.examiner.com/strange-news-in-national/london-opera portrays-life-of-anna-nicole-smith/.

Gladwell, M. (1997). "The Coolhunt." *New Yorker*, March 17, 78–84.

Goff, K. (2011). "Dear Feminists, Will You Also Be Marching in N***erwalk? Because I Won't." *Huffington Post*, October 3. http://www.huffingtonpost.com/ keligoff/slutwalk-new-york_b_993261.html.

Goffman, E. (1963). *Stigma.* Englewood Cliffs, NJ: Prentice-Hall.

Goldstein, R. (2002). "The Eminem Shtick: What Makes a Bigot a Genius? Presiding over Guilty Pleasures." *Village Voice*, June 11.

Goodchilds, J., and G. Zellman. (1984). "Sexual Signaling and Sexual Aggression in Adolescent Relationships." In N. M. Malamuth and E. Donnerstain (eds.), *Pornography and Sexual Aggression*, 233–243. Orlando, FL: Academic Press.

Goodman, B., and R. Dretzin. (2001). *The Merchants of Cool. Frontline.* Boston: WGBH Educational Foundation. Videorecording.

Hall, A. C., and M. J. Bishop (eds.). (2007). *Pop-Porn: Pornography in American Culture.* Westport, CT, and London: Praeger.

Harvey, H. B., and K. Robinson. (2007). "Hot Bodies on Campus: The Performance of Porn Chic." In A. C. Hall and M. J. Bishop (eds.), *Pop-Porn: Pornography in American Culture*, 57–74. Westport, CT, and London: Praeger.

Haug, F. (1987). *Female Sexualization: A Collective Work of Memory.* London: Verso.

Helyar, J. (2003). "Hooters: A Case Study 'This Thing Has Incredible Legs', an Early Investor Said. Twenty Years Later, the Restaurant Chain Has Finally Hit Its Stride." *Fortune Magazine*, September 1.

Herbert, E. (2010). *Lady Gaga: Behind the Fame.* New York: Overlook.

Hite, M. (1988). "Writing—and Reading—the Body: Female Sexuality and Recent Feminist Fiction." *Feminist Studies* 14 (1): 121–122.

Hoffman, J. (2011). "POISONED WEB: A Girl's Nude Photo, and Altered Lives." *New York Times*, March 27.

Holland, S., and F. Attwood. (2009). "Keeping Fit in Six Inch Heels: The Mainstreaming of Pole Dancing." In F. Attwood (ed.), *Mainstreaming Sex: The Sexualization of Western Culture*, 165–182. London and New York: I. B. Taurus.

Hollander, A. (1975). *Seeing through Clothes.* Berkeley: University of California Press.

Hooters. (n.d.). *Hooters Employee Handbook.* Atlanta, GA: Hooters.

Horyn, C. (2010). "What Do Girls Want?" *New York Times*, August 24.

Howard, H. (2011). "Vibrators Carry the Conversation." *New York Times*, April 20.

Hurt, B. (2006). *Hip-Hop: Beyond Beats and Rhymes.* Northampton, MA: Media Education Foundation. Videorecording.

Jackson, H. O., and G. S. O'Neal. (1994). "Dress and Appearance Responses to Perception of Aging." *Clothing and Textiles Research Journal* 12 (4): 8–15.

Jacobs, A. (2007). "Campus Exposure." *New York Times*, March 4.

Jeffreys, S. (2005). *Beauty and Misogyny: Harmful Cultural Practices in the West.* London and New York: Routledge.

Jhally, S. (2003). *Wrestling with Manhood.* Northampton, MA: Media Education Foundation. Videorecording.

Johnson, K. P. (1995). "Attributions about Date Rape: Impact of Clothing, Sex, Money Spent, Date Type and Perceived Similarity." *Family and Consumer Sciences Research Journal* 23 (3): 292–310.

Johnston, J. E. (1997). "Appearance Obsession: Women's Reactions to Men's Objectification of Their Bodies." In R. F. Lavant and G. R. Brooks (eds.), *Men and Sex*, 61–83. New York: John Wiley and Sons.

JOS. (2011). "SlutWalk Redux with Rebecca Traister and Feministing Writers." *Feministing*, July 22. http://feministing.com/2011/07/22/slutwalk-redux-with-rebecca-traister-and-feministing-writers/.

Justice. (2010). http://www.shopjustice.com/. Accessed September 9.

Kaiser, S. B. (1989). "Clothing and the Social Organization of Gender Perception: A Developmental Approach." *Clothing and Textiles Research Journal* 7 (2): 46–56.

Kaiser, S. B. (1997). *The Social Psychology of Clothing: Symbolic Appearances in Context.* New York: Fairchild.

Kaiser, S. B., and J. L. Chandler. (1984). "Fashion Alienation: Older Adults and the Mass Media." *International Journal of Aging and Human Development* 19: 199–217.

Katz, J. (2006). *The Macho Paradox: Why Some Men Hurt Women and How All Men Can Help.* Naperville, IL: Source Books.

Katz, J. (2009). "Eminem, Misogyny, and the Sounds of Silence." *Rosalind Wiseman: Creating Cultures of Dignity*, July 9. http://rosalindwiseman.com/2009/06/09/eminem-misogyny-and-the-sounds-of-silence/.

Katz, J., A. Heisterkamp, and M. Fleming. (2011). "The Social Justice Roots of the Mentors in Violence Prevention Model, and Its Application in a High School Setting." *Bystander Special Issue: Violence against Women* 17 (6): 684–702.

Kennedy, D. (1993). *Sexy Dressing Etc: Essays on the Power and Politics of Cultural Identity.* Cambridge, MA: Harvard University Press.

Kilbourne, J. (1999). *Can't Buy My Love: How Advertising Changes the Way We Think and Feel.* New York: Simon and Schuster.

Kilbourne, J. (2010). *Killing Us Softly 4: Advertising's Image of Women.* Boston: Media Education Foundation. Videorecording.

Kimmel, M. (2008). *Guyland: The Perilous World Where Boys Become Men.* New York: Harpers Paperbacks.

Kirkpatrick, D. (2010). *The Facebook Effect: The Inside Story of the Company That Is Connecting the World.* New York: Simon and Schuster.

Kirn, W. (2010). "Little Brother Is Watching." *New York Times Magazine*, October 17. http://www.nytimes.com/2010/10/17/magazine/17FOB-WWLN-t.html?_r=1.

Kornblum, J. (2006). "Now Playing on YouTube." *USA Today*, July 18.

Korthase, K. M., and I. Trenholme. (1982). "Perceived Age and Perceived Physical Attractiveness." *Perceptual and Motor Skills* 54: 1251–1258.

Lamb, S., and L. M. Brown. (2006). *Packaging Girlhood: Rescuing Our Daughters from Marketers' Schemes.* New York: St. Martin's Griffin.

Lenhart, A., M. Madden, and P. Hitlin. (2005). "Teens and Technology." Pew Internet and American Life Project, July 27. http://www.pewinternet.org/

Lenhart, A., L. Rainie, and O. Lewis. (2001). "Teenage Life Online: The Rise of the Instant Message Generation and the Internet's Impact on Friendships and Family Relationships." Pew Internet and American Life Project, June 21. http://www.pewinternet.org/

Lennon, S. (1997). "Physical Attractiveness, Age and Body Type: Further Evidence." *Clothing and Textiles Research Journal* 15 (1): 60–64.

Lennon, S., K. P. Johnson, and T. L. Schultz. (1999). "Forging Linkages between Dress and Law in the U.S., Part I: Rape and Sexual Harassment." *Clothing and Textiles Research Journal* 17: 144–156.

Levin, D., and J. Kilbourne. (2008). *So Sexy So Soon: The New Sexualized Childhood and What Parents Can Do to Protect Their Kids.* New York: Ballantine Books.

Levy, A. (2005). *Female Chauvinist Pigs: Women and the Rise of Raunch Culture.* New York: Free Press.

Lips, H. (1981). *Women, Men and Psychology of Power.* Englewood Cliffs, NJ: Prentice-Hall.

Lisak, D., and P. Miller. (2002). "Repeated Rape and Multiple Offending among Undetected Rapists." *Violence and Victims* 17 (1): 73.

Litewka, J. (1974). "The Socialized Penis." *Liberation* 18 (7): 61–69.

Lovell, L. (n.d.). "Lil's Story." http://www.coyoteuglysaloon.com/history.html.

Lyall, S. (2011). "A Star Turn for a Lady in Waiting." *New York Times*, May 6.

Lynch, A. (1999a). *Dress, Gender, and Cultural Change: Asian American and African American Rites of Passage.* Oxford and New York: Berg.

Lynch, A. (1999b). *Transforming Gender through Critical Research: An Analysis of Enacted Attractiveness among Undergraduate Women.* Citrus Heights, CA: International Textile and Apparel Association.

Lynch, A. (2006). "Facebook: Cultural Construction of Gender through Cyber Identity among College Students." Paper presented at the International Textile and Apparel Association Annual Meeting, San Antonio, Texas.

Lynch, A. (2007). "Expanding the Definition of Provocative Dress: An Examination of Female Flashing Behavior on a College Campus." *Clothing and Textiles Research Journal* 25 (2): 184–201.

Lynch, A. (2009). "It Was Style, with a Capital S." In P. McNeil and V. Karaminas (eds.), *The Men's Fashion Reader*, 443–453. Oxford and New York: Berg.

Lynch, A., M. Stalp, and E. Radina. (2007). "Growing Old and Dressing (Dis) Gracefully." In D. C. Johnson and H. B. Foster (eds.), *Senses and Sentiments of Dress*, 144–155. Oxford and New York: Berg.

Lynch, A., and M. D. Strauss. (2007). *Changing Fashion.* Oxford and New York: Berg.

MacKinnon, C. (1982). "Feminism, Marxism, Method and the State: An Agenda for Theory." *Signs* 7: 515–533.

Macmillan, C. D., A. Lynch, and L. A. Bradley. (2011). "Agonic and Hedonic Power: The Performance of Gender by Young Adults on Halloween." *Paideusis: Journal for Interdisciplinary and Cross Cultural Studies* 5: E1–E30.

Maddison, S. (2009). "Choke on It, Bitch!": PornStudies, Extreme Gonzo and the Mainstreaming of Hardcore." In F. Attwood (ed.), *Mainstreaming Sex: The Sexualization of Western Culture*, 37–54. London and New York: I. B. Taurus.

Maisano, L. (2006). "Growing Up with Pop Music and MTV." *Yahoo Voices*, January 3. http://voices.yahoo.com/growing-pop-music-mtv-13559.html.

Marshall, P. (2009). "Generation Sexting: What Teenage Girls Really Get Up To on the Internet Should Chill Every Parent." *MailOnline*, March 18.

Mathes, E. W., S. M. Brennan, P. M. Haugen, and H. B. Rice. (1985). "Ratings of Physical Attractiveness as a Function of Age." *Journal of Social Psychology* 125 (2): 157–168.

Max, T. (2006). *I Hope They Serve Beer in Hell.* New York: Citadel.

Max, T. (2010). *Assholes Finish First.* New York: Gallery Books.

Max, T. (n.d.). "Frequently Asked Questions." *TuckerMax.com.* http://www.tuckermax. com/about/faq/.

McNair, B. (2002). *Striptease Culture: Sex Media and the Democratisation of Desire.* New York: Routledge.

Mead, R. (2002). "Endless Spring: How Much Spring Break Can Anyone Stand?" *New Yorker*, April 1, 50–56.

Mills, E. (2010). "Rude Awakenings: How Internet Porn Is Deforming the Sexual Development of a Generation of Teenagers." *Sunday Times Magazine*, December 19, 16–23.

Mitchell, J. (2010). "Madonna and Child Launch Material Girl Fashion Line for Teens." *Popeater*, August 6. http://www.popeater.com/2010/08/06/madonna-material-girl/.

Morgan, E. (1972). *The Descent of Women.* New York: Stein and Day.

Morris, D. (2004). *The Naked Woman: A Study of the Female Body.* New York: Thomas Dunne Books.

Myung-Ok, M. L. (2011). "Perverse Incentives." *The Atlantic*, June.

Navarro, M. (2004a). "Arrest Startles Saleswomen of Sex Toys." *New York Times*, January 16.

Navarro, M. (2004b). "The Most Private of Makeovers." *New York Times*, November 28.

Nowak, D. A. (1975). "The Appearance Signal in Adult Development." PhD diss., Wayne State University, Detroit.

O'Brien, L. (2007). *Madonna: Like an Icon.* New York: Harper Entertainment.

Odzer, C. 1997. *Virtual Spaces: Sex and the Cyber Citizen.* New York: Berkley Books.

Opplinger, P. (2008). *Girls Gone Swank: The Sexualization of Girls in American Culture.* Jefferson, NC, and London: McFarland.

Owen, K. (2010). "An Education beyond the Classroom: Excelling in the Realm of Horizontal Academics." Unpublished PowerPoint presentation.

Paul, P. (2005). *Pornified: How Pornography Is Damaging Our Lives, Our Relationships and Our Families.* New York: Henry Holt.

Pederson, A. (1998). *What about Hooters.* New York: New Park Press.

Philips, M. (2007). "Eye Candy." *Newsweek*, October 28.

Pipher, M. (1994). *Reviving Ophelia: Saving the Selves of Adolescent Girls.* New York: Berkeley Publishing.

Playboy Enterprises. (2007). *The Bunny Book: How to Walk, Talk, Tease, and Please like a Playboy Bunny.* San Francisco: Chronicle Books.

Playboy Productions. (1992). *Hugh Hefner: Once Upon a Time.* Chicago: Playboy Productions. Videorecording.

Powers, A. (2009). "Frank Talk with Lady Gaga." *Los Angeles Times*, December 13.

Quart, A. (2003). *Branded: The Buying and Selling of Teenagers*. New York: Basic Books.

Radina, M. E., A. Lynch, M. C. Stalp, and L. K. Manning. (2008). "'When I am an old woman, I shall wear purple': Red Hatters Cope with Getting Old." *Journal of Women and Aging* 20 (1–2): 99–114.

Raha, M. (2005). *Cinderella's Big Score: Women of the Punk and Indie Underground*. Emeryville, CA: Seal.

Reichert, T., and C. Carpenter. (2004). "An Update on Sex in Magazine Advertising: 1983 to 2003." *Journalism and Mass Communication Quarterly* 81: 823–837.

Reid, E. (1994). "Cultural Formations in Text-Based Virtual Realities." Master's thesis, University of Melbourne.

Riordan, E. (2001). "Commodified Agents and Empowered Girls: Consuming and Producing Feminism." *Journal of Communication Inquiry* 25 (3): 279–297.

Roberts, D. F., U. G. Foehr, and V. Rideout. (2005). *Generation M: Media in the Lives of 8–18 Year Olds*. Menlo Park, CA: Henry J. Kaiser Family Foundation.

Robertson, J. (2010). *50 Years of the Playboy Bunny*. San Francisco: Chronicle Books.

Rosenfeld, D. L. (2011). "Who Are You Calling a 'Ho'? Challenging the Porn Culture on Campus." In M. T. Reist and A. Bray (eds.), *Big Porn Inc: Exposing the Harms of the Global Pornography Industry*, 41–52. North Melbourne, Australia: Spinifex.

Roszak, T. (1970). *The Making of a Counter Culture*. New York: Faber.

Rudoren, J. (2006). "The Student Body." *New York Times*, April 23.

St. John, W. (2006). "Dude: Here's My Book." *New York Times*, April 16.

Sarracino, C., and K. Scott. (2008). *The Porning of America: The Rise of Porn Culture, What It Means, and Where We Go from Here*. Boston: Beacon Press.

Sawicki, J. (1991). *Disciplining Foucault: Feminism, Power, and the Body*. New York and London: Routledge.

Schechner, R. (1995). *The Future of Ritual: Writings on Culture and Performance*. London: Routledge.

Schor, J. (2004). *Born to Buy: The Commercialized Child and the New Consumer Culture*. New York: Charles Scribner's Sons.

Schouten, J. W. (1991). "Selves in Transition: Symbolic Consumption in Personal Rites of Passage and Identity Reconstruction." *Journal of Consumer Research* 17: 412–425.

Scott, L. M. (1993). "Fresh Lipstick: Rethinking Images of Women in Advertising." *Media Studies Journal* 7: 141–155.

Scott, L. S. (1998). *The Bunny Years*. Los Angeles and London: Pomegranate Press.

"Sexual Health: My Guy Wants Me to Try a Bikini Wax That Leaves Me Totally Bare. Is That Safe?" (n.d.). *Cosmopolitan*. http://www.cosmopolitan.com/sex-love/sexual-health/bikini-wax-safe.

Singer, M. (2011). "Betsey Johnson, Spring 2012." *Style.com*, September 12. http://www.style.com/fashionshows/review/S2012RTW-BJOHNSON.

Sisson, P. (n.d.). "College Sex Magazines *H Bomb* and *Boink* Chronicle the Real Sexual Education of Today's Coeds." *Boston Nightclub News.* http://www.bostonnightclubnews.com/bostonaffiliates/boinkmagazine/.

SlutWalk Toronto. (n.d.). "Why." http://www.slutwalktoronto.com/about/why.

Sorell, G. T., and C. A. Nowak. (1981). "The Role of Physical Attractiveness as a Contributor to Individual Development." In R. M. Lerner and N. A. Bush-Rossnagel (eds.), *Individuals as Producers of Their Development: A Life-Span Perspective,* 389–446. New York: Academic Press.

Stalp, M. B., R. Williams, A. Lynch, and M. E. Radina. (2008). "Conspicuously Consuming: The Red Hat Society and Midlife Women's Identity." *Journal of Contemporary Ethnography* 38 (2): 225–253.

Stalp, M. C., M. E. Radina, and A. Lynch. (2008). "We Do It Cuz It's Fun: Gendered Fun and Leisure for Midlife Women through Red Hat Society Membership." *Sociological Perspectives* 51 (2): 325–348.

Steele, V. (1985). *Fashion and Eroticism: Ideals of Feminine Beauty from the Victorian Era to the Jazz Age.* New York and Oxford: Oxford University Press.

Sterling, A. C. (1995). "Undressing the Victim: The Intersection of Evidentiary and Semiotic Meanings of Women's Clothing in Rape Trials." *Yale Journal of Law and Feminism* 7: 87–132.

Stern, H. (1995). *Miss America.* New York: Harper Collins.

Stollar, D. (1999). "Sex and the Thinking Girl." In M. Karp and D. Stollar (eds.), *The BUST Guide to the New World Order,* 75–84. New York: Penguin.

Stone, G. (1965). "Appearance and the Self." In M. E. Roach and J. B. Eicher (eds.), *Dress, Adornment and the Social Order,* 216–245. New York: John Wiley & Sons.

Straczynski, S. (2009). "Probing the Minds of Teenage Consumers." *ADWEEK,* September 23.

Sullivan, G. L., and P. J. O'Connor. (1988). "Women's Role Portrayals in Magazine Advertising: 1958–1983." *Sex Roles* 18: 181–188.

Tetzlaff, D. (1993). "Metatexual Girl: Patriarchy, Postmodernism, Power, Money, Madonna." In C. Schwichtenberg (ed.), *The Madonna Connection: Representational Politics: Subcultural Identities, and Cultural Theory,* 239–264. Boulder, CO: Westview.

Tommasini, A. (2011). "Va-Va-Voom Goes the Soprano." *New York Times,* February 17.

Traister, R. (2011). "Ladies, We Have a Problem." *New York Times Magazine,* July 20.

Turner, J. (2005). "Dirty Young Men." *The Guardian,* October 22.

Vassar Student Association. (n.d.). "Organizations." http://vsa.vassar.edu/activities/organizations.

Walker, R. (2005). "Middle-Age: Bring It On." *New York Times Magazine,* January 30.

Waskul, D. D. (2003). *Self-Games and Body-Play: Personhood in Online Chat and Cybersex.* New York: Peter Lang.

Waskul, D. D. (ed.). (2004). *net.SeXXX: Readings on Sex, Pornography, and the Internet.* New York: Peter Lang.

Waskul, D. D., M. Douglass, and C. Edgley. (2004). "Outercourse: Body and the Self in Text Cybersex." In D. D. Waskul (ed.), *net.SeXXX: Readings on Sex, Pornography, and the Internet*, 13–34. New York: Peter Lang.

White, M. (2011). "A Tabloid Star Is Joining the Sisterhood of the Fallen." *New York Times*, February 11.

Whitely, S. (2000). *Women and Popular Music: Sexuality, Identity, and Subjectivity.* London and New York: Routledge.

Wilcox, C. (2004). *Vivienne Westwood.* London: Victoria and Albert Publications.

Williams, H. (2002). "Pornography and Light Sadism with Ian Fleming." *Times Literary Supplement*, March 22.

Wilson, E. (1990). "Deviant Dress." *Feminist Review* 35: 68–74.

Wilson, E. (2005). "Fashion Refigured." *New York Times*, May 12.

Wolf, J. (2006). "And You Thought Abercrombie and Fitch Was Pushing It?" *New York Times Magazine*, April 23, 58–63.

Wolfe, T. (2004). *I Am Charlotte Simmons.* New York: Farrar, Straus and Giroux.

Workman, J. E., and R. Orr. (1996). "Clothing, Sex of Subject, and Rape Myth Acceptance as Factors Affecting Attributions about an Incident of Acquaintance Rape." *Clothing Textiles Research Journal* 14 (4): 276–284.

Zinoman, J. (2010). "For Lady Gaga: Every Concert Is a Drama." *New York Times*, January 23.

Zissu, A. (2011). "Who Are You Calling Grama?" *New York Times*, May 11.

Index